Business Intelligence
Success Factors

Wiley & SAS Business Series

The Wiley & SAS Business Series presents books that help senior-level managers with their critical management decisions.

Titles in the Wiley and SAS Business Series include:

Business Intelligence Competency Centers: A Team Approach to Maximizing Competitive Advantage, by Gloria J. Miller, Dagmar Brautigam, and Stefanie Gerlach

Case Studies in Performance Management: A Guide from the Experts, by Tony C. Adkins

CIO Best Practices: Enabling Strategic Value with Information Technology, by Joe Stenzel

Credit Risk Scorecards: Developing and Implementing Intelligent Credit Scoring, by Naeem Siddiqi

Customer Data Integration: Reaching a Single Version of the Truth, by Jill Dyche and Evan Levy

Enterprise Risk Management: A Methodology for Achieving Strategic Objectives, by Gregory Monahan

Fair Lending Compliance: Intelligence and Implications for Credit Risk Management, by Clark R. Abrahams and Mingyuan Zhang

Information Revolution: Using the Information Evolution Model to Grow Your Business, by Jim Davis, Gloria J. Miller, and Allan Russell

Marketing Automation:Practical Steps to More Effective Direct Marketing, by Jeff LeSueur

Performance Management: Finding the Missing Pieces (to Close the Intelligence Gap), by Gary Cokins

Performance Management: Integrating Strategy Execution, Methodologies, Risk, and Analytics, by Gary Cokins

Credit Risk Assessment: The New Lending System for Borrowers, Lenders, and Investors, by Clark Abrahams and Mingyuan Zhang

For more information on any of the above titles, visit **www.wiley.com**.

Business Intelligence Success Factors

Tools for Aligning Your Business in the Global Economy

OLIVIA PARR RUD

WILEY

John Wiley & Sons, Inc.

Published by John Wiley & Sons, Inc., Hoboken, New Jersey.

Published simultaneously in Canada.

For general information on our other products and services, or technical support, please contact our Customer Care Department within the United States at 800-762-2974, outside the United States at 317-572-3993 or fax 317-572-4002.

Wiley also publishes its books in a variety of electronic formats. Some content that appears in print may not be available in electronic books.

For more information about Wiley products, visit our Web site at http://www.wiley.com.

Library of Congress Cataloging-in-Publication Data:

Rud, Olivia Parr.
    Business intelligence success factors : tools for aligning your business in the global economy / Olivia Parr Rud.
        p. cm.
    Includes index.
    ISBN 978-0-470-39240-9 (cloth)
        1. Business intelligence. 2. Globalization. I. Title.
HD38.7.R83 2009
658.4–dc22

2009005656

Printed in the United States of America

10 9 8 7 6 5 4 3 2 1

*To Brandon, Addam, and Vanessa, for whom I hope
to make a difference*

Contents

About the Contributors

Dr. Marie Amey-Taylor, Director, Human Resources Department, Learning and Development Division, Temple University, has a rich and varied career history that includes professional experiences as an educator, program administrator, internal and external training and organizational development consultant, group facilitator, theater troupe founder and artistic director, and public speaker. She is co-coordinator of the University's Leadership Academy and specializes in leadership, management and supervisory skill development and interpersonal skills including diversity, communication, team building and conflict resolution. She holds a doctoral degree in Psycho-Educational Processes/Adult and Organizational Development, College of Education, Temple University. She is also qualified to administer the Myers-Briggs Type Indicator.

Eric Brunner, SPHR is a Manager in the Learning & Development Division of Temple University's Human Resources Department. He is responsible for designing and delivering many of Temple University's, competency based Performance Management, Communication, Diversity, Conflict Resolution and policy based Anti Harassment/Anti Discrimination training programs. He is also responsible for coordinating, designing, and delivering Temple's New Hire Orientation for administration and faculty.

As an independent learning and development consultant, Eric has worked with Glaxo Smith Kline, Astra Zeneca, Novartis Pharmaceuticals, Ranbaxy Pharmaceuticals, ARAMARK, Continental Airlines, USIS, Norfolk Southern Railroad, Syracuse University, Temple University, Community College of Philadelphia, The University of Medicine & Dentistry of

New Jersey, and Bryn Mawr College. Eric has performed for improv groups both locally and nationally and is a founding member of a company, Playback for Change.

Eric had one of his training designs, *Improvisational Skills: Achieving Workplace Success* published in *The Best of Active Training II: 25 One Day Workshops Guaranteed to Promote Involvement, Learning, and Change*, Edited by Mel Silberman, Pfieffier Publishing, 2007.

Eric has performed in and/or facilitated over 200 improvisational theater performances in the last fifteen years.

John Castagnini is best known as the creator of the Thank God I . . . book series, seminars, and world community. He is a speaker, author, entrepreneur, and teacher whose original and often iconoclastic thinking has put him at the cutting edge of the personal development industry.

To his rapidly growing worldwide following, John teaches a way of experiencing actuality that transcends emotional charges. Specifically, he teaches a technique of calibrating opposite emotions to the point of equilibrium. This enables people to overcome and transcend *any* life challenge and live in a state of inspiration and gratitude.

Castagnini was born in New York City, has a degree in biology from California State University, and attended chiropractic school. Dedicated to uniting mind, body, heart, and soul toward masterful expression, John is the author of several books: *Treasures Within—Meditation with a Friend* (co-authored with Halley Elise), *Making Love with Poetry, Between Angels and Devils* (poems written between the ages of 31 and 34), *Profit with Purpose* (a practical workbook on creating wealth), a forthcoming third book of poetry, and a soon-to-be-released book *How to Say I Love You in EVERY Language*.

Carl Gaertner earned his bachelor's degree in psychology from Michigan State University in 1981. He achieved the Charter Property Casualty Underwriter designation in 1995. He has 22 years of experience applying psychological principles appropriately in business settings. He uses interviewing strategies to reveal the deep decision-making abilities of subject matter experts. The knowledge gained from those interviewed is applied to create applications for knowledge transfer between employees and when turnover of employees occurs. Currently, he is working for an insurance and financial service corporation as a business analyst leading the knowledge management initiative in the systems department.

Jalma Mesnick Marcus RN, BS, MS, CBP, PaRama Practitioner and Certified Access Trainer holds a BS and MS from Boston University, and completed post graduate work in Organizational Systems from MIT and the University of Pennsylvania. A seasoned executive and leadership coach, educator, organizational consultant, entrepreneur, and speaker with more than 35 years of experience, she combines her corporate understanding and skills in complexity science with BodyTalk, Reiki, Shamanic healing, and NLP to measure and improve adaptability and alignment in both individuals and their work environment. She has held faculty positions at Boston College and Villanova University and used her talents as principal and executive in such industries as commercial real estate, advertising, healthcare, architecture, and IT.

Her latest publication is "Adapt or Die: Uncovering Your Organization's Hidden Patterns."

John Reddish works with entrepreneurs and other leaders who want to master growth, transition, and succession to get results faster, less painfully, and in ways that work for them. Reddish has served as vice president of the Presidents Association of the American Management Association, with RA Group Advertising, the New York State Nurses Association, IBM, Edison Electric Institute, and the Civil Service Employees Association.

He has written and spoken widely and is the author of *The Professional Services Firm Bible* (John Wiley & Sons, 2004), a contributing author to "Heart of the Holidays" and "Heart of a Mother," and "New Techniques for Motivation and Discipline" (Dible, 1983). John is a member of the National Speakers Association and the International Coach Federation.

John speaks to and works with entrepreneurs and leaders who want to master growth, transition, and succession to get results faster, less painfully and in ways that work for them. Contact John at 1-800-726-7985 or e-mail johnr@getresults.com.

Jim Riordan became conscious that environments can be both healing and highly productive in the early 1970s as a result of teaching yoga. For ten years he designed, manufactured, and installed solariums and skylights transforming residential environments. Extensive research resulted in reducing customer's energy consumption as much as 50 percent, while improving indoor quality. Then while designing and building 80 custom homes over the next 20 years, he developed the MORE Program and founded Perpetual Prosperity Pumps Foundation. He is passionate about designing and promoting free-enterprise models that are self-regenerative environments. "We only need to understand the principles of nature and apply them."

Julie Roberts, Ph.D. helps individuals to move into their full potential and overcome obstacles to productivity. She developed CLEAR™ (an energy psychology method) to help individuals remove blocks and move forward in their lives. She teaches graduate courses and conducts workshops that improve leadership skills, and she teaches CLEAR. She is currently helping Women for Women International bring CLEAR to women in Afghanistan, Bosnia, the Democratic Republic of the Congo, Iraq, Kosovo, Nigeria, Rwanda, and Sudan. Dr. Roberts has written a how-to book describing CLEAR, and is certified by the Association for Comprehensive Energy Psychology. Reach her at www.changeworksinc.com.

Brian Robertson is known internationally for pioneering Holacracy™, an innovative approach to organizational governance and management he developed while leading Ternary Software, an award-winning fast-growth software consulting company he founded in 2001. In 2008 he left his position as CEO of Ternary Software to join HolacracyOne full-time, a new organization he founded to further develop and spread Holacracy beyond Ternary Software. Brian currently spends most of his time with HolacracyOne, where he leads many of the organization's trainings, outreach programs, and other initiatives, and his writings and speaking engagements provide a voice to the Holacracy movement across the world. He can be reached via www.holacracy.org.

Michael Sussman is the founder of the nonprofit organization, On TrackAmerica (www.ontrackamerica.org), which is helping the North American rail industry and government collaborate across agencies, companies, regions, and stakeholder groups. Mr. Sussman and his consulting company, Strategic Rail Finance (www.strategicrail.com), apply collaborative principles to financing the most challenging situations, creating funding breakthroughs for their clients that incorporate multiple lenders and government entities. Mr. Sussman's career in railroad finance, government consulting, and multiparty relations is designed to forge new ground in aligning commercial activity and related public policy to support the long-term, best interests of the common good.

Mr. Sussman can be reached at msussman@strategicrail.com.

Antanas Vainius is a visionary pioneer, inspirational speaker, consultant, educator, and writer whose work is devoted to helping organizations embrace alternative cultures and business models that place human wellbeing and learning at the center of the enterprise. Current projects include gRawnola and Gentle Living, two organizations dedicated to nurturing and empowering the body and restoring the role of imagination and creativity in business.

Antanas studied pre-med, theater, leadership, and religion at Brown University, movement and performing arts at California Institute of the Arts, community building and psychology at Tamalpa Institute, and holistic cooking at Living Light Institute of Culinary Arts.

Prior to forming Gentle Living, Antanas worked with Cross Cultural Studies Program, a non-profit foundation, documenting and facilitating cultural exchange between North and South American shamanic traditions. His Web site is www.AntanasVainius.com.

Dave Wells is a consultant, mentor, and teacher in the field of Business Intelligence (BI). He brings to every endeavor a unique and balanced perspective about the relationships of business and technology. This perspective—refined through a career of more than 35 years that encompassed business and technical roles—helps to align business and information technology in the most effective ways. Contact Dave at dwells@infocentric.org or visit www.visualcv.com/dlwells to keep up-to-date with his BI activities and interests.

Cherry Woodburn is the founder of Borderless Thinking™ LLC, a consulting firm helping businesses break free from business-as-usual thinking to re-invent what they can accomplish in today's highly competitive marketplace. She's had her own business for over two decades, providing process consulting and innovative solutions. She writes a monthly column on Innovative Thinking in the Eastern Pennsylvania Business Journal and was featured in the Special 11th Edition of Mission Possible! along with Stephen Covey and Brian Tracy. Her URL is www.borderlessthinking.com.

Preface

O ver the last few decades, the growth of Business Intelligence (BI) has enabled companies to streamline many processes and expand into new markets on an unprecedented scale. In addition, new BI technologies are enabling mass collaboration and innovation. However, the implementation of these BI solutions often gives rise to new challenges. Most of these challenges can be turned into opportunities through the development of new competencies. According to Jim Davis, Gloria J. Miller, and Allan Russell: "A company's success in managing its information assets is a function of infrastructure, process, people, and culture, all working in concert."[1]

The purpose of this book is to enhance understanding of the current business climate along with the tools necessary to thrive in the new global economy. It begins by linking cutting-edge scientific research to organizational dynamics. The connections that are unveiled suggest areas for organizational development and restructuring. Anyone interested in moving beyond mere survival to breakaway success in this new global economy will find value in this book.

The book is presented in four parts. Part One describes the current business landscape as well as the latest scientific research. Chapter 1 details many of today's business realities and how they can lead to chaos in many organizations. Chapter 2 delves into the newest research in science to explain why we are experiencing chaos, how it works, and why it is becoming more intense. Other scientific discoveries in the areas of

---

[1] Jim Davis, Gloria J. Miller, and Allan Russell, *Information Revolution: Using the Information Evolution Model to Grow Your Business* (New York: John Wiley & Sons, 2006), xxiii.

quantum physics, evolutionary biology, and field theory offer powerful opportunities for organizations to connect, adapt, and thrive.

Part Two explores five essential competencies that, if mastered, improve an organization's ability to leverage the new opportunities in a volatile global economy. The competencies are communication, collaboration, innovation, adaptability, and leadership. A chapter is devoted to each of these topics. While entire books are devoted to these important topics, here the focus is on emphasizing the connection to the current situation and exploring some new ideas that support success in our current business climate.

Part Three presents some new models for viewing BI in terms of the new science as well as an organizational practice to support high adaptability. Chapter 8 looks at business analysis through the lens of systems thinking. Chapter 9 introduces Holacracy, an organizational practice that supports adaptability.

Part Four presents some possibilities beyond corporate borders, given the mastery of these essential competencies. It is a mixture of seeing the potential of Holacracy, the role of the visionary, and profiles of several amazing leaders that are working to make a difference.

Within each chapter, invited contributors offer a wealth of knowledge and experience through cutting-edge research or case studies. Further reading and resources for each of these areas are found in the appendixes.

Acknowledgments

First, I would like to thank all of the wonderful people who have encouraged me to continue exploring this knowledge over the last 20 years. I always appreciated knowing that I was not alone in my view that there must be a better way to be in the corporate world.

I want to give special thanks to Dr. Jacqueline Russell, who kept my body aligned after long hours of working each week and writing each weekend. You also helped me remove blocks that allowed my writing to flow more easily. Thanks to Barbara Friling for her healing gifts and vision for my successful completion. I want to give a heartfelt thanks to Jalma Marcus for her insights and inspiration that encouraged me to explore the world of organizational alignment and complexity science. I also appreciate her help with editing as well as her contributions. Thanks to Dr. Julie Roberts for her generosity in sharing her unpublished manuscript as well as continued encouragement. And finally, thanks to Dr. Caroline Bell for fabulous coaching that truly enhanced my self-discipline.

I thank all my contributors for their brilliant offerings and commitment to my vision. Thanks to my editors at John Wiley & Sons for their guidance, patience, and faith in me. And finally, thanks to Mike Foley and my coworkers at Cisco for their continued trust in me and the privilege to contribute to such an amazing company.

The Landscape

The Evolving Business Landscape

To say that we are living in uncertain times is an understatement. Never before has the rate of change been so swift and unrelenting. Business Intelligence, a term that encompasses all the capabilities required to turn data into intelligence, has emboldened companies to strive for the ultimate goal: getting the right information to the right people at the right time through the right channel. The result is an information explosion. New sources, channels, and applications are being created, automated, and accessed every day. This abundance of information and the new opportunities it creates places unprecedented pressure on companies to reexamine their organizational models. Traditional models of operation and styles of management often lack the agility and flexibility to fully leverage these new opportunities. This dilemma is not isolated to any one industry or geographic area. It affects companies in every industry around the globe.[1]

Most large companies have the desire to change. The typical approach is to start the process by reorganizing. The scenario is: Call a meeting; analyze the problem; assign responsibilities and accountabilities; and allocate resources to make the necessary changes. It was the old function-follows-form approach. When the need for change was occasional, this approach worked. In today's business environment, however, there are several obstacles to this approach.

The difficulty arises from the enormous complexity of redesigning processes, management structures, and measurement systems to accommodate a continuously changing business climate. And all this must be done while continuing to operate the business. Another challenge is

3

the uncertainty inherent in the climate. The organizational models that worked in the past are not flexible enough. How does a business organize to an unknown business landscape? And then how does it continue to adapt as the landscape evolves? In other words, how can we allow form to follow function?

The first step is to look at the way we define the organization. In some ways, the common definition does not fit our current landscape. For business, it implies a fixed entity made up of elements such as systems, standards, rules, and personnel designed to achieve a purpose or goal. Organizational change was a term to define the act of adjusting those elements to meet new business demands. This was adequate in an industrial economy. However, in today's service-oriented economy, it makes more sense to think of the organization as emergent.[2]

The organization that survives in the new business landscape will be flat, team-centered, and dynamic with a workforce that is self-reliant, internally motivated, and connected. According to *Fortune* magazine, the organization will be composed of

> a vertiginous pattern of constantly changing teams, task forces, partnerships and other informal structures . . . teams variously composed of shop-floor workers, managers, technical experts, suppliers and customers will join together to do a job and then disband, with everyone going off to the next assignment.[3]

To gain some perspective on the acceleration of change, consider some early inventions and the pace at which they influenced local and global economies. Historians tell us that the wheel was invented in one part of the world and used for hundreds of years before it gained universal acceptance. It took almost 100 years for the knowledge about the smelting of iron ore to move across one continent. Cultural traditions such as languages and social behaviors stayed localized for many centuries.

Compare that with a few decades ago when we landed on the moon. The knowledge of this historic achievement reached every point on the globe in 1.4 seconds. Today, when a new microchip is introduced, it gets implemented around the world within weeks. And of course, any new social or cultural idea can be transferred instantaneously through the Internet. Even the formation of life is being accelerated through genetic engineering.[4]

NAVIGATING UNCHARTED WATERS

The effect of constant change on a business can be daunting and stressful. However, understanding its underlying nature and accessing its power can unveil enormous opportunities.

In *The World Is Flat*, Thomas Friedman states that the rate of change we see today is

> happening at warp speed and directly or indirectly touching a lot more people on the planet at once. The faster and broader this transition to a new era, the more likely is the potential for disruption. To put it another way, the experiences of high-tech companies in the last few decades who failed to navigate the rapid changes brought about in their marketplace by these types of forces may be a warning to all the businesses, institutions, and nation-states that are now facing these inevitable, even predictable, changes but lack the leadership, flexibility, and imagination to adapt—not because they are not smart or aware, but because the speed of change is simply overwhelming them.[5]

Globalization is here to stay. Emerging markets in Asia, Africa, India, and South America offer new opportunities as well as competitive pressures as their economies expand their global reach. Global talent exchanges are leading to very diverse workforces.

Advances in technology over the last two decades have enabled companies to obtain, organize, analyze, store, and retrieve huge amounts of information. These capabilities allow instant communication and connection. As a result, consumers have more power to influence their buying experience than ever before. They can shop from markets anywhere in the world. As they gain access to global products and services, they demand better quality, lower prices, and faster delivery. Companies are feeling increased competition. Regulation is often insufficient and inconsistent. Corporate mergers and acquisitions are becoming more common as businesses look to expand and leverage new opportunities.

In his book, Friedman describes 10 events that flattened the world. In other words, these events enabled the creation of a truly global economy. These "flatteners" laid the groundwork for companies with viable Business Intelligence strategies to expand rapidly. As a result, they are able to make decisions faster and with more accuracy. However, the flattening effect also accelerated the need for new types of organization models to emerge, models that are agile, adaptable, and able to dynamically realign amid constant change.

Flattener 1. 11/9/89: When the Walls Came Down and the Windows Went Up

The collapse of the Berlin Wall marks the beginning of a major shift. Friedman describes how this event "tipped the balance of power across the world toward those advocating democratic, consensual, free–market-oriented governance, and away from those advocating authoritarian rule with centrally planned economies."[6] This shift had a cascading effect as it unleashed "enormous pent-up energies for hundred of millions of people in places like India, Brazil, China, and the former Soviet Empire."[7]

The power of this tremendous economic expansion served to further flatten societies within these countries by "strengthening those below and weakening those above."[8] It also "paved the way for the adoption of common standards—standards on how economies should be run, on how accounting should be done, on how banking should be conducted, on how PCs should be made, on how economics papers should be written."[9]

Just as these economies were hungry for communication, the IBM personal computer (PC), along with its Windows operating system, was ready for mass distribution. This just served to enhance the power of the individual at a time when the desire was at its peak. However, this platform has some architectural limits. The next flattening broke through those limits.

Flattener 2. 8/9/95: When Netscape Went Public

The shift from the PC-based platform to the Internet-based platform was the next big flattener. It takes little effort to imagine how organizations that use Business Intelligence would be different without this flattener. The shift to a seamless exchange of information greatly accelerated the transfer of information as well as the demand for the hardware and infrastructure to support it. The digitization of music, books, photos, and, of course, data are all instrumental in the birth of the Age of Information. This rapid expansion led to the dot-com bubble and hyperinvestment in the fiber-optic cable that turned Bangalore into a suburb of Boston. Each year, the technology at each end of the cable improves. So even after the bubble burst, the benefits are continuing.[10]

Flattener 3. Workflow Software—Let's Do Lunch: Have Your Application Talk to My Application

The next flattener is particularly powerful for the Business Intelligence community. Prior to the introduction of workflow software, the sales department recorded an order on paper, and then walked it over to the shipping department. Someone from the shipping department walked it over to the billing department, where an invoice was generated and mailed to the customer. Today, as a result of advances in workflow software along with data description languages such as XML and SLAP, every step in the sales process or any other process can be performed electronically from anywhere on the planet.

This shift has enabled the use of Business Intelligence on a global scale. The explosion in growth of companies like eBay and PayPal are showing the way. According to Friedman, this phase brings workflow automation to everyone's desktop. Workflow software connects existing Business Intelligence processes to optimize tasks, timing, and people.[11]

Flatteners 4 through 10

The remaining seven flatteners—open sourcing, outsourcing, off-shoring, supply-chaining, insourcing, in-forming, and the steroids—all share a common trait in that they take advantage of connectivity and virtual adjacencies to enable collaboration and resource sharing. To truly unleash their potential, these new capacities and capabilities demand a different type of organizational model.[12]

SHIFTING FROM REACTIVE TO PROACTIVE

Everything that has been called the IT Revolution these last 20 years— I am sorry to tell you . . . that was just the warm-up act . . . that was the forging, sharpening and distribution of the tools of collaboration. We find ourselves at the end of the beginning. What you are now about to see is the REAL IT revolution!

—CEO AT A MAJOR HIGH-TECH COMPANY

The explosion of Business Intelligence is changing the way companies operate on a day-to-day basis. Traditional approaches that forecast yearly demand and then plan production to balance inventories and budgets are being replaced by real-time sensors that continuously assess customers' needs and fill those needs at revolutionary speeds with a myriad of customized product and services. To quickly acquire the technological sophistication needed to operate at this level, many large companies that historically tried to do it all are now forming strategic partnerships or acquiring companies with complementary assets and competencies.

Over the last half century, many large industrial companies flourished within the make-and-sell paradigm. They are characterized by complex, top-down management structures with highly detailed annual budgeting systems and well-defined operational functions at every level. This structure enabled their factories to produce a variety of complex products, such as automobiles, computers, ships, and airplanes, on a massive scale with great efficiency. With such a history of success, it is difficult to look at a completely different model based on determining what the customer wants and then producing it.

In the last decade, the leading information technology (IT) firms have been the main ones to experience success in the new sense-and-respond model. Software, partially due to its virtual nature, is being developed with higher degrees of functionality and complexity in shorter and shorter time frames. The nonphysical nature of software products has also enabled developers to go one step further than "sense and respond." They have engaged virtual communities of users to literally participate in development. This preemptive feedback loop ensures that the end customer is getting what he or she wants.

STRATEGIES FOR CAPTURING VALUE

Given this relentless pressure to adapt our business models, companies are embracing innovative technologies and developing new strategies for capturing value.

Embracing the Power of the Network

The evolution of IT can be viewed as three overlapping organizational learning curves representing the introduction and maturation of three dominant technologies: centralized mainframe computers (the Data Processing Era), decentralized personal computers (the

*Microcomputer Era), and now interlinked networks of computers
(the Network Era).*

—STEPHEN P. BRADLEY AND RICHARD L. NOLAN,
SENSE & RESPOND: CAPTURING VALUE IN THE NETWORK ERA

The aforementioned "flattener," fiber-optic cables, along with broad-band and advanced routing and switching capabilities, is accelerating the move from the hierarchical organizational structure toward the more integrated network organizational structure of the future. This inte-grated structure opens up a lot of opportunities for gathering information outside the company walls through Web tracking and social network-ing. According to Stephen P. Bradley and Richard L. Nolan in *Sense & Respond*, companies can "go beyond the walls of their organizations to monitor their customers continuously, not merely sensing their needs but actually anticipating their unrecognized needs, developing new capabili-ties to meet those needs, customizing their offerings to micro-segments, and competing with each other on speed in delivering products and serv-ices."[13] These new insights invite companies to customize their offerings to niche markets and compete on speed. Many products are becoming commoditized while the ease of ordering and speed of delivery can com-mand higher prices. New and smaller companies now have an advan-tage to outperform their larger competitors. Again, this advantage leads to more collaborative partnerships, mergers, and acquisitions.

Discovering New Business Opportunities

Several years ago, Lester Thurow made this observation and posed sev-eral timely questions: "The old foundations of success are gone. For all of human history the source of success has been controlling natural resources—land, gold, oil. Suddenly the answer is 'knowledge.' The king of the knowledge economy, Bill Gates, owns no land, no gold or oil, no industrial process. How does one use knowledge to build wealth? How do societies have to be reorganized to generate a wealth-enhancing knowledge environment? How do they incubate the entrepreneurs nec-essary to bring about change and create wealth? What skills are needed? The knowledge-based economy is asking new questions, giving new answers, and developing new rules for success."[14]

This statement highlights several important characteristics of the information economy. The assets themselves are often intangible. This inherent instability makes the market even more volatile. Early movers such as America Online were able to gain a strong foothold by giving away their software and charging a monthly fee for their service. But within a few years, market pressures forced them to change their model. Luckily, they have been able to adapt and maintain their value. Other companies, such as Bloomberg, Dow-Jones, Reuters, and Quote.com, provide real-time, aggregated data for the financial services industry. News is delivered from every major news source through the Internet. And blogs have becomes sources of news as well as forums for questioning the veracity of information.

Many back-office and outsourcing businesses have grown out of virtual connectivity. Services such as bookkeeping and answering the phone that were historically performed within the same building are now done in other cities or continents. Today, some are surprised to learn that most taxes are prepared and X-rays are read in India.

Morphing Current Businesses

Many traditional businesses are adapting their business models based on customer behavior. Amazon.com, the online bookseller, has grown into an Internet giant while many brick-and-mortar bookstores have closed. The publishing world has seen a change as authors enter the market independently using print-on-demand services.

Many small businesses are now gaining access to world markets. And larger, more established retail businesses, especially those with a traditional catalog presence, are creating sophisticated shopping experiences for their customers on the Web.[15]

Why are Amazon.com, Lexus, and Disney partnering with lesser-known online companies to sell products? According to *Wired* magazine's Ian Mount, the large companies are moving toward the manufacturing-as-a-service model to stay competitive. It has become necessary to compete with the small entrepreneurs who are producing and distributing products on demand. The production of products has become a commodity. Because of the low cost of entry, anyone with a good idea can compete in this market.

New businesses that leverage this model are popping up everywhere, and many have global reach. Jeffrey Wegesin, a furniture designer, advertises his designs on the Web. Upon receiving an order, he contracts with an on-demand manufacturing service in New Zealand to create and ship each piece. He has no inventory or other up-front costs. His business is pure profit.

Designers of clothing, jewelry, robots, you name it! The model is inherently charming because of its efficiency and simplicity. Individual musicians and authors can market their goods without any up-front investment. With little more than a product idea and a good design, anyone can become an instapreneur.[16]

MOTIVATION FOR CHANGE

> *Clearly the first 40 years of the computing revolution have been a
> preamble. Much greater changes lie just ahead. The marriage of computer
> and communication networks is transforming most aspects of business and
> consumer activities. Organizations face enormous changes, many occurring
> simultaneously.*

—DONALD TAPSCOTT, *BLUEPRINT TO THE DIGITAL ECONOMY*

Seven Realities that Jeopardize Business Survival

In *Information Revolution*, Jim Davis, Gloria J. Miller, and Allan Russell discuss the "seven realities that jeopardize business survival."[17] Each reality illuminates the need for new business models as well as styles of leadership.

Business Reality 1: Business Cycles Are Shrinking   In today's Web-enabled economy, speed within all parts of the business model is the great differentiator. To accommodate changing markets and consumer preferences, product development and testing that used to take years has been shrunk to months or even weeks. Today, the first to market often enjoys the competitive edge.

This shortened cycle challenges managers to make decisions with less time for consideration or analysis. As a result, they must depend on a combination of accurate, actionable information and intuition. And their decision must be in alignment with the overall strategy of the company.

Business Reality 2: You Can Only Squeeze so Much Juice Out of an Orange   The goal of improving operational efficiency drove a majority of the investment in the last decade. Initially the returns were high and provided a competitive advantage. However, now that enterprise resource planning (ERP) software is available, the field has been leveled. The next step is greater innovation and agility.

Business Reality 3: The Rules Have Changed; There Is No More "Business as Usual"   The days of following a typical path to business success are over. The same factors apply: profitability, customer satisfaction, stakeholder value, and competition. However, the path to success is very different and is fraught with new challenges:

- Mergers and acquisitions have hindered agility and cohesiveness.
- Productivity advancements have increased expectations from both customers and management.
- Advancements in IT have overwhelmed the abilities of some companies to manage and leverage the knowledge.
- The technologies that were introduced as the key to success often failed because the human issues were overlooked.

Business Reality 4: The Only Constant Is Permanent Volatility   This is a common theme but bears repeating: The company that is most agile and adaptable will gain and maintain a competitive advantage. Instead of just relying on past results to predict the future, companies need to tap into current trends through social networking, Web analysis, and employee feedback.

Business Reality 5: Globalization Helps and Hurts   Globalization presents many advantages, especially to small companies seeking a worldwide presence. Any company that is connected to the Web can strategically partner, outsource, or insource with relative ease. The downside is increased complexity when dealing with international languages, standards, and cultures. Strong communication skills are essential for navigating this terrain.

Business Reality 6: The Penalties of Not Knowing Are Harsher than Ever   In the new era of billion-dollar corporate scandals, personal accountability at the highest levels is not only prudent, it is now legally mandated. The Sarbanes-Oxley Act was designed to systematize ethical behavior. In addition to the need for strong, honest leadership, information systems to handle this complex business data are essential.

Business Reality 7: Information Is Not a By-Product of Business; It Is the Lifeblood of Business   The seventh business reality is a direct result of the first six. Due to shrinking business cycles, level playing fields, changing rules, volatility, globalization, and the cost of ignorance, information has become the lifeblood of many businesses. Today, accurate, accessible, actionable information is necessary to compete in the global economy. There are strong pressures to achieve more results while spending less time and money. Companies need up-to-the-minute information about their customers, suppliers, competitors, and markets.

These realities also point to the need for new business models as well as visionary leadership. With the complexity of business today, decisioning throughout the entire organization has to operate like a well-oiled machine.

Parts Two and Three expand on optimal organizational structures as well as the core competencies, or success factors, necessary to operate at this level.

Information Evolution Model

As companies build their infrastructure and move into more sophisticated levels of Business Intelligence, certain human and organizational competencies are critical to success. These core competencies are discussed within the context of the Information Evolution model described by Davis, Miller, and Russell in *Information Revolution*. The model is based on the belief that a company's success is a function of its infrastructure, process, people, and culture. The model presents a phased maturation of an organization through evolutionary stages.[18]

To unveil the subtleties of the Information Evolution model, each level is examined over four major dimensions:

1. *Infrastructure.* This dimension addresses all of the hardware, software, and networking tools and technologies that handle every phase of the information process. The assessment, purchase, implementation, and use of these components should be part of the overall Business Intelligence strategy. Therefore, a high level of clarity is required in the communication of needs and intentions to ensure that all decisions are optimal.

2. *Knowledge process.* This dimension focuses on the strategic as well as specific uses of the information infrastructure. Included are the policies, best practices, standards, and governance of all aspects of the information cycle. Also included are performance metrics, reward systems, and the commitment to strategic use of information at the highest levels. For this dimension to operate smoothly, a cohesive, collaborative leadership team is essential.

3. *Human capital.* This dimension speaks directly to the success factors, as it is defined by the level of competency of every employee along with the hiring practices and the training and evaluation systems established by the company.

4. *Culture.* Within the Information Evolution model, this dimension is defined as the "organizational and human influences on information flow—the moral, social, and behavioral norms of corporate culture (as evidenced by the attitudes, belief, and priorities of its members) related to information as a long-term strategic asset."[19] When considering culture in terms of the success factors, this dimension is broadened to include organizational and human influences on every activity within the company.

The five levels of the Information Evolution model are hierarchical and reflect aspects of maturity across the four dimensions. Generally, companies fluctuate within different levels across the four dimensions during this evolution. The five levels of the Information Evolution model are operational, consolidation, integration, optimization, and innovation.

According to Davis, Miller, and Russell, 70 percent of today's organizations are operating below Level 3. Future competitive pressures deem it necessary to develop the competencies and achieve the strategic alignment required to evolve to Level 3 and beyond.

Level 1: The Operational Enterprise Most small businesses, start-ups, and silo-based companies operate at this level. The *knowledge process* is uniquely individual, which allows "information mavericks" to emerge. With a focus on day-to-day tactics, information access, analysis, and implementation are not standardized. Information management positions are structured to compete. Job security is gained through individual control.

Level 1 people (*human capital*) tend to thrive in unstructured environments. The information technicians are often self-motivated risk takers. They tend to strive for differentiation and recognition, which might serve a company that is still operating at an entrepreneurial level. However, they resist change and loss of control, which may inhibit maturing to the next level.

Level 1 *culture* is well suited for charismatic leaders and self-starters. There is little consistency in how information is shared or used. With the right talent, a business can thrive at this level up to a certain point or in a limited market. As it tries to grow, the individual focus can lead to inefficiencies, redundancies, and errors. Since there is little intention to coordinate silos, alignment does not play an important role. Skills in social interaction and teamwork are of little value.

Level 2: The Consolidated Enterprise Organizations at this level have integrated information management within a silo or department. Typically, knowledge processes are optimized to support operations within the functional areas.

Level 2 *infrastructure* features all data management hardware and software that is designed to optimize information and decision processes at a departmental level. Departmental discrepancies and duplication of effort are common pitfalls.

Level 2 *knowledge process* supports decision-making at the department level. This may result in inconsistencies and suboptimal outcomes on an enterprise level.

Level 2 *human capital* and *culture* dimensions are not managed with an intention toward integration. Teamwork may be encouraged in small, homogenous areas, but strategic and interdepartmental collaborative efforts are challenged by the competitive structure of the organization. Communication may also be challenging without the benefit of a shared vision or enterprise-level goals.

Level 3: The Integrated Enterprise   An enterprise-wide approach to data management and decisioning characterizes organizations at this level. Integrated knowledge systems generate value by standardizing processes that promote coordinated marketing efforts. Resources are mobilized around market and customer relationships that optimize long-term value.

Level 3 *infrastructure* features a seamless, enterprise-wide system of hardware, software, and networking that supports data reporting, analysis, and auditing while delivering a single version of the truth.

Level 3 *knowledge process* enables the company to optimize reporting and analysis to meet enterprise-wide goals and objectives. The focus shifts from a product focus to a customer or market focus with emphasis on relationships and long-term value. All information access and quality is aligned and standardized. Performance management is automated. This level of interdepartmental cooperation requires highly developed communication and collaboration skills.

Level 3 *people* are able to balance their departmental goals with those of the enterprise. Their holistic view and emotional intelligence allows them to contribute to and champion the efforts of enterprise.

Level 3 *culture* views Business Intelligence as a corporate asset and essential strategy. Training and organizational development focus on the importance of enterprise-wide access and intelligent use of information.

As the gains of rapid decision-making, enhanced customer relationships, and shorter time to market are realized, alignment become crucial as departments strive to coordinate the actions to achieve enterprise goals. As the enterprise promotes cross-functional collaboration, competencies in the areas of communication and collaboration become even more critical.

Level 4: The Optimized Enterprise   Adaptability is the distinguishing competency of organizations at this level. The ability to constantly realign with changing markets allows Level 4 organizations to maintain a competitive edge.

Level 4 *infrastructure* enhances Level 3 by linking internal business systems across the supply chain, from back-office functions through customer touch points. This enhances communications, data exchange, and connection to partners and customers across functional areas.

Level 4 *knowledge process* focuses on bringing the information systems to a higher level of quality, access, and relevance. All work-flow patterns have been modeled across the entire information value chain to optimize continuous measurement, decision-making, and real-time analytics leading to consistent and immediate customer response. Closed-loop feedback processes ensure continuous evaluation and improvement.

Level 4 *people* have many similarities to the people in Level 1. They are independent, adaptable, innovative, and driven, and take calculated risks. However, their approach to the organization is more holistic. They, along with their peers, are focused on enterprise-level goals. So along with being innovative and adaptable, they must be highly skilled in the areas of communication and collaboration.

Level 4 *culture* empowers individuals across the organization to take on leadership roles. Along with access to rich quantitative information, they are given the autonomy to continuously fine-tune the business model by making incremental improvements. Doing this requires clear communication of the goals and vision from top management as well as the willingness and skills to collaborate and share ideas across departments. Change-readiness is an inherent part of the culture.

Level 5: The Adaptive, Innovating Enterprise   Innovation is the distinguishing competency of organizations at this level. These organizations are continuously seeking ways to reinvent and transform their value proposition. This proactive model, based on Business Intelligence and creative energy, allows organizations to stay continuously competitive.

Level 5 *infrastructure* is designed to be an "intelligence architecture" with the ability to integrate and expand quickly and seamlessly based on the needs of the organization. An advanced combination of analytic tools allows new ideas to be tested and perfected in a virtual environment, thus reducing the time to market. Innovation is systematically fostered and supported through information access and sharing.

Level 5 *knowledge process* is designed to encourage innovation at the highest levels. Extensive analytics are used to model the future while minimizing risk. As a way of stimulating new ideas, collaboration is encouraged and facilitated on an enterprise-wide basis. The entire innovation process is documented, analyzed, and communicated throughout the organization.

Level 5 *people* are whole-brain thinkers (described in Chapter 2). With a keen eye for the bottom line (left brain), they are proactive, creative thinkers (right brain). They thrive on juggling many roles and activities. They actually enjoy change and get bored if things start to feel stagnant. They know that their competitors are able to reach Level 4 with cutting-edge technology. But at Level 5, they can always outpace their competitors by continuing to innovate.

Level 5 *culture* embraces whole-brain thinking. All ideas, even the most absurd, are encouraged. Processes are designed to facilitate creativity and support an intuitive flow of ideas. Constant change is the norm. Inquiry and collaboration as tools for innovation are embedded in all aspects of the Information Model to ensure sustainable and consistent success.

According to Davis, Miller, and Russell, no organization has truly reached Level 5. Some have pockets of Level 5 competencies, but most organizations find it difficult to deal with constant change.[20]

The Evolving Organization

In the mid-1990s, an issue of Fortune magazine had an unusually arresting cover. It was two pictures, actually one above the other. The upper picture was a group of half-dozen or so men in bathing suits, sitting disconsolately with their backs to each other on a raft-like contraction that was obviously sinking. The picture below it was of a similar group on a raft, only this time they were happily facing each other as they paddled their buoyant and well-constructed craft across a lake.

The story inside was about new ways of conducting executive development programs in corporations. The two groups on the cover were all executives from one Fortune 50 company. They had each been given identical sets of materials and time limits to build a raft that would take them across the lake. There was only one difference: To build their raft, one team was required to follow all of the company's policies about new product development, planning, budgeting, and organizational structure. The other team—the happy crew of the seaworthy raft—had been left free to proceed in the best way they saw fit.

—PETER VAILL, FOREWORD TO EDWIN E. OLSEN
AND GLENDA H. EOYANG, *FACILITATING ORGANIZATIONAL CHANGE*

The lesson from this exercise is described succinctly by Peter Vaill in the foreword of Edwin E. Olsen and Glenda H. Eoyang's book *Facilitating Organizational Change*:

> The lessons are about the power of participation; about the energy that is released when command-control top-down management is reduced or removed; about the innovations that emerge when formal structures are made more flexible and responsive; and about the capacity of teams to gel around a shared vision and to exhibit extraordinary determination to fulfill that vision.[21]

This creative exercise easily illustrates the limitations and risks of a highly regimented management style. While it may be difficult to pinpoint each team to a level on the Information Evolution model, it is easy to determine which management style is more suitable for a highly volatile business environment.

So what impedes a company from reaching Level 5? What does a company need to address? How can it transform to support this evolution? New models from science and nature are emerging that offer understanding and frameworks for creating and managing a company that is adaptable and innovative.

▧ NOTES

1. Gloria J. Miller, Dagmar Bräutigam, and Stefanie V. Gerlach, *Business Intelligence Competency Centers* (Hoboken, NJ: John Wiley & Sons, 2006), 3.
2. Stephan H. Haeckel, *Managing the Information Intensive Firm* (Boston: Harvard Business School Press, 1994), 340–342.
3. Brian Dumaine, "The Bureaucracy Busters," *Fortune*, June 17, 1991.
4. Dee Hock, "Transformation by Design," *What Is Enlightenment*, No. 22 (Fall/Winter 2002), 132.
5. Thomas Friedman, *The World Is Flat* (New York: Farrar, Straus and Giroux, 2005), 46.

6. *Id.*, 49.
7. *Id.*, 51.
8. *Id.*, 51.
9. *Id.*, 52.
10. *Id.*, 56–58.
11. *Id.*, 71–73.
12. *Id.*, 81–172.
13. Stephen P. Bradley and Richard L. Nolan, "Capturing Value in the Network Era," in *Sense & Respond: Capturing Value in the Network Era*, ed. Bradley and Nolan (Boston: Harvard Business School Press, 1998), 7–8.
14. Lester Thurow, "Building Wealth," *The Atlantic*, June 1999, http://www.theatlantic.com/issues/99jun/9906thurow.htm.
15. Bradley and Nolan, *Capturing Value in the Network Era*, 7-8.
16. Ian Mount, "Upside of the Downturn: 5. The Rise of the Instapreneur: Manufacture and Sell Anything in Minutes," *Wired* (April 2008), 129.
17. Jim Davis, Gloria J. Miller, and Allan Russell, *Information Revolution* (Hoboken, NJ: John Wiley & Sons, 2006), xv.
18. Donald Tapscott, *Blueprint to the Digital Economy* (San Francisco: McGraw-Hill, 1998), 1.
19. Davis, Miller, and Russell, *The Information Revolution* 13.
20. *Id.*, 11–23.
21. Edwin E. Olsen and Glenda H. Eoyang, *Facilitating Organizational Change* (San Francisco: Jossey-Bass/Pfieffer, 2001), xxiii–xxiv.

CHAPTER 2

Models from Science and Nature

If we, on our most fundamental level, are packets of quantum energy constantly exchanging information with this heaving energy sea, it means that all of us connect with each other and the world at the level of the very undercoat of our being. It also means that we have the power to access much more information about the world than we realize.

—LYNN McTAGGART, *LIVING THE FIELD*

The seemingly continuous creation, destruction, and evolution of organizational frameworks are best understood by exploring models in science and nature. When examining the underlying principles, there are many parallels to models in physics, biology (living systems, ecology, and evolution), and complexity theory. In an attempt to explain what we are experiencing—constant change, chaos, and unpredictability—the new scientific models challenge us to rethink how we view organizations and ourselves as leaders. "'The New Science,' a radical shift in our world view, is replacing the image of organizations as machines with a living systems model that offers awe, creativity, and greater cosmological connection."[1]

QUANTUM PHYSICS

Quantum theory introduces yet another level of paradox into our search for order. At the quantum level we observe a world where change happens in jumps, beyond our powers of precise prediction. This world has also challenged our beliefs about objective measurement, for at the subatomic level the observer cannot observe anything without interfering or, more importantly, participating in its creation. The strange qualities of the quantum world, and especially its influence in shaking our beliefs in determinism, predictability, and control, don't seem to offer any hope for a more orderly universe. But our inability to predict individual occurrences at the quantum level is not a result of the inherent disorder. Instead the results we observe speak to a level of quantum interconnectedness, of a deep order that we are only beginning to sense. There is a constant weaving of relationships, of energies that merge and change, of constant ripples that occur within a seamless fabric. There is so much order that our attempts to separate out discrete moments create the appearance of disorder.

—MARGARET WHEATLEY, *LEADERSHIP AND THE NEW SCIENCE*

Right now, scientists are debating two worldviews, one offered by classical physics and the other offered by quantum physics. Classical physics, based on Newton's laws of gravity and motion, states that all objects move in three-dimensional space across the dimension of time. Matter is considered solid, with fixed boundaries. Heat, cold, and force from another object are the only influences that can affect change.

These theories form the basis of our philosophical view of the world—namely, that we live in a physical universe and things exist independently of each other. However, these theories began to unravel in the early twentieth century, when a few quantum physics pioneers were able to peek inside some of the tiniest bits of the universe. They discovered that subatomic particles were not solid and stable. In fact, they appeared to be tiny clouds of probability or simply potential of their future selves. They finally determined that a quantum particle was not just a particle, nor was it just a wave; it was both.

Quantum physics explores the world of the subatomic particles of light: atoms, electrons, photons, and protons. It also explores the larger world of lasers, neutron stars, and physical and biological systems. Max Planck (1858–1947) pioneered quantum theory in 1900 with the idea that energy exchange is "discrete," that reality is composed of discrete "quanta." This discreteness may not be visible to the naked eye, but it exists nonetheless.

The smallest unit of energy in a given subatomic event is called a quantum. Observations of subatomic particles reveal that energy moves from one orbit to another in "quantum leaps." The distance they jump is determined by how much "quanta" (plural for quantum) of energy they contain. Later, these little packets of energy were called photons. Niels Bohr, Werner Heisenberg, Ernest Rutherford, and Erwin Schrodinger were a few of quantum physics' pioneers. Albert Einstein also did much to pioneer the new science, although he had difficulty accepting quantum theory.

Physical science is based on a world made up of atoms. Atoms are very, very small—one breath contains about 1 million billion billion atoms. To understand this microscopic world, it is helpful to picture an atom as a minute solar system. There is a nucleus that is made up of protons and neutrons, and it is surrounded by electrons that orbit the nucleus in its stable position. Electrical forces bind the system together much like gravity binds our solar system together.

When atoms become unstable, for whatever reason, electrons move to different orbits. When an electron jumps to a different orbit, light is emitted with a certain frequency (which determines its color). Electrons interact by exchanging photons, which are particles of light. If an electron absorbs a photon, it gets an energy boost, which moves it to a new place. If it discharges a photon, it recoils, which also lands it in a new place. The movements that occur at the quantum level are random and unpredictable.[2]

The theories of Bohr, Heisenberg, and other quantum physicists completely contradicted the Newtonian view of matter as discrete, self-contained, and independent. In fact, they suggested that at its most fundamental level, matter cannot be separated into independent units, nor can it be independently observed. "Things had no meaning in isolation; they had meaning only in a web of dynamic interrelationships."[3]

Another surprising and important discovery is the ability of quantum particles to influence each other, regardless of their position. If quantum particles were ever in contact with each other and then separated, they maintained influence on each other across vast distances. In fact, at a subatomic level they continue to exchange little packets of vibrating energy. "The universe was not a storehouse of static, separate objects, but a single organism of interconnected energy fields in a continuous state of becoming."[4]

Experiments in the 1990s demonstrated that the amount of energy contained in a photon is uncertain, and this uncertainty allows it to pop in and out of existence. Photons and protons can collide in this state and create a rain of particles. So it appears that light shifts from matter and back to light, again demonstrating the *both/and* orientation. This actually follows relationship logic because light is both particles *and* waves, but it surely seems contrary and inconceivable from a rational, Newtonian, empirical point of view.

Another interesting observation of quantum systems shows us that electrons and photons shift as they interact with the environment. Experiments that dramatically demonstrate this are the famous two-slit experiments. These experiments are conducted by emitting photons from a precision light source. The photons are shot at a screen that has two slits in it, through which the photons travel. On the other side of the screen are measuring devices to observe the photons, either particle detectors or a wave detector. If particle detectors are used for observation, the photons travel through *one* of the slits. However, if the photons are measured collectively with a screen, the photons travel through *both* of the slits and are registered as waves.

Quantum experiments demonstrate the relationship between what is observed and the observer—that the presence of the researcher has an impact on the results of the experiment. Before the photons in the experiment are measured, they are neither waves nor particles, although they have the potential to be both. The way the experiment is set up (with devices that detect either particles or waves) calls forth either one response or the other. The response is based on the way that the experimenter decides to look at the experiment.

The results of these experiments, replicated over and over and in many different ways, indicate that electrons and photons interact constantly with their environment, changing as a result of this interaction with their surroundings. Subatomic particles have little meaning in isolation—they can be fully understood only as interconnections or correlations. The analogy is that, in the physical world, relationships determine who we are and interaction with others impacts our identity and our behavior.[5]

What brings energy into form, based on quantum physics, is the involvement of the observer. In her 2007 book, Lynn McTaggart recalls the results of an experiment, "The moment we looked at an electron or took a measurement, it appeared that we helped to determine its final state. This suggested that the most essential ingredient in creating our universe is the consciousness that observed it. Several of the central figures in quantum physics argued that the universe was democratic and participatory—a joint effort between the observer and observed."[6]

For over 30 years, prestigious scientific institutions around the world have been proving that our thoughts have their own energy, with the power to influence our environment. In other words, our thoughts are capable of affecting everything from the simplest machines to the most complex living beings.

If the observer affects reality or what comes into form, this suggests that nothing in the universe exists independent of our perception. It suggests that our very consciousness creates our reality. This concept presents a conundrum for mainstream scientists whose current scientific view of consciousness, based on the theories of seventeenth-century philosopher René Descartes, is that mind is separate and different from matter and that our consciousness is limited to the physical brain. However, quantum theory is mathematically verifiable. And it is very successful at explaining the subatomic world. It is the basis for the atom bomb and lasers, which makes it hard to ignore. But because its implications are unsettling at a larger level, mainstream scientists have generally ignored quantum physics as it relates to our perception of the world.

Quantum Organizations

In the quantum world, there is a question of whether there is more influence from the system or the individual. According to Wheatley's interpretation of the quantum world, the answer is "It depends." This speaks to the fluctuating nature of this new paradigm. "What is critical is the *relationship* created between the person and the setting. That relationship will always be different, will always evoke different potentialities. It all depends on the players and the moment."[7]

This concept has powerful implications for how we structure and run our businesses. If the focus of a business is manufacturing with stable production cycles and markets, then control is advantageous if not essential. However, in most Business Intelligence (BI)–intensive companies, the organizational structures are based on ever-changing products and markets. Instead of seeking control, adaptability becomes essential. If the company adopts a top-down, Newtonian style of management in all arenas, it cannot adapt quickly enough to changes in the market.

However, to see organizations from a quantum viewpoint, it is clear that new models, skills, and competencies are needed. Rather than telling people what to do, management will need to clearly communicate the purpose of the business and facilitate processes to achieve that purpose. Management will accomplish this through interactions via strong relationships. Each group or team will become its own entity as it creates a strategy to work toward the goal. The team, the department, the individual will reach its goals by birthing ideas, nurturing these ideas, and watching them grow. The loner or rugged individual will not have the same role in this new model. Instead, he or she will act like an unstable particle that destabilizes the structure for a while. The new energy this creates will stimulate innovation and the need for the reevaluation of many assumptions. At this point, the need for clarity of language and effective facilitation are paramount.

Relationships fuel the energy of the organization. These relationships are enabled through face-to-face contact as well as phone and Internet. However, with or without being conscious of it, employees have a relationship through the quantum field. If organizational leaders understand this fact and create an environment of connection and focus, the interconnectedness can be leveraged in very positive ways. These concepts are developed more thoroughly in Part Two.

EVOLUTIONARY BIOLOGY AND LIVING SYSTEMS

Nature gives us a perfect model of a living system that is constantly evolving and adapting. Every part is interconnected. There is no central control. Power is dispersed throughout the system, which gives it resiliency and flexibility. As a connected system, it easily adapts to change.

Organizations have this same capacity. Understanding what is possible gives rise to amazing potential.

Hive Mind

As we seek to understand how people connect within organizations, we find evidence of the quantum field in nature. Consider what biologists call "hive mind." It describes the seemingly invisible interconnectedness of a swarm of bees. It also explains how a flock of birds can fly in perfect formation or a school of fish can turn at once as if following an external cue. This excerpt from Kevin Kelly's *Out of Control* describes an experience of 20,000 people connecting through hive mind.

In a darkened Las Vegas conference room, a cheering audience waves cardboard wands in the air. Each one is red on one side, green on the other. Far in back of the huge auditorium, a camera scans the frantic attendees. The video camera links the color spots of the wands to a nest of computers set up by graphics wizard Loren Carpenter. Carpenter's custom software locates each red and each green wand in the auditorium. Tonight there was just shy of 5,000 wandwavers. The computer displays the precise location of each wand (and its color) onto an immense, detailed video map of the auditorium hung on the front stage, which all can see. More importantly, the computer counts the total red or green wands and uses that value to control software. As the audience waves the wands, the display screen shows a sea of lights dancing crazily in the dark, like a candlelight parade gone punk. The viewers see themselves on the map: they are either a red or green pixel. By flipping their own wands, they can change the color of their projected pixels instantly.

Loren Carpenter boots up the ancient video game of Pong onto the immense screen. Pong was the first commercial video game to reach pop consciousness. It's a minimalist arrangement: a white dot bounces inside a square: two movable rectangles on each side act as virtual paddles. In short, electronic ping-pong. In this version, displaying the red side of your wand moves the paddle up. Green moves it down. More precisely, the Pong paddle moves as the average number of red wands in the auditorium increases or decreases. Your wand is just one vote.

Carpenter doesn't need to explain very much. Every attendee at this 1991 conference of computer graphic experts was probably once hooked on Pong. His amplified voice booms in the hall, "Okay guys. Folks on the left side of the auditorium control the left paddle. Folks on the right side control the right paddle. If you think you are on the left, then you really are. Okay Go!"

The audience roars in delight. Without a moment's hesitation, 5,000 people are playing a reasonably good game of Pong. Each move of the paddles is the average of several thousand players' intentions. The sensation is unnerving. The paddle usually does what you intend, but not always. When it doesn't you find yourself spending as much attention trying to anticipate the paddle as the incoming ball. One is definitely aware of another intelligence online: it's this hollering mob.

The group mind plays Pong so well that Carpenter decides to up the ante. Without warning the ball bounces faster. The participants squeal in unison. In a second or two, the mob has adjusted to the quicker pace and is playing better than before. Carpenter speeds up the game further; the mob learns instantly.

Kelly goes on to describe the audience's experience with forming numbers as well as flying, rolling, and landing a jet. He then relates it to nature:

The conferences did what birds do: they flocked. But they flocked self-consciously. They responded to an overview of themselves as they co-formed a "5" or steered the jet. A bird on the fly, however, has no overarching concept of the shape of its flock. "Flockness" emerges from creatures completely oblivious of their collective shape, size, or alignment. A flocking bird is blind to the grace and cohesiveness of a flock in flight.[8]

In almost all organizations, the power of this interconnectedness is a huge untapped resource. Interconnectedness may be a function of the age of the company or a result of many years of consistent teams. With today's changing workforce, it is even more imperative that companies are conscious of this interconnectedness and know how to leverage it.

Collective Wisdom

Another benefit of this interconnectedness is the ability of a group to unveil the truth. Considerable research shows how groups of people, when asked a question, often get the wrong answer a majority of the time. But many times the average of the answers is very close to the truth. Interest in this research emerged as a result of an innocent experiment by an arrogant scientist.

In 1906, the British scientist Francis Galton set out to a country fair to gather data for his research. He had dedicated his life to two areas: the measurement of physical and mental qualities, and breeding. His interest was driven by his opinion that very few people had the intelligence and wisdom to keep societies healthy. His extensive experiments left him believing in "the stupidity and wrong-headedness of many men and women being so great as to be scarcely credible."[9]

While strolling around the fair, Galton came across a competition: Pay a small fee, guess the weight of an ox, and win prizes. Based on his evaluation of the crowd, Galton surmised that the average of the guesses would be way off. To verify his hypothesis, Galton borrowed the tickets from the organizer and ran a series of statistical tests. The average weight determined by 787 guesses came to 1,197. The correct weight was 1,198. Galton writes later, "The result seems more creditable to the trustworthiness of a democratic judgment than might have been expected."[10]

Translate this to tasks within an organization. Based on this theory, employees could predict the number of widgets their company is going to sell in the next year. Or the probability that a drug will be approved by the Food and Drug Administration. Or the amount of total sales a team will bring in over the next year. Companies that solicit feedback are tapping into a wealth of knowledge, not just from each individual but from the collective wisdom.

Our Evolving Brain

Many of the stresses we experience in our lives come from a gap between what our culture requires of us and the structure of our brain. Our brain's structure has stayed the same for 50,000 years, while the number of tasks we must do in a day, the number of social interactions we experience, and the amount of information we must process has increased exponentially. Cultural evolution is much faster than biological evolution.

The way to close the gap is to work with and develop our brain to adapt to the challenges of modern life. Fortunately, neuroscience shows this is possible through the brain's "plasticity"—its ability to change its actual structure with experience. We can train our brain to have greater attention capacity, to hold more in working and long-term memory, to process information more efficiently, to maintain a state of relaxed productivity, and even to experience time differently. What it takes is practice.

—ANDREA SULLIVAN, *BRAINSTRENGTH SYSTEMS*

The human brain is one of the most complex, if not *the* most complex, entity in the universe. "The typical brain consists of some 100 billion cells, each of which connects and communicates with up to 10,000 of its colleagues. Together they forge an elaborate network of some one quadrillion (1,000,000,000,000,000) connections that guides how we talk, eat, breathe, and move."[11]

The National Institutes of Health declared the 1990s to be the decade of the brain. The first half of the twenty-first century is the age of brain–mind science.[12]

It is common knowledge that the brain has two hemispheres. For many years, scientists believed that the left brain—the rational, analytical, and logical half—set humans apart from animals because it contains the language center. The right brain, characterized as mute, instinctual, and nonlinear, was considered something that humans no longer needed.

In the 1950s, a Caltech professor named Roger W. Sperry unveiled that in fact the right brain was "the superior cerebral member when it came to performing certain kinds of mental tasks. . . . There appear to be two modes of thinking represented rather separately in the left and right hemispheres, respectively."[13] The left brain functions sequentially and excels at analysis. The right brain operates holistically, reads emotions, and recognizes patterns. Based on more recent research and the experience of Dr. Jill Bolte Taylor, a neuroanatomist, the right brain may be what allows us to access more expansive thinking or hive mind.[14]

The effective use of both hemispheres is necessary to survive in our rapidly evolving business landscape. The ability to quickly make good decisions is a competitive advantage. This ability taps into what researchers call the "adaptive unconscious." It is like a giant computer that integrates a lot of data very quickly. The adaptive unconscious has allowed us to survive as a species. And now it can be leveraged for organizational survival.[15]

The frontal lobes, a more recent evolutionary addition, are considered to hold the chief executive position in the brain. "As the seat of intentionality, foresight, and planning, the frontal lobes are the most uniquely 'human' of all the components of the human brain."[16]

Most recently, the frontal lobes have been the subject of intense scientific research. While much of the functioning is still unexplained, it has been determined that "the prefrontal cortex plays a central role in forming goals and objectives and then in devising plans of action required to implement the plans, coordinate these skills, and applies them in a correct order. Finally, the prefrontal cortex is responsible for evaluating our actions as success or failure relative to our intentions."[17]

The frontal lobes have great cognitive power that allows humans to look to the future and be proactive. This power gives humans the ability to seek goals, make plans, dream—basically conjure up and manipulate models to represent and predict the future. "[T]he generative power of language to create new constructs may depend on this ability as well. The ability to manipulate and recombine internal representations critically depends on the prefrontal cortex, and the emergence of this ability parallels the evolution of the frontal lobes. If there is such a thing as 'the language instinct' it may be related to the emergence, late in evolution, of the functional properties of the frontal lobes."[18]

More insights into the brain are discussed in Chapter 5.

COMPLEXITY SCIENCE AND CHAOS

Our global ecosystem is a superb example of a highly adaptable evolutionary system.

> Order arises spontaneously all the time from complex, irregular, and chaotic states of matter. It is no accident that the chaos of the Big Bang evolved into atoms, molecules, elements, stars, and galaxies; it is no accident that life eventually organized into cells, tissues, organs, organisms, species, and ecological communities. A defining feature of complexity is that order arises naturally from the evolution of vast aggregates of simple subunits.[19]

Evolution is a process that is both open and decentralized. Our ecosystem is always importing energy from the environment and exporting entropy (the inverse of a system's ability to change).

> Open systems, which receive energy from the outside, tend to produce order, not disorder; they self-organize. Interactions among a collection of objects tend to produce aggregates that have stable spatial patterns or temporal rhythms. Higher-order behaviors emerge from the interactions of many simple components, and they do so without a central controller. No agent does the organizing; structure arises even

though none of the interacting units has a plan or a goal for how the overall system should behave.[20]

In order to remain viable and strong, our ecosystem does not seek equilibrium, which is, by definition, a state that leads to contraction and eventual death. "In classical thermodynamics, equilibrium is the end state in the evolution of isolated systems, the point at which the system has exhausted all of its capacity for change, done its work, and dissipated its productive capacity into useless entropy."[21]

As in any complex system, our ecosystem organizes through the interaction of nonlinear components that lead to positive feedback loops. Some interactions are reinforced while others die off. Even the smallest change, through this continuous feedback, can have a huge effect on the entire system.

While these changes seem random and unpredictable, the shape of their movement is finite. It is determined by what scientists call "attractors," forces that exert a magnetic pull.[22]

There is no overall plan for how the process should execute. The resulting pattern is designed or controlled without any central organizing agent. In this open, viable system, the value of resiliency replaces the value of stability. Within complex systems, natural selection gives rise to both fitness and adaptability. By staying out of balance or on the edge of chaos, our ecosystem is able to continuously adapt and evolve.

Chaos Theory

Chaos theory, or dynamic systems theory, grew out of the fields of mathematics and physics over the last several decades. It is a body of knowledge generated by the understanding of many disciplines and their connectedness. Chaos theory created a revolution in the scientific world, because it impacts anyone interested in science and natural systems. It created a shift in emphasis from the quantitative with an emphasis on mechanistic structures to the qualitative, where relationships and patterns are observed. With the discovery of the chaos theory, scientists from different specialties, such as physics and mathematics, who often preferred to work separately, began to exchange information. Eventually, scientists from many other disciplines, including biology, chemistry, ecology, economics, and astronomy, contributed to the understanding of chaos.

One of the initial contributors to the chaos theory was a meteorologist and mathematician named Edward Lorenz. The "Lorenz attractor," discovered in 1961, was the result of a data entry error. While entering a relatively long number into the computer, Lorenz left a few digits off, set the computer to print, and left the room. He assumed that their absence would be so insignificant that they would barely impact the results. He was wrong, and that mistake led him to the discovery of infinitely complex patterns that never exactly repeat themselves, but that stay within very clear boundaries and create a distinct pattern. These Lorenz attractors were later called strange attractors.

The picture of the Lorenz attractor printed by the computer looked like the wings of a butterfly, thus the term the "butterfly effect." The butterfly effect means that small initial deviations or changes (e.g., Lorenz leaving off the last few digits in his number) have substantial impact on a system. In terms of the weather, the draft created by the wings of a butterfly in the United States could create a hurricane in Japan, and it is why Lorenz said that it would be impossible to predict the weather. The discovery of Lorenz attractors was the beginning of the chaos theory, which emerged as a new science in the 1970s.[23]

Two different but enlightening definitions of chaos are "The qualitative study of unstable periodic behavior in deterministic nonlinear dynamical systems,"[24] and "behavior that produces information (amplifies small uncertainties) but is not utterly unpredictable."[25]

The theory of chaos resulted from the study of nonlinear systems. A "system" is a collection of processes or objects that has a *figurative* framework drawn around it for the purpose of study.[26] A system could be one person, it could the population of birds in a given area, it could be a cell under a microscope, it could be the sun and the planets, or it could be an organization. "Nonlinear" systems express relationships that are not exclusively uniform.

Nonlinearity means rules are not constant—there are many dimensions to nonlinearity. Systems are unpredictable, and the smallest variation can create large changes (the butterfly effect). Most systems in nature are nonlinear. A system is a model that depicts behavior over time using mathematical formulas. The application of chaos theory in organizations is the study of complex, unpredictable systems that, in spite of their apparent random nature, exhibit predictable patterns over time.

Universality: Order Out of Chaos

Through the study of numerical functions, the particle physicist Mitchell Jay Feigenbaum discovered a theory that shook the foundations of science for many practitioners: a "universal" theory. He discovered that when observing nonlinear systems, different systems may appear similar if they are examined in a certain way. This phenomenon is known as Universality. With the aid of computers that can quickly track a system's evolution, natural systems can be simulated to unveil their *patterns and relationships*. When observed over time, seemingly random movements in a system can display incredibly structured patterns. Systems are "universal" because of the common nature of these patterns. Examples of universality are ant colonies, swinging pendulums, and dripping faucets; they all have predictable qualities that create certain patterns called "strange attractors."

Strange attractors pull a system into visible shape once it has begun to move into a state of chaos. These strange attractors have been discovered by tracking systems on computers. Attractors occur in "phase space," a space in which all possible states of a system are represented. In phase space, a computer creates a multidimensional map of the history of a system by plotting points that represent the long-term behavior of the system. Movement in phase space converges on a set of points, making a strange attractor visible. Pictures of attractors in phase space show us that chaos does not move outside the bounds of the strange attractor, and the attractors create order from turbulence. (See Exhibit 2.1.) Strange attractors are described by a few simple mathematical equations, although they depict complex and random behavior. Even data from a dripping faucet produces patterns that indicate the presence of strange attractors creating order from the random disorder of the real data.

As a system interacts with its environment, it shifts and moves into disorder; it becomes chaotic, existing far from equilibrium although within certain boundaries. In this place it generates information, and if effective feedback loops exist, new forms of order emerge. Information is a source of order. Order is inherent in living systems, and rises naturally from chaos. Natural systems are *self-organizing*—they transform chaos into ordered, dynamic patterns. Chaos is, therefore, a *necessary part of change* for systems. Healthy systems maintain a balance between chaos and a lack of it. They are most efficient when they are poised at the edge of chaos,

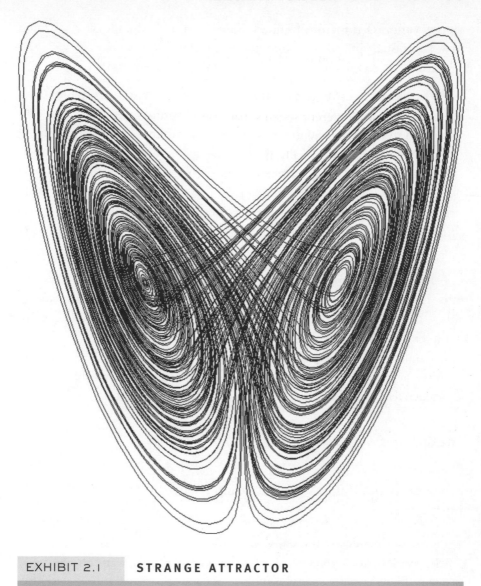

| EXHIBIT 2.1 | **STRANGE ATTRACTOR** |

Source: www.turnex.dk

between disorder and stability. Too much disorder, and the system is torn apart; too much order, and the system dissipates or is diffused.

Barbara Mossberg, president of Goddard College, believes that "Chaos Theory applied regularly serves to keep chaos at bay." She says, "The theory's premise is that even when things seem out of control, if you step back far enough in space or time, there is order."[27]

Certain characteristics of chaos are useful to keep in mind:

- As energy, positive or negative, enters the system, there is a temporary destabilization. It is best to act quickly and often.
- Control works only in the short term. Stability emerges over time.
- Every component of the system, no matter how small, plays a role. Diversity feeds long-term stability. Connection and inclusion facilitate cohesion.
- A holistic view of the system is necessary to provide guidance to the system. The integrity of the system is "the congruent harmony of parts working together in a state of aligned action."[28]

Complexity science offers a theoretical framework for research into fundamental questions about living and working within adaptable, changeable systems. Viewing the organization through the lens of complexity science and chaos theory can shed light on behaviors that undermine resilience. Leaders who view their organizations as complex adaptive systems will build adaptability and resilience. Tools, techniques, and practices for facilitating this approach are discussed in Part Two.

The Chaordic Age

Consider the characteristics and capabilities of a company built using an evolutionary model that surfed the tension between chaos and order. Visa International

> espouses no political, economic, social or legal theory, thus transcending language, custom, politics and culture to successfully connect a bewildering variety of more than 21,000 financial institutions, 16 million merchants and 800 million people in 300 countries and territories. Annual volume of $1.4 trillion continues to grow in excess of twenty percent compounded annual. A staff of about three thousand people scattered in twenty-one offices in thirteen countries on four continents provides . . . around-the-clock operation of two global electronic communication systems with thousands of data centers communicating through nine million miles of fiber-optic cable. Its electronic systems clear more transactions in one week than the Federal Reserve System does in one year.[29]

Dee Hock, the founder of Visa International, built his company using the principles of chaos theory without even knowing it. After years of success, he retired to his ranch. Many years later, he was reading Mitch Waldrop's *Complexity* and realized that the process he used to build his company were the very principles described in the book. In the late 1990s, he wrote *Birth of the Chaordic Age*.

Hock coined the term "chaordic" to represent the dynamic tension between chaos and order. A chaordic organization can be described as

> a self-organizing and self-evolving entity, which ends up looking more like a neural network (like the Internet) than a hierarchically-organized bureaucracy in which decision-making power is centralized at the top and trickles down through a series of well-regulated departments and managers. Chaordic organizations do not fear change or innovation. They are, by their very nature, supremely adaptive. They also tend to be inclusive, multicentric, and distributive and, ultimately, strongly cohesive due to their unshakable focus on common purpose and core principles.[30]

SYSTEMS THEORY AND SYSTEMS THINKING

Systems theory is an interdisciplinary field of science and the study of complex systems in nature, society, and science. Systems thinking is the application of systems theory, or "a discipline for seeing wholes."[31] The inherent variability within the system provides an opportunity for it to be seen as a collection of parts (or subsystems) that are highly integrated to accomplish an overall goal.

Systems Thinking for Business Intelligence

Adaptability and resilience are crucial competencies for thriving in a dynamic global economy. Applying the new science principles to organizations with a focus on Business Intelligence provides a powerful framework for building adaptability. Because complex systems are so highly dependent on the flow of information, knowledge-driven organizations are uniquely poised to leverage the benefits of systems thinking. "In the new science, the notion of information is intimately linked with the degree of complexity of a system."[32]

In an article on the Business Intelligence Network, an online journal that covers all aspects of business intelligence, business analytics expert Dave Wells makes this observation:

> Many of today's Business Intelligence programs focus intensely on analytics. The business wants scorecards, dashboards and analytic applications, and the technology to deliver them is mature. Still we struggle to deliver high-impact analytics that are purposeful, insightful and actionable. The key to high-impact analytics is a strong connection with cause and effect—the essence of understanding *why* and deciding *what next*. Systems thinking offers the cause-and-effect connection. It holds the key to real analytic value that is derived through insight, understanding, reasoning, forecasting, innovation and learning.[33]

To embrace systems thinking, knowledge-based organizations must become proficient at skills and support infrastructures that build connections, foster innovation and collaboration, improve clarity, ensure adaptability, and allow self-organization to emerge. Part Two delves into these essential competencies, or "success factors," as they relate to knowledge-based organizations. Chapter 8 expands on systems thinking and its uses in business analytics.

◼ NOTES

1. Carol S. Pearson, Cover, *InnerEdge* 1, No. 4 (October/November 1998), 1.
2. Julie Roberts, Ph.D., "Leading with Heart and Soul," manuscript, 5.
3. Lynn McTaggart, *The Intention Experiment* (New York: Free Press, 2007), xix.
4. *Id.,*
5. Roberts, "Leading with Heart and Soul," 6.
6. McTaggart, *The Intention Experiment,* xx.
7. *Id.,* 34.
8. Kevin Kelly, *Out of Control,* (Reading, MA: Addison-Wesley, 1994), 8–10.
9. James Surowiecki, *The Wisdom of Crowds* (New York: Doubleday, 2004), xi.
10. *Id.,* xii–xiii.
11. Daniel Pink, *A Whole New Mind* (New York: Riverhead Books, 2005), 13.
12. Elkhonon Goldberg, *The Executive Brain* (Oxford: Oxford University Press, 2001).
13. Quoted in Pink, *A Whole New Mind,* 14.
14. www.ted.com/index.php/talks/jill_bolte_taylor_s_powerful_stroke_of_insight .html.
15. Malcolm Gladwell, *Blink* (New York: Little, Brown, 2005), 11.
16. Elkhonon, *The Executive Brain,* 23.

17. *Id.,* 24.
18. *Id.,* 25.
19. Philip Anderson, "Seven Levers for Guiding the Evolving Enterprise," in *The Biology of Business,* ed. John Henry Kipplinger III (San Francisco: Jossey-Bass, 1999), 117–118.
20. *Id.,* 118.
21. Margaret Wheatley, *Leadership and the New Science* (San Francisco: Barrett Koehler, 1992), 76.
22. Thomas L. Guarriello, "Emergence of a Living Systems–Inspired Organizational Culture," *InnerEdge* 1, No. 4 (October/November 1998), 16.
23. James Gleik, *Chaos: Making a New Science* (New York: Penguin Books, 1987).
24. Stephen H. Kellert, *In the Wake of Chaos* (Chicago: University of Chicago Press, 1993).
25. Gleik, *Chaos.*
26. Kellert, *In the Wake of Chaos.*
27. Barbara Mossberg, *Why I Wouldn't Leave Home Without Chaos Theory, InnerEdge* 1, No. 4 (October/November 1998), 5.
28. Jalma Marcus, personal communication.
29. Dee Hock, "Transformation by Design," *What Is Enlightenment,* No. 22 (Fall/ Winter 2002), 130.
30. *Id.*
31. Peter M. Senge, *The Fifth Discipline* (New York: Currency, 1990), 68.
32. Christopher Laszlo and Jean-François Laugel, *Large-Scale Organizational Change* (Boston: Butterworth Heinemann, 2000), 131.
33. Dave Wells, "A Systems View of Business Analytics, Part 1," 2008, www.b-eye-network.com/view/8143.

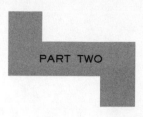
PART TWO

The Success Factors

CHAPTER 3

Effective Communication

*If the seat of the soul is not inside a person, or outside a person, but the
very place where they overlap and meet with their world, then the voice is
as good a candidate as any for getting the measure of our soul life.*

—DAVID WHYTE, *THE HEART AROUSED*
REFERRING TO GERALD DE NERVAL'S CONCEPTS

In a global economy of increasing complexity and interdependency,
effective communication is an essential core competency. Companies
that are striving for or have achieved world-class Business Intelligence
are dealing with great complexity while managing a highly specialized
and multicultural workforce. This chapter focuses on the many aspects and
components of interpersonal communication as they relate to success for
organizations in the global economy.

BENEFITS OF EFFECTIVE COMMUNICATION

*Innovation occurs for many reasons, including greed, ambition, conviction,
happenstance, acts of nature, mistakes, and desperation. But one force
above all seems to facilitate the process. The easier it is to communicate,
the faster change happens.*

—JAMES BURKE, *CONNECTIONS*

Many leaders have the notion that communication is a "soft" issue,
having very little effect on profit. The enormity of communicating in

today's interconnected economy can be overwhelming, given the number of different languages, technologies, industries, and markets across the globe.

Consider the experience of a measurement instrument company that hired a consulting company to improve its process of getting new products to market. The research began with a meeting of about 40 senior engineers.

The meeting was designed to gather information from the engineers on what they considered to be the main barriers to getting their products to market. They divided themselves into small groups and began to create lists. Then, as a group, they labeled the barriers as either technical or social.

After tallying the chart scores, they determined that 81 percent of their barriers were social. One manager said, "We're always trying to take waste out of our technical processes, but in 22 years I've been here, we have never even looked at taking waste out of our interactions with people."[1]

The engineers worked on their communication skills and cut their development cycle in half. The project's sponsor commented that if they had made these changes five years earlier, they would have saved $50 million.

There are numerous examples of costly failures as a result of poor communication. The *Challenger* disaster is a tragic example. The banking failures beginning in 2008 can be highly attributed to a lack of information being shared with deserving parties.

Statistics on the success of mergers, acquisitions, and alliances also show that today's leaders are no better at communicating than they were many years ago. Studies by some of the top accounting firms show that most mergers and acquisitions fail. The average statistics are:

- 60 percent of merged companies lose value after five years.
- 30 percent have no increase in value.
- 10 percent are successful at increasing value.

This is after billions have been spent on Business Intelligence software and hardware systems to connect, integrate, disseminate, and more.

While the risk of this problem is higher in companies involved in mergers and acquisitions, there are similar challenges within more stable organizations. Consider interdepartmental conversations such as the exchange of information, needs, and ideas between information technology (IT) and marketing. Some people experience the other department as speaking a different language.

These chasms of understanding exist between many departments with specialized workers whose thinking patterns may be different. Similarly, important conversations take place with entities outside the organization, such as vendors, suppliers, investors, auditors, and authorities. The style of communication may vary among all these interested parties.

Mickey Connolly and Richard Rianoshek, in *The Communication Catalyst*, offer a three-part conversational model that is useful for enhancing important activities such as "teamwork, planning, accountability, and learning":

1. *Align.* Conversation facilitates the sense of shared purpose, enhances creativity, and promotes smart planning.
2. *Act.* Conversation clarifies accountabilities and initiates action.
3. *Adjust.* Conversations evaluate performance and acknowledge successes or launch corrective action.

When these three related elements are effective, work is meaningful, satisfying, and fast. We infuse work with meaning, galvanize teams, and inflame loyalty among customers, employees, and investors. When these elements are ineffective, we decelerate our high-speed ambitions. We render work meaningless, destroy teamwork, and inflame discontent among customers, employees and investors.[2]

PRINCIPLES OF COMMUNICATION

Five basic principles of communication are generally accepted by scholars.[3] These principles provide a solid base for understanding the concepts in this chapter.

1. *Human communication is symbolic.* In an attempt to communicate, humans send messages to each other. Communication happens in the interpretation. The sender uses an encoding process, turning "thoughts, feelings, beliefs, and experiences into the words, sounds, and gestures"[4] that help the receiver to decode the message and interpret the meaning.

2. *Communication is personal.* Since the meaning is not conveyed directly, the same words can have different meanings to different people. It is important to understand the context and anticipate possible areas of misunderstanding to avoid confusion or worse.

3. *Communication is a transactional process.* For communication to be successful, both parties much engage and have the intention of understanding the other. "The sender–receiver roles occur simultaneously not alternately."[5] Residual impressions or feelings may carry through to subsequent conversations. Communication is not static but continuously in flux.

4. *Communication is not always intentional.* It is impossible to *not* communicate. Silence, absence, and lateness are all forms of communication, albeit nonverbal. Gasps and sounds of anger are forms of communication that may not be intentional. Body language, a strong form of communication, is often unconscious and therefore unintentional.

5. *Communication involves content and relationship dimensions.* The content dimension is the "what" of the communication. It relays the idea, subject, or belief of the message. The relationship dimension is the "how" of the communication and refers to the attitudes, views, or relationship to the receiver or receivers. Both content and relationship play an important role in the effective delivery of the communication.

Role of the Receiver

The effective delivery of information goes beyond simple agreement. It requires a mutual understanding, which depends on the receiver's ability and willingness to process the information or message.

People grasp information through three primary modes:

1. *Visual.* Receive information through pictures or visual displays of information.
2. *Auditory.* Listen to information through lecture or music.
3. *Kinesthetic.* Feel or sense, grasp by experience, or imagine feeling.

Most individuals are better at one mode than the other two. When communicating with a group, the challenge is to find a mode of presentation that is the best fit for everyone.

Speakers can improve the rate at which the information is received by incorporating all three communication styles:

1. Verbalize the information.
2. Display the information.
3. Involve the receiver in the process, whenever possible.

COMMUNICATION IN A HIGH-TECH ECONOMY

The highly technical and global nature of business today presents specific communication challenges.[6] Many companies are hiring top technical and business talent from around the globe and equipping them to work virtually to save on travel. This section discusses some of the challenges presented by the style of communication and the changing nature of the workforce.

Computer-Enabled Communication

In today's global economy, many companies are using technology to hold virtual meetings and trainings. *Computer-mediated communication* (CMC) is the term for using computers to interact through the Internet. CMC comes in many forms, including electronic mail (e-mail), chat rooms, instant messaging, electronic bulletin boards, list-servs, as well as audio and videoconferencing.

A *net conference* is a conference that is "electronically mediated by net-worked computers." Teleconferences are very common applications in companies using Business Intelligence. Video capabilities to share docu-ments are widely utilized.

There are some challenges to virtual meetings for obvious reasons. It is not possible for participants to read others' facial expressions and body language. This fact may limit communication or make some participants less comfortable. Exhibit 3.1 compares the strengths of teleconferences to face-to-face meetings.

Ease with virtual meetings develops over time. A well-trained modera-tor can greatly enhance the experience.

Communication Challenges for the Technical Professional

In an organization that is Business Intelligence intensive, the largest or fastest-growing sector of the workforce tends to be technical professionals.[7]

EXHIBIT 3.1   **COMPARISON OF STRENGTHS OF TELECONFERENCES AND FACE-TO-FACE MEETINGS**

Teleconferences	Face-to-Face Meetings
Good for information sharing and routine meetings.	Better when group cohesiveness and interpersonal relationships are important.
Quantity and quality of ideas are equal to face-to-face meetings.	Group organization is easier to maintain.
In negotiations, evidence has more weight than personality.	Participants can exchange more messages more quickly.
Participants may pay more attention to what is said.	Important nonverbal information (body language, facial expression) is available.
In the event of conflict, opinions may change more easily.	Participants are more confident of their perceptions.
More cost effective.	Generally preferred by participants.

For a majority of technical professionals, communication in general and with nontechnical people in particular can be difficult, given their specialized education and linear style of thinking. In addition, the influx of persons from other cultures has added to the challenges of effective communication.

The technical skills of a professional are very important to the organization. But the skills to communicate results, explain concepts and concerns, and engage in dialogue with nontechnical workers are equally important. Therefore, it is useful to have a balance of both the technical skills and interpersonal skills.

Technical professionals tend to be task–oriented rather than people-oriented. If their focus is on precision and solution, with little concern for dealing with various perceptions or emotional reactions, the true value of their research or analysis may never generate value. At some point, the information must be sold to the business decision makers.

Another challenge is the potential complexity of findings, which may be hard to translate into everyday business language. The ramifications of this complexity of findings on the functioning of a team, department, or organization may be significant, resulting in the loss of the value of the work and the worker.

There may be a desire to overanalyze, seeking higher complexity or perfection. The best analysis may be the one that is simpler and easier to communicate and therefore implement.

Liz Haggerty, program manager for business and manufacturing-process improvements for the Carrier Corporation in Hartford, Connecticut, commented on the importance of communication for scientific and technical professionals:

> Scientific and technical professionals need to understand business. We all need to be cognizant of the fact that there are many aspects of business, finance, and marketing that have an impact on what we are doing in our chosen field. We must understand that many people think differently than we do, and we must expose ourselves to different types of training that will help us to communicate more effectively, do a better job of accepting and receiving criticism, and giving feedback to others. We must help scientific and technical professionals see how they fit into the big picture. Training on understanding others and increasing communication effectiveness can be very helpful in broadening the skills of those of us in these professional areas. This is especially critical for those who have ambitions to move up in the organization.

Nonverbal Communication

> *Our brains were responding to nonverbal cues long before we had language. So whether we are aware of it or not, our brains are hard wired to pay attention to nonverbal communication. And in a communication interaction, it's our nonverbals that manage the other person's behavior. That's why the awareness of the effect of our nonverbals on others is so important.*

—Robert Knowlton, *Success Options*

Albert Mehrabian, a UCLA professor, conducted studies and concluded that 55 percent of our face-to-face communication is visual, 38 is tonal and tempo, and 7 percent is the actual words.[8] The emergence of a virtual community has introduced added complexities and considerations in communication.

Functions of Nonverbal Communication

Nonverbal communication is the communication that takes place outside of speaking. It has six basic functions.[9] Awareness of these functions allows for more intentional use and understanding.

1. *Supplementing the verbal.* Nonverbals supplement verbal communication in many ways. Hands are often used to draw attention to someone or something that the speaker wants noticed. Inflections in the voice can place emphasis or denote excitement or hesitation. Physical position and eye contact can send a powerful message.

2. *Substituting for words.* Hand gestures often replace words for certain effect. It is considered polite to raise your hand when you want to get the attention of a group. Facial expressions such as nods or smiles can communicate an affirmative response.

3. *Contradicting verbal messages.* Body language and facial expressions can send a mixed message if it is incongruent with the verbal response. Requesting clarification or insights from someone sending these signals helps to avoid confusion or disappointment later.

4. *Expressing emotions.* Message delivery can vary significantly depending on the emotions of the sender. Tone of voice, facial expression, and other aspects of communication are strongly affected by emotions. The importance of emotions in communication is highlighted by the fact that clever symbols have been created with a combination of keystrokes to express emotions in e-mail.

5. *Regulating interaction.* The rhythm or cadence of a conversation between two people or in a group is often regulated by body gestures, audible breathing, nods, or eye contact. This is a bit more challenging on phone meetings, where facial expressions and body language are not discernible.

6. *Indicating status relationships.* Position at a table or self-placement in a group can imply implicit or explicit authority. Voice loudness or penetrating stares can also involve a grab for power. A relaxed demeanor often signals openness, vulnerability, and a sense of equality. Those with explicit authority often appear more relaxed and comfortable.

Forms of Nonverbal Communication

Given the role that nonverbals play in communicating, there is a real need for self-awareness. To facilitate understanding and management of each part of communication, it is useful to look at the three categories: paralanguage, kinesics, and proxemics.

Paralanguage   *Paralanguage* is the vocal or tonal quality and pitch as well as the speed and emphasis of our words. It plays a role in face-to-face communication and in telecommunication. Paralanguage is the "how" of our speaking and can be broken down into several areas:

- Increasing loudness or softness and high or low pitch can designate a question or convey emotion.
- Timing variation and changes in pitch can provide emphasis or convey meaning.
- Vocal constriction versus openness can imply tension or emotion.
- Drawling or clipping is evident in various accents, where someone either drags out certain syllables or skips letters entirely.
- Emotion reflects how the speaker's feelings affects the delivery. Crying versus laughing while speaking will almost always convey a different meaning.[10]

Kinesics   *Kinesics* is the study of body language. Whether speakers are aware of it or not, their bodies communicate messages. The ability both to manage these messages as a speaker as well as to understand them as a listener is invaluable in business. Effective speaking engages the emotions of the audience, and the use of body language is a powerful aspect of that communication.

A story told about President Franklin D. Roosevelt demonstrates his belief in nonverbal communication. One evening he decided to have some fun while greeting people. Many of them said, "Good evening, Mr. President, and how are you?" to which he responded with a warm smile, "I'm fine, thank you. I murdered my mother-in-law." Not one person reacted to his comment. It is possible that no one even heard it because his body language was so contradictory to his statement. Because body language is typically unconscious, it is believed to be the most genuine form of communication.

Because body language is based on feelings, it is valuable to read the recipient's body language when communicating. More important, it is possible to leverage the use of body language as well as other nonverbals to enhance the delivery of a message. A list of the most common body actions that can lead to intended or unintended impressions follows.

- *Erect posture.* Power, confidence, control
- *Two people sitting in similar positions.* Harmony, agreement
- *Leaning forward.* Interest in other, confidence
- *Open hands.* Sincerity, openness
- *Crossed arms.* Defense, closed
- *Head tilting toward the speaker.* Agreement or interest
- *Smile.* Pleasure, compassion, trust, desire for connection[11]

There are certainly exceptions to this list, particularly when considering other cultures. It is best to consider body language in combination with cultural behaviors before drawing conclusions.

The use of the hands to guide the eyes is one of the most powerful body language techniques to convey or guide attention.

Proxemics   *Proxemics* relates to the space in which we operate and its effect on our level of comfort.[12] There are two general aspects to proxemics:

1. *Physical territory*, such as the orientation or characteristics of furniture or surroundings, can have an effect on our comfort. For example, a desk facing a window versus a dingy wall can affect a worker's mood. Or a presentation in a poorly lit room might change the experience of the audience.
2. *Personal territory* reflects our comfort level in proximity to others. Depending on the level of intimacy, there are basic ranges for each level.

   a. *Public space.* The distance maintained between an audience and a speaker is generally 12 to 25 feet.
   b. *Social space.* The distance between business associates in communication or strangers in public settings is 4 to 10 feet.
   c. *Personal space.* The distance between close friends or family members, or between strangers waiting in line, is 2 to 4 feet.

Cultural differences can lead to variations in these distances. Becoming familiar and respecting these cultural differences will improve cross-cultural relations and build connection. Distances can also vary by gender, age, and personal preferences. Reading body language and observing reactions are the best way to determine the best distances.

THEORY OF RELATIONAL COORDINATION

In highly complex organizations, work processes are often highly interdependent. In contrast to the hierarchical model where processes are sequenced or pooled, an organizational model that allows order to emerge requires that the processes are well connected. In this way, the environment is sensitive and responsive to the needs of others. Jody Hoffer Gittell describes these relationships in the theory of relational coordination: "The theory of relational coordination suggests that coordination of highly interdependent work is facilitated by high-quality connections, specifically by high-quality communications carried out through relationships of shared goals, shared knowledge, and mutual respect."[13]

There are several dimensions to the theory of relational coordination.

High-Quality Communication

High-quality communication comes in many forms, all of which play an important role.

Frequent Communication   Effective communication is necessary to exchange information in highly interdependent organizations. Frequent communications are important for building familiarity and trust, which leads to increased sensitivity and responsiveness.

Timely Communication   Organizations that thrive on turning information into knowledge understand that timing is everything. As speed to respond has grown in importance, delays can lead to waste and increased costs. Timely communication facilitates the smooth transition of information in highly interdependent organizations.

Accurate Communication   In an information-driven economy, accurate communication is essential. However, as an integral part of relational coordination, accuracy often suffers when organizations become more complex and greater speed is encouraged. Business Intelligence systems provide a solid framework to ensure accuracy.

Problem-Solving Communication   Highly interdependent organizational processes can run flawlessly until a problem arises. However, when members of these complex organizations face problems and are not skilled in dealing with them, conflict often arises, leading to blame and loss of communication. Organizations that focus on developing communication skills will benefit from the increased quality and depth of connection.

High-Quality Relationships

High-quality relationships are the lifeblood of an organization that seeks to leverage complexity and emergent knowledge. Once a set of solid communication practices are in place, relationships begin to form. To use these relationships effectively, however, the dissemination of crucial information, such as the goals of the business and the knowledge needed to attain those goals, is essential. As relationships form through effective communication practices, a culture of mutual respect will emerge.

Shared Goals   Traditionally, goals are shared within functional teams. The overall goals of the organization, however, are less well known. In an organization with a highly interdependent framework, each member of the organization must focus on the overall goal. Since the framework is designed to allow structure and process to emerge, the shared goal of the organization is the unifying force that empowers that emergence.

Shared Knowledge   Sharing knowledge goes hand in hand with shared goals for any organization using a highly interdependent framework. Knowledge shared between teams from different functional backgrounds creates connections that foster cross-functional support while reducing competition and conflict.

Mutual Respect   Highly interdependent organizations thrive on mutual respect. Effective communication practices as well as shared knowledge and goals go a long way to create a culture of mutual respect. Within a respectful dialogue, differences in opinions unleash energy and creativity.

Problems are minimized when the involved parties feel respected. This behavior is best learned by watching those in positions of power.

PRINCIPLES OF DIALOGUE

Communication works for those who work at it.

—JOHN POWELL, CREATOR OF THE FIVE LEVELS
OF COMMUNICATION

Dialogue goes beyond communication to describe a style of conversation that taps into the energy of an organization through shared intention. Jalma Marcus, executive coach and energy healer, shares her perspective on dialogue.

What Is Dialogue?

Dialogue is "a conversation with a center, not sides."[14] It is a way of taking the energy of differences and channeling it toward the creation of something new. It lifts us out of polarization and into a greater understanding. In essence, it is a means for accessing the innate intelligence and previously untapped power of the organization.

Dialogue is "a flow of meaning."

Dialogue is "a conversation in which people think together in relationship." Rather than holding on to their own position, the participants relax their grip on certainty and listen to the possibilities.

Dialogue is "about exploring the nature of choice."

The intention of dialogue is to reach new understanding and, in so doing, form a totally new basis from which to think and act. In dialogue, problems are not just solved, they are dissolved. The goal is not merely try to reach agreement but to create a context from which many new agreements emerge. By unveiling a base of shared meaning, the group's actions and values come into alignment.

Dialogue seeks to address the problem of fragmentation not by rearranging the physical components of a conversation but by uncovering and shifting the organic underlying structures that produce it.

Dialogue requires thinking, not just reacting. It requires a deep awareness of personal feelings as well as other's reactions.

Key Building Blocks—Practices and Principles

Dialogue can be learned. It requires a set of practices based on theory and principles. A "'practice' is an activity you do repeatedly to help bring about an experience."[15] A practice based on principles establishes a tradition. It is intentional and designed to create choices.

The Practice of Listening: "The Principle of Participation"

- Develop an inner silence; listen with all the senses
- Notice the self; "attend to both words and the silence between the words";[16] be aware of thought.[17]
- Let go of the inner clamor.
- Slow down; be still.
- Stick to the facts; suspend judgment.
- Stay in the present; do not jump to conclusions based on the past; look for evidence that challenges any convictions.
- Find the gaps.
- Listen together; question self and others.

The Practice of Respecting: "The Principle of Coherence"

- Observe, honor, and defer to others. See others as legitimate.
- Honor people's boundaries; do not intrude; do not withhold the self or distance the self. Imposing is not honoring; sharing personal experience is.
- Accept that others have something to teach us.[18]
- Pay attention to connections in differences; look for the relationship among the parts.[19]
- Look for the whole; find the hub, the center in order to slow down and stay in the present.
- Notice the internal disturbance; suspend the desire to fix it or tell others to change. Find your own center and focus on yourself as part of the whole.
- Look for the elephant in the room and name the feeling. Make deliberate space for those who have a different point of view.
- Hold the tension; do not react to it.

The Practice of Suspending: "The Principle of Awareness"

- Suspend opinion and judgment, and the certainty that lies behind them.
- Acknowledge and observe thoughts and feelings as they arise without being compelled to act on them; avoid "shoulds."
- Access your ignorance; recognize and embrace things you do not already know.
- Be courageous in the face of fear.
- Understand what is happening *as* it is happening; you do not hear and know by turning up the volume.
- Put on hold the temptation to fix, correct, or problem solve. Suspension allows us to inquire into what we observe.
- Question; one good question is better than many answers. Tolerate the tension to *not knowing*. Ask "What are we missing? What haven't we said?"
- Resist holding onto positions that polarize. Be willing to expand the conversation to hold beliefs other than your own.

The Practice of Voicing: "The Principle of Unfoldment"

- Notice your reactions, suspend judgment, honor your intuition and cherish your choices. Listen to yourself.
- Be willing to be still.
- Be confident that what you are thinking is valid and relevant.
- Choose consciously before you speak. Ensure that what you say is related to you and not a directive to diminish, change, or dismiss the other.
- Be patient with your self and during silences. Trust the emptiness, the sense of not knowing what to say or do. Sometimes just beginning to speak without determining the words brings forth opportunity.
- In speaking you can create. Give yourself permission to voice what is in the moment.[20]

Maintain the Relationship: Look for the Similarities in the Differences

- Clarify intentions.
- Acknowledge each participant's uniqueness, perceptions, beliefs.

- Create a container, an intentional space for safe communication.
  - *Hear and understand me.* Identify what you want.
  - *Even if you disagree, please don't make me wrong.* Support dreaming. No one gets to be wrong.
  - *Acknowledge the greatness within me.*
  - *Remember to look for my loving intentions.* Deepen the listening.
  - *Tell me the truth with compassion.*[21]
- *Attend.* Pay attention, observe, be aware.
- *Ask.* Gather information, withhold criticism, be respectful, honor the self.
- *Act.* Authentically do something that is consciously determined to be the best of all. Offer support; provide feedback. Maintain connection even if you disagree.
- *Amend.* Create restitution. Being human means making mistakes. Be courageous. The intention is to keep a connection that is respectful for all. This is an obligation for promoting successful results.[22]

ART OF LISTENING

> *Listening may or may not be an "act of love" or way to "tap into people's dreams," but it sure as hell is (1) an uncommon act of courtesy and recognition of worth from which (2) you will invariably learn amazing stuff . . . and (3) it will build-maintain relationships beyond your wildest dreams.*

—TOM PETERS, BEST-SELLING AUTHOR

To be a strong leader, you must be able to influence others. In highly complex organizations, everyone plays the role of leader from time to time. And communication is an essential mechanism for the exchange of knowledge and intentions. Mastering the art of listening is essential to the success of all participants in an interdependent organization.[23]

Those who are good listeners greatly increase their influence on others. Although listening is passive in nature, when someone feels heard, he or she feels inspired and validated. Sadly, many leaders fail to listen because they are biased, impatient, bored, or rigid in their views. This prevents the critical exchange of knowledge, insights, and intentions.

Listening skills are rarely taught. Communication training in business schools typically focuses on argument and persuasion. These skills fit the old management model with its top-down, authoritative approach. Managers had little reason to listen. They communicated down the chain of command, and the workers followed orders.

As stated earlier, as organizations embrace new business models, listening is becoming an integral part of the communication process. Two-way interaction helps to clarify and prevent confusion, aid comprehension, and improve connection.

Listening goes beyond just hearing. Hearing usually triggers a reflexive response without any thought or reflection. Listening is deliberate and requires interpretation. A good exercise in listening is to ask recipients to reflect back what they heard.

Bad listeners:

- *Interrupt.* They are impatient and may like to dominate the conversation.
- *Are inattentive.* They are easily distracted, perhaps even multitasking.
- *Exhibit mind-drift.* They are easily bored, perhaps even self-centered.
- *Are biased.* They have strong marginal views (out of the mainstream) and cannot expand their thinking.
- *Have closed minds.* They have already drawn a conclusion or stay with their own beliefs.

Good listeners:

- *Are quiet.* They talk less than the speaker.
- *Are patient.* They never interrupt the speaker.
- *Are unbiased.* They avoid prejudgment.
- *Are curious.* They ask clarifying and open-ended questions.
- *Pay attention.* They sit attentively, take notes, concentrate.
- *Employ nonverbals.* They smile, maintain an open posture and eye contact.
- *Reflect back.* They verify and reinforce what was heard through summary comments.

Skillful listeners are natural leaders in the new business landscape with their ability to influence, engage, and inspire.

STORYTELLING

> *Story telling . . . is one of the world's most powerful tools for achieving astonishing results. For the leader, storytelling is action oriented—a force for turning dreams into goals and then into results.*

—PETER GUBER OF MANDALAY ENTERTAINMENT GROUP

Storytelling has always been a powerful method for teaching and inspiring. In many cultures, it is the primary method of sharing and retaining knowledge through the generations. It is also an effective way to communicate to various stakeholders at every level of the organization. A gifted salesperson gains acceptance by telling a story that sets a product or service up as the hero. A manager rallies direct reports to make short-term sacrifices as they work towards a long-term goal. A talented chief executive translates the company mission statement into an emotional narrative that attracts investors and partners while inspiring employees. When a problem arises, it is also a powerful technique for creating calm and inspiring hope.

Four Truths of Storytelling

Unlike fantasy storytelling, the practice in business is built on truth and authenticity. To be effective, the storyteller must be seen as someone with integrity. According to Peter Guber of Mandalay Entertainment Group, there are four kinds of truth found in effective storytelling.[24]

Truth to the Teller   As mentioned earlier, authenticity is critical to the success of the story. The storyteller "must be congruent with his story—his tongue, feet, and wallet must move in the same direction. The consummate modern shaman knows his own deepest values and reveals them in his story with honesty and candor."

The power of storytelling comes from its ability to tap our emotions. Whether you are aware of it or not, most opinions are formed, decisions are made, and reactions are triggered at this level. So the secret is to get to the heart of the listener. To do this successfully, the storyteller must speak from the heart.

Truth to the Audience Storytelling may evoke a sense of leisure. However, when using this technique in business, the storyteller must consider that time may be the scarcest resource. So a commitment to efficacy and value is the essence of this truth.

The goal of the process is to induce an altered emotional state. This requires that the storyteller build suspense and stimulate curiosity. The storyteller can take a few steps to assist the process:

- Practice on a group of colleagues who still need convincing. Study the nonverbal responses to detect the emotional power of the story.
- Identify the audience's emotional needs and deliver with accuracy and integrity. Manage expectations throughout the story, and conclude with an unexpected twist or insight that leaves the audience convinced and delighted.
- Involve the audience in the storytelling experience. Guide the listeners to see themselves as the heroes of the story. Elicit suggestions or strategies as you guide them to your conclusion.

Truth to the Moment Never tell a story the same way twice. Given the dynamic nature of business, as described in Chapter 1, as well as the changing audience, an effective story is one that sounds different each time. In addition, the more the storyteller involves the audience, the more unique the process becomes.

There is an inherent paradox here. A great storyteller is both well practiced and flexible enough to improvise. A skilled storyteller can vary the story without "losing the thread of the focus."

Truth to the Mission A great storyteller conveys that the mission of the story is greater than the self. To evoke a real desire for change, the storyteller has to weave a tale that advocates for the good of all. This brings passion and emotion to the group to take action.

> Even in today's cynical, self-centered age, people are desperate to believe in something bigger than themselves. The storyteller plays a vital role by providing them with a mission they can believe in and devote themselves to. As a modern shaman, the visionary business leader taps into the human learning to be part of a worthy cause. A leader who wants to use the power of storytelling must remember this and begin with a cause that deserves devotion.[25]

The Heart of Storytelling

Technology has provided many new venues for storytelling. Beyond the physical gathering of people, stories are shared through print, radio, television, and movies.

> State-of-the-art technology is a great tool for capturing and transmitting words, images, and ideas, but the power of storytelling resides most fundamentally in "state-of-the-heart" technology.

> At the end of the day, words and ideas presented in a way that engages listeners' emotions are what carry stories. It is this oral tradition that lies at the center of our ability to motivate, sell, inspire, engage, and lead.[26]

■ NOTES

1. Mickey Connolly and Richard Rianoshek, *The Communication Catalyst*, (Chicago: Dearborn Trade Publishing, 2002), xii.
2. Ibid., xi–xiii.
3. The discussion about communication is based on Gloria J. Galanes, Katherine Adams, and John K. Brilhart, *Effective Group Discussion* (New York: McGraw-Hill, 2004), 50–54.
4. *Id.*, 51.
5. *Id.*, 52.
6. *Id.*, 54–56.
7. Harry E. Chambers, *Effective Communication Skills* (Cambridge, MA: Perseus Publishing, 2001), 7–23.
8. Businessballs.com. "Professor Albert Mehrabian's communications model." www.businessballs.com/mehrabiancommunications.htm (accessed January 22, 2009).
9. Gloria Galanes, Katherine H. Adams, and John K. Brilhart, *Effective Group Discussion,* 89–92.
10. Robert Bacal, "What Is Paralanguage?" www.work911.com/communication/nonverbparalanguage.htm (accessed January 22, 2009).
11. Patricia Ball, "Watch What You Don't Say." www.speaking.com/articles_html/PatriciaBall,CSP,CPAE_592.html (accessed January 22, 2009).
12. Mike Sheppard, "Proxemics." www.cs.unm.edu/~sheppard/proxemics.htm (accessed January 22, 2009).
13. Jody Hoffer Gittell, "The Theory of Relational Coordination," in *Positive Organizational Scholarship,* Kim S. Cameron, Jame E. Dutton, and Robert E. Quinn, eds. (San Francisco: Barrett-Koehler Publishers, 2003), 281–283.
14. William Isaacs, *Dialogue: The Art of Thinking Together* (New York: Currency Book Doubleday, 1999), 19–20.

15. *Id.,* 79.
16. *Id.,* 86.
17. Jiddu Krishnamurti, *Talks and Dialogue* (New York: Avon Books, 1968), 93.
18. Isaacs, *Dialogue,* 86–116.
19. Christopher Alexander, "The Nature of Order," Ms., 120.
20. Isaacs, *Dialogue,* 122–166.
21. Hyler Bracey, *Managing from the Heart* (New York: Dell Publishing, 1990), 192.
22. Jean Isley Clark, *Connections* (Center City, MN: Hazeldon Books, 1999).
23. William F. Kumuyi, "Sir, Listen Up!" http://findarticles.com/p/articles/mi_qa5391/is_200806/ai_n27900527/print?tag=artBody;col1 (accessed January 22, 2009).
24. Peter Guber, "The Four Truths of the Storyteller," *Harvard Business Review* 85, No. 12 (December 2007), 53–59.
25. *Id.,* 59.
26. *Id.,* 59.

CHAPTER 4

Collaboration

The new promise of collaboration is that with peer production we will harness human skill, ingenuity, and intelligence more efficiently and effectively than anything we have witnessed previously.

—DON TAPSCOTT AND ANTHONY D. WILLIAMS, *WIKINOMICS*

COLLABORATING FOR THE FUTURE

Cisco, the world's largest provider of Internet networking and communication equipment, is powered by collaboration. With 22 current worldwide initiatives, chief executive John Chambers claims that it would be impossible to manage his company using his old style of command and control.[1] Collaboration enables Cisco to foresee changing trends and act quickly.

According to Chambers, one of Cisco's strengths is its ability to foresee impending market transitions. "Cisco is able to predict trends six to eight years ahead even in the highly volatile technology market by recognizing early-warning signals its customers unwittingly put off. To capitalize on these 'market shifts,' Chambers gave up his command-and-control style and made decision-making highly collaborative."

Cisco organizes for collaboration in several ways.

No Hierarchy

Chambers claims that he found it difficult to let go of his usual command-and-control style, but he disciplined himself to change his behavior. Specifically, in meetings, he gave his team time to think. He began to see that his team often made decisions that were just as good, if not better, than his. And because they were involved in the process, the members of the team were much more invested in the execution. However, not all managers were able to make the adjustment. When this collaborative leadership style was implemented throughout Cisco, 20 percent of the top management team went elsewhere.

State-of-the-Art Technologies

Among Cisco's offerings are several technologies that enable collaboration. PC software for online meetings is powerful and efficient. But the real collaborative power comes from the company's next-generation videoconferencing that connects customers and team members worldwide.

Collaborative Teams

Cisco has a highly matrixed structure of cross-functional teams called councils and boards that collaborate on projects. Because of the highly sophisticated conferencing software, Cisco employees collaborate in real time much like social networking groups. "The power of collaboration is not in adding more people to the process but in getting immediate input from smart people and thinking through the problem as a group." This is critical to the success of the company. Individuals and teams from anywhere in the world can gather quickly for an intimate virtual meeting using their state-of-the-art videoconferencing technology.

Verbal and Financial Motivation

To begin a project, Cisco puts people together who speak a common language and engages them in reaching their goal. The leader then drives the team through execution. People are motivated to engage with strong leadership and compensation tied to team performance.

Clear and Consistent Communication

Chambers states: "Clear and consistent communication was and is very, very important to making this whole thing work." Top management has developed a clear and consistent vocabulary to ensure that information is dispersed and shared consistently worldwide.

Quick Alignment of Resources

When resources are low, flat management and collaboration may save the day. Team members are encouraged to help each other and reallocate resources. Risk taking is also necessary to make a quick change of direction. Team members must be tolerant of failure.

Chambers claims that the new challenges keep him motivated and competitive. His passion for collaboration and willingness to share decision-making infuses the whole system with new energy to fuel the vision and stimulate innovation.

CREATING A COLLABORATIVE CULTURE

In his award-winning book *The Culture of Collaboration*, Evan Rosen defines collaboration as "working together to create value while sharing virtual or physical space."[2]

Expanding on that, the new science based on quantum physics and field theory suggests that the value created by collaboration is greater than the total possible value from the individual contributions. The energy released from the interaction and feedback increases the total value from the system.

Cultural Elements of Collaboration

For collaboration to flourish, the organization must take steps to create a collaborative culture. Rosen suggests that there are ten cultural elements of collaboration.[3] Many of these elements are inherent qualities of an adaptive company:

1. *Trust.* Trust is a foundational feature of any team. Members who trust each other feel safe in sharing ideas. If people are afraid their ideas will be stolen or they will be criticized for mistakes, collaboration is difficult. Look for more discussion of trust later in the chapter.
2. *Sharing.* Some individuals resist sharing because they fear they will lose their value. It is important to demonstrate that by sharing, everyone's value is increased.
3. *Goals.* Commonly created and shared goals are essential for vital collaboration.

4. *Innovation.* Collaboration stimulates innovation, which then fuels more collaboration.
5. *Environment.* The physical and virtual environment represents the nonverbal language of the company. Spaces that facilitate informal congregation lead to the natural sharing of ideas and issues. Virtual collaborative environments through technology advances are as important as real environments and are discussed in a later section.
6. *Collaborative chaos.* Chaos energizes the system. By facilitating the unstructured exchange of ideas, innovation flourishes.
7. *Constructive confrontation.* Respectful disagreement fuels the system to generate new ideas. When individuals feel safe to challenge each other's ideas, innovation is unleashed.
8. *Communication.* Effective communication skills are fundamental to collaboration. Communication is the channel that builds trust while facilitating inquiry and sharing.
9. *Community.* A sense of community is a natural outcome of collaboration. Shared goals, invigorating idea exchanges, and group problem solving build trust and community.
10. *Value.* Value from collaboration is realized in numerous ways. Companies have experienced business benefits, such as reduced processing times, shortened product development cycles, new markets identification, and more. There are also considerable cost savings realized through human benefits. When individuals feel engaged and valued as part of something larger than themselves, they have a more positive attitude about work. This leads to increased productivity, lower absenteeism, and more.

Instilling a Culture of Collaboration

Many organizations spend large amounts of money on state-of-the-art collaboration software. However, success is elusive if the culture does not support collaboration. Some approaches for instilling a culture of collaboration are as follows:[4]

- *Establish a mentoring system.* A natural complement to collaboration, mentoring helps support team effort by providing assistance to members in learning and development. A formal structure with top-level commitment and participation goes a long way to support system-wide collaboration.

- *Invite constructive confrontation.* Disagreement and conflict in a safe and trusting environment infuse the system with energy, leading to innovation within and evolution of the system.
- *Integrate collaborative tools into work styles.* Technology that facilitates collaboration is transforming the workplace. System-wide support and advocacy that consider individual styles as well as organizational goals ensure high adoption rates and benefits.
- *Facilitate cross-functional brainstorming.* Bringing diverse individuals together in a safe, informal environment to share ideas and concerns taps into the wisdom of the organization, leading to expansive thinking and breakthrough solutions.
- *Reward people for collaborative behavior.* Effective collaboration leads to efficiencies across the organization. Discouraging internal competition by rewarding individuals who collaborate helps to ingrain the behavior. The goal is create a new norm where collaboration is the natural tendency.
  - *Reward people for gaining broad input.* Evaluate and reward individuals for seeking input and advice from others.
  - *Reward people for sharing information.* Evaluate and reward individuals who share their knowledge and resources freely.
  - *Reward people who use collaboration to innovate.* Evaluate and reward those who initiate and inspire cross-functional teams that innovate.
  - *Promote collaborators.* Promote individuals who demonstrate their understanding of that concept that considering multiple perspectives leads to better decisions.
- *Practice collaborative leadership.* Modeling behaviors such as engaging people, asking questions, listening, and building consensus sends a powerful message that encourages similar behavior at all levels. Using positive nonverbal communication such as an accepting and curious tone elicits trust, sharing, and consensus.

Building Collaboration through Appreciative Inquiry

Traditionally, organizations look to change behavior by focusing on detecting errors, performing gap analyses, and fixing problems. This deficit-based theory of change may work for the top-down, hierarchical organization. But for dynamic organizations with a continual need to adapt, these models are not sufficient. With their focus on problems and crises, they may even be deleterious to the change process. In 2000 David Cooperrider, a pioneer of Appreciative Inquiry proposed that "While researchers have demonstrated the potential for increased organizational understanding when members focus on opportunity rather than threat . . . deficient inquiry continues to guide many in their quest for change."[5]

Conversely, the new science suggests that when the focus and intention are directed toward that which is positive, a creative power is unleashed that facilitates adaptation with unprecedented ease and efficiency. Appreciative Inquiry, a technique that focuses on positive outcomes, is based on the premise that humans are naturally drawn toward that which is positive. The practice of Appreciative Inquiry suggests that by searching within an organization for what works, what motivates, and what evokes positive energy, the organization will evolve in a positive direction. "Appreciative Inquiry involves the coevolutionary search for the best in people, organizations, and the world around them. It involves systematic discovery of what forces are at work when a system is its most effective, compassionate, and capable in economic, ecological, and human terms."[6]

The practice of Appreciative Inquiry has unveiled a new theoretical framework for viewing change. Its protocol has an inherent ability to tap into the positive energy that is created by the relationship of the group. The resulting change is often spontaneous, natural, and successful beyond all expectations. "Conspicuously absent from this process are the vocabularies of deficit-based change (e.g., gap analysis, root causes of failure, unfreezing, defensive routines, variances, diagnosis, resistance, and flaming platforms)."[7] The theoretical framework offers a deeper understanding of the power of this approach.[8]

Four Phases of Appreciative Inquiry

By asking positive questions, members of the organization begin to build a collective vision of what is possible. The future is designed through a self-organizing process that solicits the best from every member of the organization. The process generally consists of four phases.

Discovery Phase   The discovery phase is based on the theory that "human systems are drawn towards their deepest and most frequent explorations."[9] This phase is characterized by interviews that are designed to determine the optimal capacity of the organization. In contrast to many discovery interviews that bring in outside consultants to uncover problems, the discovery phase is usually done in house with most members of the organization participating. It really becomes a "system-wide analysis of the positive core by its members."[10] As members of the organization are exposed to the possibilities expressed by other members, their level of appreciation and hope increases. The result is the discovery of themes and patterns.[11]

Dream Phase   The dream phase[12] guides participants into a transformational state by asking them to imagine what is possible for the organization. By tapping into the creative energy of the group, an imaginary future emerges for the organization. The dream usually contains "three elements: a vision of a better world, a powerful purpose, and a compelling statement of strategic intent." As a result, participants feel a deeper connection and sense of shared purpose for their organization.

Design Phase   The power of the dream fuels the design phase. In a typical change process, the directive is top down and often met with great resistance. The design and strategy necessary to bring the dream into reality emerges out of the new system of cooperation, mutual respect, and shared vision. In most cases, participants enter the design phase with a desire to change.

Destiny Phase   Initially, the fourth phase was known as delivery because it was considered a more traditional stage of planning and implementation. However, after several years of working with the process, practitioners discovered that it felt more like a major transformation. Participants were realizing that their interpretation of the world has an effect on the process. As discussed in Chapter 2, their intention was creating their reality. So rather than focusing on planning and implementation, practitioners just let the participants guide the process. They completely gave up control. What seemed like a recipe for chaos turned into a perfect container for dynamic transformation and organization. Cooperrider and Whitney describe the Destiny Phase as follows:

> Appreciative Inquiry accelerates the nonlinear interaction of organization breakthroughs, putting them together with historic, positive traditions and strengths to create a "convergence zone" facilitating the collective re-patterning of human systems. At some point, apparently minor positive discoveries connect in accelerating manner and quantum change, a jump from one state to the next that cannot be achieved through incremental change alone, becomes possible. What is needed, as the "Destiny Phase" of AI (Appreciated Inquiry) suggests, are the network-like structures that liberate not only the daily search into qualities and elements of an organization's positive core but the establishment of a convergence zone for people to empower one another, to connect, cooperate, and co-create. Changes never thought possible are suddenly and democratically mobilized when people constructively appropriate the power of the positive core and . . . let go of accounts of the negative.[13]

Appreciative Inquiry is successful because every member of the organization has an equal voice. This has the effect of breaking down common communication barriers and inspiring full participation. It does not require any exceptional knowledge. Each member is asked to share his or her view of past and present organizational competencies. "The focus is on achievements, assets, potentials, innovations, strengths, elevated thoughts, opportunities, benchmarks, high-point moments, lived values, traditions, strategic competencies, memorable stories, and expressions of wisdom."[14] The sharing of positive aspects brings the members into a sense of wholeness from which the insights, visions, and future dreams can emerge. Appreciative inquiry is based on the concept that every member has value in the process.

BUILDING COLLABORATIVE TEAMS

Teams are the backbone of a collaborative culture. In the contribution that follows, John Reddish, succession planning expert, speaker, author, and consultant, discusses the characteristics of effective teams in the new business landscape.

Effective Teams for Today's Business Landscape

Work teams can be very effective. They can also be a disaster, as anyone with even a passing knowledge of organizational dynamics understands. In today's world of instant information, many of these impediments to real team performance are being overcome, while new challenges are emerging. New teams must be highly communicative, collaborative, mutually supportive, multitalented, and quick to respond, often without having a complete picture of the "facts." New teams must be able to act with relative autonomy, demanding higher levels of accountability, unparalleled access to information, and commensurate authority. Team leadership can shift as demands for expertise change, although accountability remains with the titular team leader. The new team leader, therefore, must be both highly talented and politically savvy to survive and thrive as organizations adapt to new models. He or she must either have the stature or authority to withstand great pressure to avoid producing the "same old stuff," which is tantamount to team failure.

In organizations with traditional structures and loyalties, teams are easily compromised by the often divergent pull from multiple constituencies that provide lip service to team success while providing minimum support or even actively working to sabotage team efforts. Teams that cannot pull themselves loose through the efforts of a strong, grounded leader or who have a patron high up in the organization often are teams in name only.

Organizations that want to embrace the increasing demands of emerging world market dynamics must become "flat." New teams flourish in flat organizations, but leaders must be willing to embrace the transparency that accompanies increased initiative and accountability where disparate, often remote, teams, including ones with members operating from multiple locations and communicating largely electronically, take almost instantaneous action in the furtherance of organizational goals. Through convergence, the technology is developing to more fully support such remote collaboration and control. Management and team members/leaders must be willing to embrace this new dimension of work.

A current definition for successful team leadership might be:

> As I see it, leadership is goal oriented, and effective. My leadership skills help me to release my own creative potential and the potential of individuals around me (both on my team and in support of our team

efforts). These skills also help to tap the productive capacity of group actions, whether I'm the "active" leader or not.

11 Ways to Avoid Failure with Collaborative Teams

The following list details 11 reasons for team failure in traditional organizations and how they are avoided in collaborative organizations.

1. Failure to delegate is being replaced by multitalented peer-level team members with spunk and access to the same information as the team leader and/or organization.
2. Conflict with and among the team is being replaced by greater acceptance of the role of psychology and soft skills in organizations large and small.
3. Conflict with organizational, customer, and/or stakeholder leadership is being handled by increased transparency and clarity at all informational levels.
4. Excessive detail orientation is being replaced by a growing acceptance of pattern recognition (still being resisted in many quarters) as a viable alternative to detailed fact analysis.
5. Lack of meaningful management controls (responsibility/authority) is being replaced by the use of online tools for project management and collaboration in real time for organizations of all sizes.
6. Decision avoidance is being replaced by peer-level participation and resolution.
7. Failure to embrace new technology and methods is diminishing as Gen X, Gen Y, and New Millenniums are playing increasingly important roles in teams.
8. Noninclusion (ignoring the ideas and feelings of other team members and/or stakeholders) is being replaced by peer-level participation in teams and a breakdown in the perceived value of selective "loyalty."
9. Hoarding information is being replaced by technologically astute team members developing open systems that make hoarding more difficult.
10. Emphasis on process rather than people is being replaced by the growing recognition that, as teams become more democratized and populated by peers, the benefits of collaboration are realized.
11. Failure to share credit is being replaced by the acknowledgment and acceptance of collaborative contributions.

Self-Organizing through Cross-Functional Teams

In business, cross-catalytic cycles are defined as the interaction of a variety of entities, such as people, teams, divisions, or even separate companies, that lead to the birth of a new, higher-level entity made up of the contributing entities and their relationships.[15] The new entity that emerges from this process is incredibly stable and adaptable.

There is evidence of cross-catalytic cycles both within corporations and between corporations and their environment. These cycles are commonly facilitated by what organizations call cross-functional teams that coordinate and share information about sales, purchasing, product development, finance, and more. The learning that occurs through this process is essential for resilience and growth in large corporations.

Over the last few years, there has been a growth in cross-catalytic cycles between corporations. For example, a single company can be a vertical catalyst for one company through the supply chain and be a horizontal catalyst to a different company through competition. The stability of the system depends on the interaction and performance of each of the players.

The eventual outcome of cross-catalytic cycles is convergence.

> Each cycle feeds on itself, develops itself, and converges toward a cycle on the next higher level of the organization. Thus, loosely connected departments become integrated parts of divisions; divisions become subsystems of the corporation; the corporation becomes increasingly bound up in the health of the industry; and the health of the industry is inextricably linked to the natural cycles of the global economy.[16]

VALUE OF TRUST

> *There is one thing that is common to every individual, relationship, team, family, organization, nation, economy, and civilization throughout the world—one thing which, if removed, will destroy the most powerful government, the most successful business, the most thriving economy, the most influential leadership, the greatest friendship, the strongest character, the deepest love.*

> *On the other hand, if developed and leveraged, that one thing has the potential to create unparalleled success and prosperity in every dimension*

of life. Yet, it is the least understood, most neglected, and most underestimated possibility of our time.

That one thing is trust.

—STEVEN M. R. COVEY, *THE SPEED OF TRUST*

Trust is a fundamental building block for organizations that seek to build a collaborative culture. Since power is dispersed and each area is interdependent, a breach of trust can undermine the integrity of the entire system.

According to Alan Greenspan, former chairman of the Federal Reserve, "Our market system depends on trust. Trust in the work of our colleagues and trust in the word of those with whom we do business." Greenspan goes on to say that the honesty and integrity of a company are a function of the character of the chief executive officer (CEO). "If a CEO countenances managing reported earnings, that attitude will drive the entire accounting regime of the firm. If he or she instead insists on an objective representation of a company's business dealings, that standard will govern recordkeeping and due diligence."[17]

In our complex business environment, trust is built through relationships. Specifically, our behaviors build or undermine trust. And our ability to communicate forms the foundation of those relationships. Margaret Wheatley and Byron Kellner-Rogers describe the importance of trust in organizations:

> Relationships are another essential condition that engenders the organizations that we see. The forms of the organization bear witness to how people experience one another. In fear-filled organizations, impervious structures keep materializing. People are considered dangerous. They need to be held apart from one another.

> But in systems of trust, people are free to create the relationships they need. Trust enables the system to open. The system expands to include those it had excluded. More conversations—more diverse and diverging views—become important. People decide to work with those from whom they had been separate.[18]

In *The Speed of Trust*, Steven Covey discusses how trust is a new competitive advantage. In a business landscape where speed is essential, the presence of trust empowers leaders to eliminate many steps related to governance, due diligence, and so on. The organizations that depend on large volumes of data and employ Business Intelligence depend on the veracity or the data as well as the data analysts and architects.

Covey offers 13 behaviors that are based on enduring principles that govern success. Based on integrity and credibility, they apply to all areas of an organization as well as life in general.

13 Behaviors

It takes twenty years to build your reputation and five minutes to ruin it.

—WARREN BUFFETT, CHAIRMAN & CEO, BERKSHIRE HATHAWAY

As Covey describes it, the 13 behaviors reflect both character and competence.[19] This is valuable to understand because "the quickest way to decrease trust is to violate a behavior of character, while the quickest way to increase trust is to demonstrate a behavior of competence."

Behavior #1: Talk Straight

What we say is true and forthcoming—not just technically correct.

—DELL INC.'S CODE OF CONDUCT

Straight talk is really about honesty. The ability and integrity to speak the truth with great clarity is essential for success today. Too much is happening too fast to be delayed by confusion or deception.

Strong leadership is necessary to create a culture of trust. Straight talk from top management is essential for success.

Behavior #2: Demonstrate Respect

I try to treat people as human beings. . . . If they know you care, it brings out the best in them.

—SIR RICHARD BRANSON, FOUNDER AND CHAIRMAN,
THE VIRGIN GROUP

Demonstrating respect builds trust on all levels. Expansion into global markets brings exposure to new customs and manners that need to be understood and integrated. This creates the space for unparalleled innovation and collaboration.

Behavior #3: Create Transparency   Creating transparency involves telling the truth in a way that can be verified. This means not hiding mistakes and information. Leaders who come from a place of authenticity and transparency are rewarded with loyalty and trust.

Behavior #4: Right Wrongs   To be an effective leader, one must practice humility. Mistakes are expected in a dynamic, innovative company. And no one is immune from them. To admit mistakes and make restitution, when necessary, is a sign of great integrity.

Behavior #5: Show Loyalty

> *To retain those who are present, be loyal to those who are absent.*

> —STEVEN M. R. COVEY

To demonstrate and encourage loyalty, it is important to acknowledge the contributions of others and offer praise freely. Leaders who speak about people as though they were present and show respect for their privacy gain the trust of those who *are* present.

Behavior #6: Deliver Results

> *We judge ourselves by what we feel capable of doing, while others judge us by what we have already done.*

> —HENRY WADSWORTH LONGFELLOW

As a full participant in any organization, it is crucial to establish a track record of delivering results. However, it is also important to know what to deliver. This involves understanding how results will be implemented and making sure the results have value to the organization.

In a dynamic organization, individuals enjoy a lot more autonomy. Proactive behavior invigorates the system and moves the organization forward. It is good to underpromise and overdeliver.

Behavior #7: Get Better

> *The illiterate of the 21st century will not be those who cannot read and write but those who cannot learn, unlearn, and relearn.*

> —ALVIN TOFFLER, AMERICAN WRITER AND FUTURIST

A practice of continual learning is essential for the growth of both the organization and the individual. Improving skills and knowledge in your current area of expertise as well as learning through collaboration with other areas leads to exponential growth. Developing formal and informal feedback systems are essential to support learning.

Behavior #8: Confront Reality

> *Leaders need to be more candid with those they purport to lead. Sharing good news is easy. When it comes to the more troublesome negative news, be candid and take responsibility. Don't withhold unpleasant possibilities and don't pass off bad news to subordinates to deliver. Level with employees about problems in a timely fashion.*

> —JON HUNTSMAN, CHAIRMAN, HUNTSMAN CHEMICAL

When times are tough, confronting reality requires obligated courage. True leaders share the truth at all times and address the difficult issues directly.

Behavior #9: Clarify Expectations

When communicating within an organization, clarity of word and deed is very powerful. Effective communication and feedback are essential for ensuring that everyone understands what is expected. It is dangerous to assume otherwise.

Behavior #10: Practice Accountability   Personal accountability fuels trust and mobilizes an organization for growth. Leaders must set the standard by holding themselves accountable. Then they are in integrity and can hold others accountable. Avoid blaming others when things go wrong.

Behavior #11: Listen First

> *I have found that the two best qualities a CEO can have are the ability to listen and to assume the best motives in others.*

> —JACK M. GREENBERG, CHAIRMAN AND CEO, McDONALD'S

As discussed in Chapter 3, truly listening is an art that takes intention and effort. But the value of this practice is significant. To understand someone, it is necessary to listen with your eyes, ears, and heart. Seek to learn what is important to others. This is the first step toward accessing the plethora of untapped wisdom in organizations.

Behavior #12: Keep Commitments

> *Stand up for what's right, in small matters and large ones, and always do what you promise.*

> —REUBEN MARK, CHAIRMAN AND CEO, COLGATE-PALMOLIVE

Covey calls this the "Big Kahuna" of all behaviors. It is a fundamental building block of trust and is essential for effective collaboration.

Behavior #13: Extend Trust

> *Trust men and they will be true to you; treat them greatly and they will show themselves great.*

> —RALPH WALDO EMERSON

Great leaders demonstrate a propensity to trust. When members of an organization extend trust to others, it fosters a collaborative environment. Learn from those who break the bond of trust.

COLLABORATIVE TECHNOLOGIES

The telephone might be considered the first collaborative technology, followed by fax and e-mail. However, in the last few years, the advances in newer forms of collaborative technology are transforming business efficiency and accessibility worldwide. The use of collaborative software enhances the ability of an organization to adapt quickly in a volatile economy.

Collaborative Technology Adoption

In *Collaboration 2.0*, David Coleman and Stewart Levine offer five stages of collaborative technology adoption that are typical in any large enterprise. The stages of growth resemble those of any enterprise-level technology adoption cycle.[20]

Stage 1: Traditional collaboration. Typical technologies that fall into this group are phone, face-to-face meetings, e-mail, and fax. They enable the quick distribution of material but lack the ability to unite a team in real time.

Stage 2: Specific application. As limitations appear in Stage 1, individual business units and departments adopt tools that enable group interaction and sharing online. This might include audio, video and data conferencing, instant messaging, chat and presence detection, and virtual team spaces (online meeting space).

Stage 3: Collaborative proliferation. As collaboration grows, adoption increases across the company. Unfortunately, there is very little coordination around which technology to use, leading to security issues and problems for information technology (IT).

Stage 4: Consolidation and standardization. To improve overall efficiency, IT takes the lead of selecting a company-wide vendor that meets the needs of the organization. Measurements of users, meetings, and minutes provide insights for the adoption cycle.

Stage 5: Virtual work environment. In this final stage, collaboration is fully embraced and adds value as it connects the organization with customers, suppliers, and partners as well as other organizations. Usage is continuously analyzed to improve flow and functionality.

Research suggests that very few organizations have reached stage 5.

Steps to Collaborative Technology Adoption

Step 1: Assess the environment. This step involves analyzing the infrastructure and collaborative technologies as well as the existing collaborative behaviors. Additional analysis on the potential affect of the application of technologies is recommended. Managers and key stakeholders need to understand the value proposition that improved collaboration will bring as well as how to phase in the technology. A global assessment in conjunction with IT is important to understand the complete ramifications and develop "a corporate-wide strategy for the successful deployment of collaboration technologies going forward."[21]

Step 2: Identify collaborative business processes. Some business processes are more conducive to collaboration. The next step is to identify business processes that will benefit from "collaborative leverage." These processes typically include sales and marketing, customer service and support, research and development, training, decision support, and crisis management.

Step 3: Build a collaborative vision. Creating a shared vision and extolling the benefits of collaboration is the next step. It can be done through workshops and trainings. The use of case studies and examples built around critical business processes is most effective.

Step 4: Build a business case for collaboration. This step involves estimating the costs, benefits, and risks involved in implementing the vision. It must specify the business problems being addressed, the value of the collaboration platform, and who will fund the initiative. Total cost of ownership should be used to determine the net benefit of the project, including direct and indirect costs. The benefits that factor in include but are not limited to shorter cycle times, increased productivity, revenues, profitability and market share, fewer errors, and better-quality products and services.

Step 5: Identify a sponsor. Identification of an executive sponsor who believes in the project and will allocate funds to see it through to its final stages is an essential step in the success of any project. The sponsor should be someone who is likely to benefit from collaboration and will be a champion for the project within the organization.

Step 6: Develop a collaboration strategy. A strategy for implementation should be developed that supports the overall goals of the project.

This strategy involves determining which technologies already exist and if they should be replaced or integrated into the larger network. Process maps are useful in determining which business processes can be improved. A gap analysis is recommended to find areas where:

- The infrastructure may need to be upgraded.
- Security policies may need to be revised.
- Training and education will improve adoption rates.
- Processes may need to be streamlined.

The strategy should include initial projects where collaboration delivers quick wins. Strong project management and communication around progress are essential to successful implementation.

Step 7: Select collaboration technology. The next step is a careful vendor analysis that addresses the appropriateness of the offerings as well as the vendor's financial viability, track record, training, and support. A return on investment analysis that details the actual costs and benefits is strongly recommended.

Step 8: Pilot project. A pilot project is a good next step to get the project off and running. The application that is selected should be one that will have a substantial impact and positive results. This success can be used to sell the concept throughout the organization.

Step 9: Enterprise rollout. This step leverages the success and learning from the pilot project. The steps for enterprise rollout are to:

- Prioritize the business units.
- Identify necessary resources.
- Define the education and training process.
- Define the support process.
- Define the metrics.

It is easy to underestimate the complexity of this process. It is important to facilitate communication so that issues and delays will surface quickly.

Step 10: Measure and report. To achieve the greatest value from the entire process, it is critical to continually monitor, measure, and report the adoption and usage of collaborative technologies for each business case. Publicity about successes as well as compensation for adoption and usage should be considered as ways to ensure success.

As collaboration technology improves, the pressure to adopt will only increase. Organizations that embrace collaboration are going to raise the competitive bar. The use of technology is essential to survival in a dynamic organization.

Crafting Collaboration

Informal collaborative communities are springing up across the globe as people from a variety of industries share best practices around a common interest. Such communities, or networks, are shown to have substantial benefits when they succeed in solving huge problems or generating valuable ideas.

> Despite the huge potential returns, few managers adequately invest in developing these kinds of networks (or) deliberately design them to foster measureable business results. One reason for this is the misperception that networks, which are essentially self-governing communities, draw their energy from common enthusiasms and a shared sense of purpose and this cannot be managed.[22]

However, real-world evidence suggests that there is benefit to actively managing some aspects of collaborative communities, albeit not in a typical style. Top-down directives and individual performance incentives have the potential to undermine these communities. "Success comes from applying the same rigor, time, and attention to the 'soft issues' of designing and managing human connections that managers ordinarily apply to structural decisions about capital investment, logistics, and technology."

Cartography of Connections   The first step in managing collaborative communities is to map the relationships within the community and look for patterns. The patterns of collaboration are given visibility using an organizational network analysis, a type of analysis that originated in the 1930s, "when Jacob Moreno set out to map the relationships of people in social groups in an attempt to reliably represent the ways in which group dynamics (like friendships, ostracism, popularity, and unpopularity) emerge." The approach used today is based on complex mathematics and probabilities.

Moreno pioneered the sociogram, a network analysis tool that maps interactions and offers quantitative insights into the community. A typical map displays "network density" of the system, which reveals the number of actual connections compared to the total possible connections (everyone to everyone). Another detectable measure is "community cohesion," which averages the shortest paths and the smallest number of connections between any two people, thus showing how close or distant the connections are overall. The members who tend to be found on the short paths are known as natural brokers.

Strategic Emergence   A baseline sociogram can reveal existing problems and areas where network connections can be strengthened. For example, companies that are organized into silos can connect individuals around a common expertise.

A database containing this information, as well as demographics and hobbies, is a worthwhile investment. These data can be leveraged in numerous ways to encourage collaboration. For example, event planners can use these data for seating designs or to assign individuals to breakout work groups. At one event, a technology company used the data to code each participant's badge with a radio frequency identification (RFID) chip. As attendees mingled, their badges glowed when they neared someone with similar interests. The computers tracked the connections in real time and built a sociogram on a large projection screen. By the end of the evening, "a poorly connected network had evolved into a richly linked community of practice."

Leveraging Natural Brokers   Increased connectivity will always improve collaboration. Nevertheless, there are ways to strategicly leverage the placement of natural brokers to maximize the improvement.

One effective tactic is to identify natural brokers and offer them incentives to reach across organizational silos. In one case study, a company identified five natural brokers and asked them to get to know two specific people in other parts of the organization. They also participated in regular calls with each other to share learning. A comparison of the sociogram before and after the process show improved cohesion of the network by 22 percent. In *The Craft of Connection*, Laseter and Cross describe how communities of practice are built with natural brokers:

> Better communities of practice can be built not only by leveraging natural brokers who already exist, but also by increasing or amplifying the personal network connections of critically placed people. Research has shown that one of the consistent differentiators of high performers

is their tendency to maintain ties outside their unit and outside their organization. Using coaching, mentoring, or career development efforts to help a greater number of strategically important people diversify their networks can have a powerful impact on the individual and on the community as a whole.

Global Connection   The use of social network analysis holds great promise for understanding and managing collaboration in highly interconnected and increasingly global communities of knowledge works. "Naturally occurring communities of practice offer a powerful vehicle for this. Managers can directly shape the relationships and information flows by providing better information access, by assigning roles such as formally designated 'Global advisors,' and by working with individual informal 'brokers.'"

COLLABORATION IN ACTION: A CASE STUDY

Competition has been the driving force behind the U.S. freight rail industry and related public policy since the first railroad began operations in 1830. This is a curious phenomenon for a contiguous "network" of railroads within a transportation "system." With competition in the marketplace and competition for government attention as the prevailing influences, the system continues to underutilize rail technology, even though railroads move freight on one-third the amount of fuel and consequent air pollution as trucks moving on the highway. In the following section Michael Sussman, founder of OnTrackAmerica, describes how collaboration is helping to rebuild and strengthen the national railway system.

Power of Collaboration in the Railroad Industry

Railroads are energy, capital, and space efficient. Yet their market share of an otherwise growing transportation demand has continually declined since the early twentieth century. What is it about this competition-based system that suppresses the use of efficient modes of transportation?

Competition, as a commercial and regulatory principle, often rewards better-operated companies. But it is usually ineffective at preventing companies that enjoy more financial and political clout from dominating the marketplace. How often in recent years has that domination had a detrimental impact on our greater communal interests? The country needs a rail system that advances in concert with our national needs; instead, it has developed according to its corporate needs.

In 1995 it became apparent that many smaller freight railroads across America were undersupported by policy makers and lending institutions. This threatened the long-term economic vitality and overall quality of life in America.

The railroad industry was cost-cutting by consolidating service to higher-volume components of the rail system. This path, while leading to greater profitability for the industry, contributed to a far less efficient transportation system than was called for by post–World War II demographic and business trends. The years since have been characterized by dramatic population growth, steadily increasing freight traffic, ongoing growth of rural and urban communities, and the proliferation of small businesses, distribution centers, and time-sensitive shipping needs. The trucking industry, in spite of its inherent fuel disadvantage, has filled this service gap ably. But with the increase in fuel prices and its uncertain future availability, the question becomes "Now what?"

To satisfy the imperative for collaboration between government and private sector, a broad network of relationships with government representatives at the federal and state levels was established. The success in bridging the public-private sector communications divide led to the founding of OnTrackAmerica, a nonprofit organization dedicated to creating new methods and forums for the multistakeholder development of better policies and more effective private initiatives.

This collaborative approach has proven to be been highly effective in creating financing breakthroughs for smaller freight railroads. Project and industry funding options typically are offered by individual entities competing *against* other funding sources. This alternative approach leads to benefit for all involved by facilitating cooperation among multiple banks and government agencies. In practice, it has resulted in significantly higher capitalization levels with better terms than if those funding sources were made to compete for the entire project.

Even the clients' existing bankers, who previously had declined further lending, are included in this collaborative approach. Rather than being pitted against other banks, the current bank is urged to offer what it can and what it prefers, as its part of an overall strategy for helping the client grow.

In the case of the Iowa Northern Railway, a corn-hauling railroad that was suddenly in the heart of the alternative energy belt, additional capital was required that outstripped the lending limits of its local bank. A collaborative approach provided bankers at Iowa's Lincoln Savings Bank with the understanding and assurance they needed to expand the railroad's credit from $150,000 to over $1.5 million. This facility became the anchor for $30 million in additional funds secured from a Federal Railroad Administration loan program, a Chicago regional bank, several equipment lenders, and even the railroads' customers and suppliers.

The basic orientation of competition is toward individual gain. Yet so much of what occurs in business involves multiple parties, with all parties benefiting if success is shared. Shared benefit and the resulting gain are the foundation of collaboration. What if our "for individual gain" concept of competition was reoriented to a competition (or striving) to make the greatest contribution to the community? That model of competition would naturally lead to a refocus of business plans and activities toward "collaboration for the common good."

While competition is a useful tool in certain elements of regulating private interests in the marketplace, it can be a dangerously wasteful force in public policy discourse and formulation. Competition, unfortunately, is now the overarching principle of interaction, not just between political parties but also among agencies, legislative offices, committees, think tanks, universities, and other entities that influence and produce public policies. The marketplace of ideas should continue to accommodate competing ideas. But the *process* for thinking and teasing out competing ideas requires our best collaboration.

Our world and our economies are undergoing changes at a rate that demands we upgrade public-sector management processes. OnTrackAmerica has taken on the challenge of bringing forward a new method for large-scale industrial policy, planning, and implementation. By lowering antagonism and increasing trust among businesspeople, academic and industry experts, the community, and policy developers, the potential emerges for unveiling the best solutions and resulting public policy. Just as cooperative multimodal relations among transportation providers are now clearly needed to advance the efficiency of the overall system, collaboration among public policy creators is the necessary ingredient for improving our national transportation policy.

Design improvements for intelligence and efficiency at the level of governance do not have to wait for the crucible of crisis. No law or regulation mandates that business must depend only on competitive, vested-interest lobbying of government legislators and policy makers. All well-intentioned citizens are entitled to advance leadership and cooperation in government and commerce. Contrary to what is expressed in popular culture, many people in Washington and beyond are anxious to participate in productive collaborative engagement. A new model of leadership that convenes and facilitates that collaboration is the missing ingredient.

■ NOTES

1. Interview of John Chambers by Bronwyn Fryer and Thomas A. Stewart, "Cisco Sees the Future," *Harvard Business Review* 86, No. 10 (November 2008), 72–79.
2. Adapted from Dan Rosen, *The Culture of Collaboration* (San Francisco: Red Ape Publishing, 2007), 9.
3. *Id.,* 9–15.
4. *Id.,* 212–213.
5. David Cooperrider, "Appreciative Inquiry and the Conscious Evolution of Chaordic Organizations," *Inneredge* 3, No. 1 (February/March 2000), 13.
6. *Id.,* 13–14.
7. David L. Cooperrider and Leslie E. Sekerka, "Toward a Theory of Positive Organizational Change," in *Positive Organizational Scholarship,* ed. Kim S. Cameron, Jane E. Dutton, and Robert E. Quinn (San Francisco: Barrett-Koehler Publishers, 2003), 231.
8. *Id.,* 227–231.
9. *Id.,* 227.
10. *Id.*
11. Russell K. Elleven, "Appreciative Inquiry: A Model for Organizational Development and Performance Improvement in Student Affairs," 2007, www.accessmylibrary.com/coms2/summary_0286-32297462_ITM.
12. Cooperrider and Sekerka, "Toward a Theory of Positive Organizational Change," 227.
13. D. I. Cooperrider and D. Whitney, "A Positive Revolution in Change: Appreciative Inquiry," in *Appreciative Inquiry, Rethinking Human Organizations towards a Positive Theory of Change,* ed. D. L. Cooperrider, P. F. Sorensen Jr., D. Whitney, and T. F. Yeager (Champaign, IL: Stipes Publishing, 1999), 18.

14. Cooperrider and Sekerka, "Toward a Theory of Positive Organizational Change," 231.
15. Christopher Laszlo and Jean-François Laugel, *Large-Scale Organizational Change* (Boston: Butterworth Heinemann, 2000), 30–31.
16. *Id.*
17. Patricia Aburdene, *Megatrends 2010* (Charlottesville, VA: Hampton Roads Publishing, 2007), xiv.
18. Margaret J. Wheatley and Myron Kellner-Rogers, *A Simpler Way* (San Francisco: Barrett-Koehler, 1996), 83.
19. Steven M. R. Covey, *The Speed of Trust* (New York: Simon and Schuster, 2008), 133–229.
20. David Coleman and Stewart Levine, *Collaboration 2.0* (Silicon Valley, CA: HappyAbout.info, 2008), 227–246.
21. *Id.,* 223.
22. Tim Laseter and Rob Cross, "The Craft of Connection," Autumn 2006, www .strategy-business.com/press/freearticle/06302. The quotes that follow in this section are all from Laseter and Cross's article.

CHAPTER 5

Innovation

Like water flowing from an underground spring, human creativity is the wellspring greening the desert of toil and effort, and much of what stifles us in the workplace is the immense unconscious effort on the part of individuals and organizations alike to dam its flow.[1]

—DAVID WHYTE, *THE HEART AROUSED*

The last few decades have belonged to a certain kind of person with a certain kind of mind—the computer programmers who could crank code, lawyers who could craft contracts, MBAs who could crunch numbers. But the keys to the kingdom are changing hands. The future belongs to a very different kind of mind—creators and empathizers, pattern recognizers, and meaning makers. These people—artists, investors, designer, storytellers, caregivers, consolers, big picture thinkers—will now reap society's richest rewards and share its greatest joys.

—DANIEL PINK, *A WHOLE NEW MIND*

While many organizations are still immersed in the Information Age, there is both an economic pull and a human yearning to move beyond the logical, linear, reductionist view to a more compassionate, inventive, holistic view. The economic pull stems from the business realities of a flattening world described in Chapter 1. Increasingly, the linear, process-oriented work is being automated or shipped overseas. And greed has undermined many legitimate business ventures. The human yearning stems from an experience of material abundance leading to a deeper yearning for nonmaterial riches. According to Daniel Pink, author of *A Whole New Mind*, this combination of forces is birthing a Conceptual Age, characterized by high concept and high touch.[2]

Spiral Dynamics offers another view that takes humanity through stages based on value systems called memes. A fascinating concept with broad implications for human development, Spiral Dynamics suggests a possible next level as more integrative than conceptual.[3] It suggests that organizations can evolve from the Information Age into one with high concept and high touch while staying grounded within the system through a high level of connection. Perhaps the next age is, as Don Beck, a leading global authority on value systems, calls it, an Integral Age.[4]

As these trends continue and global pressures increase, the next phase for business is one that competes on innovation. Innovation emerges from organizations that nurture creativity. So how is that done? The first step is to understand creativity.

CREATIVITY

> *A flash of inspiration can burst out anywhere. For Archimedes, it came in the bathtub and for Isaac Newton beneath an apple tree. But for Alastair Pilkington, it came one misty October evening while he was washing the dinner dishes. Staring at the soap and grease floating in the dishwater, he suddenly conceived of float glass—a way of making glass more cheaply by floating it in an oven on a bath of molten tin.*
>
> —1964 *NEWSWEEK* MAGAZINE ARTICLE

Many people in knowledge-based organizations, especially those working in analytical or technical positions, believe that right-brain creative processes are irrelevant to their line of work. They tend to favor more left-brain, linear, hierarchical thinking processes. However, evidence shows that the best way to solve complex analytical problems is to access the whole brain.

The Human Brain

The structure and processing of the human brain play an important role in creative thinking and problem solving. Basically, the brain is a highly adaptable complex system with no chief executive. It thrives on billions of connections, feedback loops, and interactions. When presented with stimulation, the only region of the brain that activates is the one needed. Meanwhile, other areas sit idle. Research suggests that people relate differently to situations based on the way their brains are wired.

Left-Brain/Right-Brain Theory of Organization   To understand the mechanics of the creative process, it is useful to have a deeper understanding of the structure of the brain. Most people are familiar with the fact that the brain has a left and a right hemisphere. Within the two hemispheres are the neocortex and limbic system. Also important are the connectors that connect these four areas and send signals to one another. Within these four areas, there are two patterns of brain functioning, situational functioning and iterative functioning. These are the components of the left-brain/right-brain theory of organization.[5]

Neocortex   Roughly 80 percent of the brain is in the neocortex. It is anatomically divided into two halves, called cerebral hemispheres. The neocortex manages "processes concerning vision, hearing, body, sensations, intentional motor control, reasoning, cerebral thinking and decision-making, purposeful behavior, language, and non-verbal ideation."[6]

Limbic System   The two halves of the limbic system are nestled into each of the two cerebral hemispheres and make up most of the rest of the thinking cortex. The limbic system has one of the richest blood supplies in the body; it "regulates eating, drinking, sleeping, waking, body temperature, chemical balances such as blood sugar, heart rate, blood pressure, punishment, hunger, thirst, aggression, and rage."[7]

The limbic system is responsible for producing emotions. It is connected to both the brain stem and the cerebral hemispheres through vast and highly developed connections. Therefore, it is in a position to mediate brain activity between the brain stem and the cerebral hemispheres. In other words, it has the power to overwhelm logical thinking with emotional energy.

Connections within the Brain   The connections within the brain fall into two categories, those within each hemisphere and those between the hemispheres and the two halves of the limbic system. The most famous of these, the corpus callosum, connects the two cerebral hemispheres. It is believed to have between 200 and 300 million fibers. Research suggests that, on average, female brains have an advantage over male brains in size, speed, and maturity rate—the rate at which the brain matures. This may explain some of the differences in male and female aptitude and behaviors.

Situational versus Iterative Functioning   To improve efficiency, the brain determines which part to activate based on the particular situation. For example, if people are listening, their language center will activate while their calculation center sits idle.

Iterative functioning, in contrast, "is a back-and-forth movement of signals among the brain's specialized centers that take place to advance work on a task."[8] Depending on the complexity of the task, it can be a single iteration or multiple iterations between or within hemispheres.

Amygdalae   Another area of the brain plays a big role in the ability to survive amid complexity as it relates to fear. The amygdalae sit at the base of the brain and serve as processors for emotions, especially fear. One of the oldest parts of the brain, their characteristics can be the most deep-seated and hard to explain. When dealing with transformation and moving in new directions, people's level of fear plays a prominent role in their ability and willingness to move forward.

Cerebellum   The latest research on the cerebellum suggests that it is a powerful mechanism with more nerve cells than the rest of the brain combined.[9] It quickly processes information from all other parts of the brain, such as motor areas, cognitive areas, language areas, and areas involving emotional functions. Its computer-like circuitry allows it to send information back out to various parts of the brain. Its connections to the cerebral cortex resemble segregated bundles, which allow it to communicate complex information. Current theories under investigation suggest that the cerebellum is involved not only in skilled motor performance but in skilled mental performance as well as "various sensory functions including sensory acquisition, discrimination, tracking and prediction."[10] Experimental evidence shows that it may also be responsible for automating repetitive processes, thereby freeing the brain for other mental activities.

Activities by Brain Function   Considering the complexity of today's volatile global economy, the role of the right brain is increasingly vital. With computers becoming more and more adept at handling the linear processes, the competitive advantage for humans is in the ability to access the power of the right hemisphere. And the skills needed to participate in an adaptive organization are also dominantly right-brained. In fact, research suggests that our right hemisphere is the only area that deals effectively with change.[11]

In general, the two halves of the brain work together to orchestrate every human activity. However, neuroscientists suggest that the two hemispheres approach every situation slightly differently. Understanding and enhancing the use of one side or the other can enhance creative endeavors.

The differences in the hemispheres can be characterized in four major ways:

1. *The left hemisphere controls the right side of the body; the right hemisphere controls the left side of the body*. This fact is well known. But it is interesting to note that in many languages the written word goes from left to right, a movement controlled by the left hemisphere. Therefore, reading and writing are controlled by the linear, logical, sequential part of the brain. Until recently, this was the source of almost all knowledge. Only since the twentieth century has information been conveyed in pictures, encouraging right hemisphere or even whole-brain synthesis.

2. *The left hemisphere is sequential; the right hemisphere is simultaneous*. As described, reading is sequential. The left hemisphere also manages other sequential processes, such as talking and interpreting speech. By contrast, the right hemisphere has the ability to interpret information simultaneously. This enables people to make sense of very complex situations. To illustrate, consider a comparison to computer software. SAS software can perform statistical calculations faster than humans can. But the most powerful software cannot recognize a human face as fast as the average person. "Think of the sequential/simultaneous difference like this: the right hemisphere

is the picture; the left hemisphere is the thousand words."[12] As the flow of complex information accelerates, frequent and proficient use of the right hemisphere becomes increasingly important.

3. *The left hemisphere specializes in text; the right hemisphere specializes in context.* In most people, both left- and right-handed, the left hemisphere is the source of language. However, the ability to comprehend language is a bit more nuanced and requires both hemispheres. Chapter 3 described the mechanics of both verbal and nonverbal communication. Within the brain, the left hemisphere interprets the words. The right hemisphere processes all of the nonverbal parts of the communication, such as tone, pace, facial expressions, and body language. In addition, the right hemisphere's ability to consider context gives it responsibility for filling in blanks, translating nuance, and interpreting metaphor.

4. *The left hemisphere analyzes the details; the right hemisphere synthesizes the big picture.* Basically, the left brain analyzes information in a linear manner. The right brain synthesizes information to create a whole. The left brain can find problems, identify parts, and grasp details. The right brain focuses on interactions and relationships. And "only the right brain can see the big picture."[13]

Ned Herrmann, a well-known brain researcher, created a list of common business functions and mapped them to the quadrant of the brain that primarily handles each one.[14]

Left Cerebral Cortex

- Gather facts
- Analyze issues
- Solve problems logically
- Argue rationally
- Measure precisely
- Understand technical elements
- Consider financial aspects

Right Cerebral Cortex

- Read signs of coming change
- See the "big picture"

- Recognize new possibilities
- Tolerate ambiguity
- Integrate ideas and concepts
- Bend or challenge established policies
- Synthesize unlike elements into a new whole
- Problem solve in intuitive ways

Left Limbic System

- Find overlooked flaws
- Approach problems practically
- Stand firm on issues
- Maintain a standard of consistency
- Provide stable leadership and supervision
- Read fine print in documents and/or contracts
- Organize and keep track of essential data
- Develop detailed plans and procedures
- Implement projects in a timely manner
- Articulate plans in an orderly way
- Keep financial records straight

Right Limbic System

- Recognize interpersonal difficulties
- Anticipate how others will feel
- Intuitively understand how others feel
- Pick up nonverbal cues of interpersonal stress
- Relate to others in empathetic ways
- Engender enthusiasm
- Persuade
- Teach
- Conciliate
- Understand emotional elements
- Consider values

Fostering Creativity

Innovation is fostered by information gathered from new connections; from insights gathered from new connections; from insights gained by journeys into other disciplines or places; from active, collegial networks and fluid, open boundaries. Innovation arises from ongoing circles of exchange, where information is not just accumulated or stored, but created. Knowledge is generated anew from connections that weren't there before. When this information self-organizes, innovations occur, the progeny of information-rich, ambiguous environments.

—Margaret Wheatley, *Leadership and the New Science*

Creativity cannot be forced. It can only be allowed. However, much can be done to increase the flow of creativity.

Actions for Stimulating Creativity   While most leaders are highly creative, many of the best ideas bubble up through the rank and file. They are the ones closest to the processes or customers where innovation has the biggest impact. Everyone loves to share ideas. So innovation is a resource that is easy to tap. One can take several actions to encourage ideas.

Offer Incentives   Most people love to share their ideas, but some may be fearful of criticism or rejection. So it is best to set rules that no idea will be judged negatively. However, the best ideas, especially those that translate into profits, should be rewarded. An organizational-level program that offers incentives and rewards for good ideas goes a long way toward fostering creativity.

Ask Inspiring Questions   Continually questioning every process is a great way to generate new ideas. Asking "what if" and questions based on curiosity can stimulate thinking. And inspiring individuals to dream or create their own department, process, or even company is a great way to get the juices flowing. Also, challenging a group to solve an impossible problem can lead to amazing breakthroughs.

Create Time and Space to Think   Most people feel so much pressure that just having time to think is a luxury. But this is exactly what is needed to nurture creativity. Some companies are creating relaxing spaces just for daydreaming. Others are allocating time and telling their workers to go for a walk in the woods or visit an art gallery to get out of their thinking rut. A change of scenery is one of the best ways to tap into the right side of the brain.

Design a Creative Workspace   There is so much that can be done to enhance the simplest workspace. Artwork and plants give a cubicle or office a more organic feel. Soft, inspiring music enhances brain function. A view of the outdoors is an ever-changing landscape of color and light.

Enhance Diversity   Creativity can be stimulated by bringing together people of different talents, backgrounds, cultures, and viewpoints. The more varied the experience of the participants, the more each person's own ideas will be enhanced.

Mistakes are the portals of discovery.

—JAMES JOYCE

Encourage Mistakes   Organizations that encourage individuals to make decisions at their own level will most likely see an increase in errors. This is natural because it is expected that the organization is changing and evolving at a much faster rate. So while there may be a concern about the increase, more mistakes may mean that more new ideas are reaching the experimentation stage. A common theme is "managers must decrease the fear of failure and that the goal should be to experiment constantly, fail early and often, and learn as much as possible in the process."[15]

Free-Form Conferences   In 1985, the organizers of the International Symposium on Organizational Transformation discovered that the participants thought the best part of the conference was during the coffee break.[16] It turned out that this time of mingling and freestyle interaction also was the part the participants liked the most. So the organizers decided to design the entire conference as a coffee break. In other words, they decided to use open space methodology to design the entire program. "The result is a conference with no agenda, no organizing committee and, surprisingly, almost no stress."

In the book *Open Space Technology: A User's Guide*, Harrison Owen[17] offers ideas for running all types of programs with minimal structure. He suggests that gathering in an open space that is outside of the day-to-day experience allows ideas to emerge. "If the aim is creativity and innovation, knocking out the stultifying drudgery is step one. Step two is removing expectations, developing trust and getting back to a sense of play," according to Professor Lizbeth Goodman, director of the SMARTlab Digital Media Institute at the University of East London. She uses theater games and voice work: shouting, singing, and laughing. "People remember some previous version of themselves that hadn't yet been taught to think in boxes. When you free up someone's body movement, you free up their mind."

One company builds a conference by bringing in top experts in their field. The attendees hear each expert in a morning plenary session. Then small teams book time with the experts for a few days. "It's this combination of structure and absolute freedom to brainstorm, along with up-close access to successful mentors, that feeds the 'anything is possible' atmosphere."

Although the format has been used primarily in the media arts industry, the model works for all types of companies. One event brought together "top-level professionals from across the biopharmaceutical, FMCG [Fast Moving Consumer Goods], petrochemical, and chemical industries." The invitation-only event allowed the participants to design "their own agenda of interactive-workshops, personal meetings, networking sessions and keynote presentations."

Several companies offer these conferences in different formats, but the overarching concept is simple: Reduce the structure and let the ideas flow.

INNOVATION IN THE MARKETPLACE

> *Engineers say that, a new idea is "invented" when it is proven to work in the laboratory. The idea becomes an "innovation" only when it can be replicated reliably on a meaningful scale at practical costs.*

> —PETER M. SENGE, *THE FIFTH DISCIPLINE*

Economics of Innovation

To remain competitive, companies must innovate.[18] Without innovation, products and services become more and more alike. In other words, they eventually become commodities. Then businesses have to compete on price, which eventually destroys profit margins. When the market stabilizes at the lower price, investors move to other markets. By contrast, innovation allows companies to differentiate. This enables premium pricing, which eventually leads to higher value. When the market stabilizes well above cost, it becomes easier to attract investors.

"The fundamental principle that drives this argument is that when innovation creates differentiation, it creates attractive economic returns." However, there are other possible outcomes for all types of innovation efforts. The ultimate goal is to calculate "return on innovation." There are four other types of innovation:

- *Differentiation.* Innovation designed to capture market share, attract investors, and gain economic advantage
- *Neutralization.* Innovation to keep up with higher-performing competitors
- *Productivity.* Innovation to lower costs, thus freeing resources for other forms of innovation
- *Waste.* Innovation that falls short of achieving any goals

Differentiation is the type of innovation that holds the most potential for economic gains. However, it is often stifled by adversity to risk. A company that is focused on risk reduction stays close to norms and tends to leverage the experience of the market leaders. This is dangerous for companies that hope to take a "value proposition to such an extreme that competitors either cannot or will not follow."

Companies who seek to be innovative must encourage collaboration. "Breakaway differentiation requires a highly coordinated effort across the entire enterprise." The idea may come from a small group. But "at the end of the day, every function in the corporation has to realign its priorities in order to amplify the innovation to breakaway status. Anything less is simply too easy for competitors to neutralize."

Successful innovation requires strong leadership. In most companies, innovation is highly decentralized with multiple projects going on at the same time. This is the best strategy for the incubation stage. But when it comes to selecting the best prospect for further investment, strong leadership is required. "If management does not take a position on innovation strategy, the company's innovation will continue to bubble up, but they will not be aligned. If all are brought to market—and that is the default option in this scenario—none will achieve breakaway status."

Taking Ideas to Market

When an organization decides to pursue innovation as a strategy, there are several aspects to consider. First, how viable is the product or service? Second, is the product or service feasible? And third, once it is developed, what is the best way to take the new product or service to market?

Rob Goldberg, an innovation consultant, specializes in helping companies take their ideas to market. He offers the following assessments when considering an innovation project.[19]

Evaluation of Viability   Goldberg uses eight dimensions to determine the viability of products and services:

1. *Size of opportunity.* What is the size of the market?
2. *Growth of market.* Is the market growing or shrinking?
3. *Strength of customer relationship.* Can existing customer relationships be leveraged?
4. *Value creating.* How do we create a competitive advantage?
5. *Degree of government involvement.* To what extent is the market regulated?
6. *Degree of competitive density.* What is the structure of the market, and who are the leaders?
7. *Value delivery.* What barriers to entry exist?
8. *Window of opportunity duration.* How much time do we have to launch successfully?

Evaluation of Feasibility   When considering entering the market, there are several questions to assist in assessing feasibility.

- *Perception.* How much pain is associated with what the company does today? Is there a need for the product or service?
- *Competitive density.* Are there any 800-pound gorillas lurking?
- *Brand image.* Can your company deliver a credible solution in this space?
- *Innovation.* Does the technology exist to develop the solution?

- *Experimentation.* Does the solution rely on proven technology?
- *Business model.* Is the company willing to pay for it?
- *Return on investment.* Does the product or service support corporate hurdles to bring the innovation to market?
- *Cost of entry.* How do we enter the market?

Taking the Innovation to Market Once the innovation is ready, Goldberg uses a four-stage process to take an idea to market:

1. Requirements analysis defines the *what.* The goal is to document all function/feature, performance, and user-interfacing requirements of the solution that meets the customer's needs.
2. Design analysis describes the *how.* Design essentially transforms the requirement into a blueprint that outlines data structures, architecture, procedural detail, and interface characterization that can be created to deliver the desired customer experience.
3. Feasibility analysis determines the *how much.* The aim of a feasibility study is to see whether it is possible to develop the solution at a reasonable cost.
4. Optimization analysis determines *what it is worth.* The goal of optimization is to establish the optimum feature set based on economic value and customer preferences.

Depending on the industry and type of product or service, there may be other considerations. But these basic concepts offer some guidelines for accelerating the innovation process within an organization.

TIPS FROM THE FIELD

All my successes have been built on my failures.

—BENJAMIN DISRAELI, BRITISH STATESMAN AND LITERARY FIGURE

Cherry Woodburn, a business innovation consultant, attributes her passion for innovation to her first manager who encouraged her to try new ideas without fear of recrimination. "If an idea didn't work," Woodburn states, "we would analyze the process and learn from the experience." Here she shares advice on creating a culture of innovation.

Innovation in Action

Most companies fail to encourage innovation. Large companies in particular tend to be risk adverse and have a mind-set geared toward exploiting ways to control their processes through standardization. Process improvement is beneficial. But a company's emphasis on reducing variation in its *present* systems can result in a lack of innovation over the long term. It is a paradox. While companies are increasing the quality of their product, they may be decreasing their ability to innovate.

Businesses need to cultivate innovation in order to compete in today's fast-paced, innovation-driven economy. Since innovation is now recognized as necessary to keep a business viable and competitive, why doesn't a culture of innovation spring up organically? Why does it need to be fostered? What keeps employees from naturally bubbling with creativity?

Obviously there are many variables, one of which is a cultural belief that there is one right answer. The natural outcome of this simplistic thinking is a reduction in the dialogue, thereby blocking the exploration of various alternate viewpoints and ideas. Meetings are held to find "the one right answer." No one really listens to anyone else. Everyone is too busy preparing an opposing response. Underlying assumptions go unquestioned and unexamined. And too often, the person who speaks up or disagrees with the majority opinion is labeled "not a team player." Add in today's hectic pace and a general disdain for meetings, and it is understandable that people look for closure rather than exposure to new ideas.

However, innovation and expansive thinking emerge from nurturing different points of view. Doing so requires the pioneering spirit of exploring new territory. Innovation by its very nature requires experimentation and failure. Thomas Edison is the classic example. After more than 1,000 attempts to invent the first long-lasting electric light bulb, he was successful inventing bulbs that stayed lit for only a few minutes. One of his colleagues asked, "Mr. Edison, don't you feel you are a failure?" Without reservation, he answered, "Not at all. Now I definitely know more than a thousand ways *not* to make a light bulb."

Sadly, the culture in many organizations dictates that mistakes are bad and should be avoided at all costs. Employees are criticized or even ridiculed for mistakes. This stems from early learning in institutions where mistakes meant a lower grade and even possible consequences at home.

Often this attitude continues into the workplace, where the aversion to mistakes is continued. Consider how these stultifying lessons continue to pile on: Sue gets reprimanded in front of peers for making errors and feels humiliated. Consequence: In the future, she will be prone to hide her mistakes and not deviate from business as usual. In the same company, Tom is written up for insubordination because he experimented with a new way of doing things, thereby not adhering to long-held company practices. As a result of these and similar incidents, people play it safe. Yet the greatest innovations can come from workers' own initiatives, not just from an initiative pushed down from the top.

The need for innovation is nothing new, but the recognition that it needs to be a core competency—permeating all departments and all levels of the organization—is relatively recent. Much as leaders once believed that quality was primarily the responsibility of the quality department, so has innovation been primarily confined within the borders of research and development. Frans Johansson, author of the successful book *The Medici Effect: Breakthrough Insights at the Intersection of Ideas, Concepts & Cultures*[20], advocates that companies also be willing to take their efforts at innovation beyond the borders of their business to include other industries and disciplines. He called this cross-fertilization of ideas the Medici effect, after the fifteenth-century banking family that broke down traditional barriers separating disciplines and cultures to ignite the Renaissance.

A culture of innovation needs to be nurtured until it is deeply rooted into the psyche of every employee. However, this cannot be done successfully with announcements, slogans, or playing on people's fear of competition. Ironically, innovative thinking is also needed to maintain traditional practices that still add value and to cultivate a daily crop of new ideas. The culture is about recognizing individual mind-sets and accepting perceived borders and limitations in order to question them. These mind-sets typically come from each employee's individual experiences and culture. They are empowered by past experiences that have become hardwired into the brain. Couple that with the fact that brains are structured to simplify and categorize massive amounts of daily stimuli, and it is no wonder people get caught in a duality of right and wrong. The pattern becomes "Success is good; failure is bad." When new information is compatible with what is known, it is accepted as the truth; when it does not mesh with preconceived ideas or past experiences, it receives little consideration. As a result, opportunities to innovate and change the status quo are missed. Research shows that the act of recognizing and surfacing unconscious beliefs offers the highest leverage for change.

Understanding and acknowledging the current situation in comparison to the desired state is the first step in any change initiative. It is impossible to change something that is not acknowledged or understood, which makes it difficult to grow into a future culture steeped in innovative thinking.

Begin with asking tough questions of everyone in the organization. Dig up deeply embedded beliefs and assumptions that are, more than likely, not in sync with the stated company vision and values. Here are some questions for starters.

- What are your own and your organization's assumptions and beliefs related to innovation, particularly innovation that deals with new practices and methods? New product ideas tend to fare better, but, again are they encouraged and tested? Begin a dialogue with employees at all levels and in all departments to learn how steeped the company is in "Business as usual" and "That won't work here."
- Has an emphasis on process improvement, standardization, and reducing variation created a myopic focus on improving what you are already doing to the virtual exclusion of creativity and innovation? Think of the demise of the fully integrated steel mills versus today's mini-mills; think of Kodak improving in film and print while virtually ignoring digital photography for years.
- What are your own and your organization's assumptions and beliefs about risk taking, mistakes, and lack of immediate positive outcomes? Ask yourself if you stick with a new idea long enough to see results. Tally the number of initiatives that started over the past five to ten years. Then honestly evaluate the number remaining—in other words, those that maintained their initial momentum. Study the gap between the organization's actual behavior and the values it espouses about vision, growth, and innovation.
- Do you encourage experimentation, testing hypotheses, or do new ideas get quashed in meetings or die a slow death as they are analyzed, dissected, and debated?

Think of the ensuing dialogue as preparatory work for growing the innovative capabilities that have been lying fallow due to traditional business practices. When transforming a garden, it is not enough to plant verbal seeds. If the ground has been depleted of creative nutrients due to years of leaching the soil with criticism, tight control, and fear, announcing a new gardening program will not be successful.

By taking time to listen carefully and allow fears to emerge, the organization can begin to prepare the soil. Fertilizing with acceptance and courage allows an innovative culture to emerge. As leaders cultivate the vision, innovation will flourish and generate new ideas for years to come.

■ NOTES

1. David Whyte, *The Heart Aroused* (New York: Currency Doubleday, 1994), 20–21.
2. Daniel Pink, *A Whole New Mind* (New York: Riverhead Books, 2005), 2.
3. Jessica Roemischer, "The Never-Ending Upward Quest," *What Is Enlightenment* No. 22 (Fall/Winter 2002), 108.
4. Don Beck, "Human Capacities in the Integral Age." Available at www .spiraldynamics.net/DrDonBeck/essays/human_capacities.htm.
5. Ned Herrmann, *The Creative Brain* (Lake Lure, NC: The Ned Herrmann Group, 1994), 32.
6. *Id.*
7. *Id.,* 33.
8. *Id.,* 38.
9. Henrietta C. Leiner and Alan L. Leiner, "The Treasure at the Bottom of the Brain," September 1997. Available at www.newhorizons.org/neuro/leiner.htm.
10. *Id.*
11. Herrmann, *The Creative Brain,* 125.
12. Pink, *A Whole New Mind,* 19.
13. *Id.,* 23.
14. Herrmann, *The Creative Brain,* 424.
15. Teresa M. Amabile and Mukti Khaire, "Creativity and the Role of the Leader," *Harvard Business Review* 86, No. 10 (October 2008), 101–107.
16. Rosanne Bersten, "Hatching Ideas," *Fast Thinking* (Summer 2007): 63–65. The quotes that follow in this section are all from Bersten's article.
17. Harrison Owen, *Open Space Technology: A User's Guide* (San Francisco: Berrett-Koehler Publishers).
18. Geoffrey A. Moore, *Dealing with Darwin* (New York: Penguin Group, 2005), 5–12. The quotes that follow in this section are all from Moore's book.
19. Rob Goldberg, "Stages of Innovation Product Development & Program Management Services Pamphlet," available by request at www.stagesofinnovation .com.
20. Frans Johanson, *The Medici Effect: Breakthrough Insights at the Intersection of Ideas, Concepts & Cultures* (Boston: Harvard Business School Press, 2004)

CHAPTER 6

Adaptability

We must remain open to change by building flexibility into our organizational structures and interactions. The more rigid we become, the less access we have to the reality of the system, and thus, the less able we are to shift as the environment demands.

—JULIE ROBERTS PH.D., PRINCIPAL OF CHANGEWORKS

For the last several decades, organizations have dealt with economic shifts using change management. Based on the new science, there are two major flaws with this approach. First, the word *change* implies an event with an ending. Second, it implies that change can be managed. In a world of economic volatility, this approach is no longer viable. The continuous climate of uncertainty and volatility demands another view, one that supports adaptability and resilience.

THE SHIFTING PARADIGM

Risk management's inability to adapt to the changing business landscape played a large role in the global financial meltdown.

—DANIEL TU, PRICEWATERHOUSECOOPERS

An adaptable organization is one that self-organizes. Most organizations appear to have order. But order is not the same as organization. Organization involves differentiation and specialization.[1]

To understand the basic reasons for the resistance to evolve, it is instructive to trace the roots of our traditional business models. The organizational model that serves as the foundation for most companies has its origins in Newtonian physics, which states that all "individual or system behavior is knowable, predictable, and controllable."[2] It operates like a machine "with each part acting on the other part with precise linear laws of cause and effect."[3] This structure brings with it many aspects of mechanistic thinking, some of which are useful. But in a highly volatile economy, most aspects of this model are inefficient. For example, most companies have rigid organizational structures with centralized command and control. Their business intelligence systems are linear and unidirectional. They utilize rigorous analysis and measurement to limit variation and drive efficiency, and, in the event of an unpredicted outcome, they search for root causes. They tend to be highly mechanized companies with highly specialized workers who receive extensive instructions. This model is useful in stable environments, such as operating rooms or highly specialized factories, where systems are closed, change is slow, and variability is low.[4]

TRADITIONAL METHODS

Traditional change methodologies designed for the mechanistic model are typically "rational, top-down, expert-driven, and planned."[5] And even though nearly three-fourths of change initiatives, such as total quality management or reengineering, fail, most organizational change initiatives still operate under these models.[6]

Total Quality Management

Total quality management (TQM), for example, is defined by the International Organization for Standardization as "a management approach for an organization, centered on quality, based on the participation of all its members and aiming at long-term success through customer satisfaction, and benefits to all members of the organization and to society."[7] "One major aim [of TQM] is to reduce variation from every process so that greater consistency of effort is obtained."[8]

This approach is based primarily on the philosophy of Dr. W. Edwards Deming, pioneered in the 1930s and 1940s. However, he later abandoned the terminology of TQM "because he believed it had become a superficial label for tools and techniques. The real work, which he simply called the 'transformation of the prevailing system of management,' lay beyond the aims of managers seeking only short-term performance improvements. This transformation [. . .] required 'profound knowledge' largely untapped in contemporary institutions."[9]

In a letter to Peter Senge, Dr. Deming (then almost 90) wrote:

> Our prevailing system of management has destroyed our people. People are born with intrinsic motivation, self-respect, dignity, curiosity to learn, joy in learning. The forces of destruction begin with toddlers—a prize for the best Halloween costume, grades in school, gold stars—and on up through university. On the job, people, teams, and divisions are ranked, reward for the top, punishment for the bottom. Management by Objectives, quotas, incentive pay, business plans, put together separately, division by division, cause further loss, unknown and unknowable.[10]

Business Process Reengineering

Business process reengineering (BPR) is based on a theory by Frederick Winslow Taylor that variation is waste. It actually makes sense for areas within a business that are highly linear and measured. Originally conceived as a way to reshape processes, it became the rationale for the massive layoffs in the 1990s that had such a disastrous effect on the economy. "Its bias toward static, written rules means it cannot handle the abstract, dynamic thinking and actions of humans in a knowledge based economy."[11] By imposing actions from outside, it ignores the knowledge of the people within the system and undermines their value in the process of realignment.

THE NEW PARADIGM

In traditional organizations, strategy management is usually static and reductionist. The focus is on short-term gain, optimal allocation of resources, process improvement, and increasing competitive advantage. The approach to change is incremental, with the assumption that a slight change in the existing strategy or variation in the organizational structure will do the job.

As mentioned earlier, two fundamentally different organizational models are offered. The traditional model, based on Newtonian science, is linear, rational, and reductionist. It is based on the idea that organizations are made up of individual units that can be managed separately. Units such as people, products, tasks, and expenses can each be optimized to support the whole. Change is predictable and controllable with a final end state characterized by stability. According to Laszlo and Laugel in *Large-Scale Organizational Change*, "This notion is rooted in calculus with which Newton expressed his immutable laws of physics—smooth, continuous, differential equations that lead toward a fixed equilibrium."[12]

The emergent model is on the opposite end of the spectrum. It sees organizations as emerging from complexity with their parts interconnected and relating as living systems. Behavior emerges and is experienced on an organizational level. It cannot be reduced to incremental units. Rather than implementing change, the emergent or living systems model is always adapting to stay in balance. Change, as defined by the old model, is continuous. The wisdom or intelligence of the organization does not just reside with leadership but is assumed to be distributed across a wide variety of people and systems.

By understanding the rules, principles, and behaviors of each model, organizations can select the best path based on the specific situation. For example, if a company needs to manufacture a product, a clear linear process with a predefined path and time frame is optimal. However, when pressures from outside or deep within an organization require adaptation, it is rarely predictable or controllable. The constant need to innovate, a pressure felt by many in the global economy, is a good example. The intelligence of the organization to meet this goal is far superior to that of the top management team.[13]

Exhibit 6.1 highlights the comparison between classical science and the new science.

The results of each of these paths are shown in Exhibit 6.2.

To illustrate how our traditional change methodologies and structures limit adaptability, Deehock, founder of Visa Corporation, asks us to imagine if traditional business rules and processes are applied to the neurons in the brain.

> Organize the neurons in your brain, the most complex, infinitely diverse organ that has ever emerged in evolution, as you would a corporation. The first thing you've got to do is appoint the Chief Executive neuron, right? Then you've got to decide which are going to be the Board of Directors neurons and the Human Resources neurons, and then you have to write an operating manual for it. Now, if you could organize your

EXHIBIT 6.1	COMPARISON BETWEEN CLASSICAL SCIENCE AND NEW SCIENCE

Classical Science	New Science
Mechanistic, linear, separate parts, events, moments.	Holistic, nonlinear, integrated.
Whole is defined as sum of parts.	Whole is greater than sum of parts.
Reality is predictable; laws determine the outcome. "Either/or" thinking.	Reality is full of possibility; nothing is predetermined. "Both/and" thinking.
Work with building blocks. Those in control dictate what is done.	Work with networks. System is emergent and self-referencing.
Chaos is suppressed; structures are taken apart to examine and control.	Natural order emerges from chaos; self-organization.
Science is objective; what is not observed does not exist.	No objective reality; our observation evolves; we cannot avoid having an impact.
Seek the truth.	Seek best approximation of reality.

EXHIBIT 6.2	RESULTS OF PATHS IN EXHIBIT 6.1

Classical Science	New Science
Closed rigid systems	Flexible open systems
Resistance to chaos	Willingness to leverage chaos
Passive hostility to being controlled	Creativity, adaptability, energy
Lack of information	Flow of information through natural connections
Low value placed on relationships	Relationships emerge and flourish
Fear during change	Support during change
Fragmentation	Harmony

brain on that model, what would happen? You would instantly be unable to breathe until somebody told you how and where and when and how fast. You wouldn't be able to think or see. What if your immune system were organized on this basis? First you'd have to do some market research to determine what virus, if any, was attacking you, right? Then you'd have to have marching orders for all the various aspects of your immune system.[14]

MODELS FOR ADAPTIVE ORGANIZATIONS

Chapter 2 offered complexity science, chaos theory, and evolutionary biology as models for understanding organizational dynamics in a volatile economy. Further exploration into various aspects of these models unveils concepts for improving organizational adaptability.

A Living Systems Model

Leading an organization based on living systems requires an understanding of organizational evolution.[15] "The focus shifts from what is to what is becoming, from structure to dynamics." The following steps describe the pattern of change in living systems:

1. Innovation
2. Complexification and Convergence
3. Bifurcation and Chaos

The steps originate in science but have a direct application in the corporate world. Their role and interrelation are critical to understanding adaptability in an emergent organization.

Innovation   Innovation is essential for maintaining adaptability and resilience. The combination of advances in technology and globalization put pressure on many organizations to adapt or die. Both of these are seen as irreversible. And the speed at which they occur continues to increase. The impact of a high level of innovation is felt through the next step.

Complification and Convergence   As advanced technologies inject new information into the system, complexity increases. However, there are limits to the complexity an organization can handle. To accommodate increased complexity, new levels of organization must be created to control and coordinate the existing levels. As a result, an organization "always converges progressively toward more embracing and coordinated multilevel structures."

Convergence is seen across the globe as many corporations are partnering, forming alliances, merging, and diversifying into multiple lines of business. Global business standards and regulations are a result of this phenomenon.

What happens when a global company reaches its limit of complexity is unknown. Based on the new science, the next step in the sequence may be chaos.

Bifurcation and Chaos   Scientists have known for decades that as complex systems evolve, chaos and uncertainty increase. Today, computer models are able to simulate the evolutionary path with mathematical precision. The models show the attractors that form the pattern of the evolutionary trajectory.

The evolutionary trajectory can be plotted to show a graphical pattern providing a visual depiction of an attractor. There are several types of attractors. A system that evolves toward a fixed point over time is defined by stable-point attractors; a cyclically recurring state is characterized by period attractors; and an emergent system of order is defined by strange or chaotic attractors, as described in Chapter 2. As chaotic attractors are plotted, a shape emerges that has definite boundaries and patterns. The beautiful shapes of the plots prove that chaotic attractors are neither arbitrary nor disorderly.

Bifurcation occurs when a complex system changes trajectory. It is characterized by a change in pattern and a shift from one set of attractors to another. In the real world, complex systems evolve out of a specific initial state until a pattern emerges. If the evolution comes to rest, the process is ruled by static attractors. If the patterns are cyclical, the system is regulated by periodic attractors. If neither of these occurs, the system is controlled by strange or chaotic attractors.

Strange or chaotic attractors are pervasive in our global economy. The recent collapse of the world's financial markets and its domino effect around the world demonstrates this pattern. Catastrophic bifurcations are occurring as many large financial institutions seek equilibrium amid the chaos.

Chaotic attractors do not operate with total randomness. Scientific analysis has unveiled a subtle order that emerges. Complex systems self-organize through a natural phenomenon known as cross-catalytic cycles. Following periods of instability and chaos, these cycles allow complex systems to return to dynamic stability where they can grow and prosper.

LEVERAGING CHAOS IN ORGANIZATIONS

As mentioned earlier, the key to leveraging chaos within an organization is to allow the vision to drive the change. Chaos manifests within organizations as an inability to find and deal with information in a useful way. If the chaos is contained within specific boundaries, and if the members of the organization can tolerate the tension, order will eventually emerge. Crisis, however, is the failure of coping mechanisms, resulting in a loss of a framework that leads to stagnation or death. In other words, the system is unable to tolerate the tension.

Vision-driven energy can create change that does not result from crisis, although chaos will still occur. Dissatisfaction with the status quo drives a vision, not crisis. Dissatisfaction is the result of examining the status quo with an open mind in relation to the environment and deciding that change is necessary. The vision provides a way of getting members of the organization focused on the future. A vision should inspire and motivate. It should entice members to move out of the current state and move toward the new state while honoring the values of the organization and its members.

Structure within Chaos

For organizations to foster adaptability, it is important to provide a structure or boundaries to guide it through the chaos. However, there is a delicate balance between providing structure and controlling the process. Recall that new patterns emerge only when the system is far from equilibrium. Providing structure in this case means utilizing the system, getting people together and providing them with ways of interacting, and sharing information. This process provides the tension that results in people feeling the need to change. In a healthy system, they would eventually create a plan *together*. "No one system dictates conditions to another. All participate together in creating the conditions of their interdependence."[16]

When an organization is in chaos, leaders typically decide they know the answers and take it upon themselves to establish the necessary structures, processes, and rules without any input from the rest of the organization. While this approach is generally easier and faster, it is antithetical to systems thinking and may impede adaptability. It actually prevents the system from rising to a higher level by way of *self*-organization. Systems thinking requires that the all parts of the system be involved in any major decision-making process.

When chaos is overwhelming the system, it is necessary to provide boundaries or simple rules to contain the chaos. Doing so entails helping people stay focused on the core purpose of the organization and values. By allowing employees to experience the underlying strength of the organization, everyone in it is able to understand and internalize the core purpose. However, it is critical to create dialogue opportunities that encourage tough questions regarding the purpose and its impact. It is common to assume that everyone understands the purpose; thus, often this step is skipped. Understanding the core purpose is crucial in self-organizing systems; this purpose provides the goals around which self-organization occurs. Dialoguing regarding purpose aligns individuals and helps them to claim the purpose as their own.

Values are guiding principles for *how to act*. They define members' behavior in reaching their goals. An example of a value is: "We will continue to learn and evolve by examining what we do and how we do it on an individual, group, and system level." Values act as the strange attractor that pulls the system into order during times of turbulence. They provide guidelines for how to interact with one another, particularly during chaos. Without clear standards for how to work and interact, change can be too risky.

It is futile to have values that mean nothing and do not define how people *actually behave*. If people hear one value and see behavior that contradicts it, they will not feel safe. For example, if an organization values self-examination and criticism to aid learning and then uses blame and punishment when something goes wrong, the self-examination will cease. In addition to consistency around behavior, it is important for leaders to model the desired organizational behavior.

Tolerance for Discomfort

Systems change when they are far from equilibrium. For this reason, it is important to resist complacency in times of success. Many organizations fail as a result of complacency. Organizations that continue to look for indicators of new shifts will maintain a competitive edge.

It is helpful to develop a tolerance for the discomfort associated with the change process. Doing so allows natural connections to develop. But when discomfort reaches high levels, some organizations hurry the process by forcing connections, coming to premature solutions, and controlling outcomes. This control impedes the formation of natural connections.

Newly formed groups, which are particularly susceptible to this urge, cope with it by jumping to solutions prematurely. During times of change, the urge to bring closure to issues and to know the answers increases. This urge needs to be managed with forethought and care by developing a tolerance for ambiguity and lack of control.

Natural Connections and Flexibility

Order rises naturally from chaos, and connections form naturally to make sense of the inherent and emerging information. Organizational structures and processes should be formed as a result of *natural* connections, and they should be adapted when necessary to ensure that the vision is achieved in the most productive and efficient manner. Jan Carlzon, chief executive of Scandinavian Airline System, made the organization legendary by (among other things) simplifying its rules. He burned thousands of pages of manuals and handbooks to demonstrate how overrun the organization was with rules.[17] If rules and processes are rigid and inflexible, the organization will not be able to shift at the appropriate time. Six guidelines for staying flexible include:

1. Be patient when allowing connections to form.
2. Avoid becoming rigid with or overrun by structures, rules, and processes.
3. Make sure the rules and processes that are in place are relevant and necessary.
4. Solicit regular feedback.
5. Stay open to new ways of doing things.
6. Make sure suggestions and ideas are fully understood before discarding them.

Evolution at the Edge

It is important to acknowledge that the discomfort created by chaos is necessary for change to occur. It is equally important to safeguard against getting lost or frozen in the midst of the chaos. Leaders need to balance on the edge of chaos, dipping in and being comfortable there in order to move themselves and the organization to higher levels of evolution. This delicate balance includes inviting members of the organization to feel the need for change while not feeling overwhelmed by it. According to Coveney and Highfield in *Frontiers of Complexity*, "[C]omplex systems that can evolve will always be near the edge of chaos, poised for that creative step into emergent novelty that is the essence of the evolutionary process."[18]

The edge of chaos is the best place to observe the patterns of order available, patterns that then may be applied to the current situation. Getting stuck in one particular state of order is not effective because, sooner or later, that state will become obsolete. It is crucial for leaders to remain open to new experiences that the environment contains and show a willingness to adapt and change based on the information received from the environment.

Emotional Distance   The ability to move gracefully in and out of change and the resulting chaos requires an ability to observe what is happening. Doing so involves being able to psychologically step back and assess what is occurring on multiple levels with detachment. If participants become emotionally involved, it becomes difficult for them to be objective.

Emotional distance allows participants to observe with an open mind, thereby enhancing the likelihood that they will hear other points of view and see what is occurring in the group. This is the reason why it is often suggested that facilitators not participate in the *content* of a discussion. They are then more able to see what is going on and make helpful interventions, dipping in when necessary to keep the group on course or help members deal with something they are avoiding.

What to Observe at the Edge   It is helpful to observe specific aspects of the group while maintaining emotional distance by asking:

- Are the goals clear?
- Are people listening to one another and communicating well?
- Are individuals involved and included?
- How are people feeling (what are their nonverbal expressions, what they are doing, how are they interacting)?

All of this information will help to identify clues regarding the health of the group, its relationships, and its interactions in the organization. If ineffective interactions are apparent, an intervention will help move the group to greater effectiveness. For example, if people are not listening, the facilitator can ask others to repeat what was just said. If goals are not clear, the facilitator can ask the group to clarify them. If the group is moving off task, the facilitator can ask if this is what the group should be doing. If someone looks angry or confused, the facilitator can ask him or her how they are doing. Another way of observing group effectiveness is to look for patterns in the organization, which is discussed in the next section.

Fractals   Discovered by Benoit Mandelbrot in the 1970s, fractals provide a guide for examining complexity and patterns. They are characterized by patterns that replicate to create the whole. In a fractal, each part is autonomous. However, the pattern of each part is embedded in every part of the whole. Some common examples of fractals are the lungs, circulatory systems, leaves, and feathers. Fractals contain a certain order that allows them to be decoded with a few rules. Complexity is the result of a given structure being repeated many times.

Fractals can be seen within the social life of an organization. Each member is autonomous while it is part of the greater whole. The organization is healthiest when members' patterns are replicated throughout the whole through effective communication.

Leaders are fractals of others in the organization. Their behavior is often mirrored throughout the organization. If the leader is collaborative, communicates openly, and attempts to learn from past mistakes, this behavior will carry through to the members.

Norms as Fractals   Norms for behaving are patterns that can be observed in the organization. Much like a fractal, an organization is seen as connected if certain norms exist throughout it. Norms are the implicit or explicit rules that guide and determine what behaviors are acceptable within a group. Although often not explicit, these are the rules by which people work on a daily basis. They determine how a group handles conflict and stress, makes decisions, listens, generates ideas, and allows certain language to prevail. In any group, norms may be effective or ineffective.

An example of an organizational norm is the way a group deals with conflict. For example, some organizations suppress tension by pretending it is not there. Nonverbal cues, such as frowns, crossed arms, and downward glances, are ignored while the group goes on to the next agenda item. This norm keeps the group from examining what is occurring, from sharing thoughts, feelings, and disagreements. As a result, these unresolved feelings and disagreements go underground and sabotage the group later because they have not been resolved. Avoiding conflict cuts off important sources of information that could possibly improve the team, the product, and the way things are done.

Healthy norms are patterns in the organization that can:

- Encourage continuous open feedback, both negative and positive
- Encourage people to share thoughts and feelings
- Encourage individuals and groups to deal with conflict
- Allow learning from mistakes, without blame or judgment
- Create a flow of information throughout the organization
- Encourage participation and involvement in decisions

Each of these norms facilitates the emergence of a truly adaptable organization. All of these norms must be aligned with and support the desired values to ensure that those values permeate the organization. These values are in harmony with the principles that support living systems. As they become institutionalized, healthy norms will come to characterize the organization.[19]

CONFLICT RESOLUTION: A LIVING SYSTEMS APPROACH

Conflict is a natural by-product of the tensions that arise in dynamic organizations. Although it is often perceived as negative, conflict that is handled effectively has the potential to inject new, creative energy into the system.

Conflict can be dealt with in a variety of ways. The use of mediation along with the practice of effective listening skills detailed in Chapter 3 is often successful. Organizations are discovering that by inviting individuals to work through their issues in new positive constructive ways that tap into the energy of the group, these techniques deepen the connections within and across their teams.

Eric Brunner, manager of Human Resources at Temple University, and his colleague, Marie Amey-Taylor, director of Temple's Human Resources Department, use a variety of training techniques that provide content in visual, auditory, and kinesthetic formats. They also design their trainings to be active, using both inductive and deductive activities to transfer learning to the participants.

For over ten years, Brunner and Amey-Taylor have been practicing a combination of improvisational theater and sociodrama to demonstrate appropriate and inappropriate conflict resolution skills and ways to work through conflict and build trust. Sociodrama is a form of improvisational theater based on the "shared central needs and issues" of the audience or participant group and involves dramatic enactments of real-life situations or conflicts so that participants can observe and develop interpersonal skills. It is presented using trained actors, occasional volunteer audience members, and a highly trained facilitator. In practice, Brunner and Amey-Taylor found that participants became very engaged in the action, would dialogue with the characters in a scene, and might even jump in to take the place of actors to "correct" inappropriate or ineffective behaviors. This unique combination of improv and sociodrama is a powerful technique and has become a staple in their work with employees at all levels within a wide variety of organizations. In the next section, Brunner and Amey-Taylor share their experience with the process.

Conflict Resolution with Sociodrama

Recently, we were asked to partner with a professor from Temple University's School of Communications and Theater who was presenting on the topic of cross-cultural communication at a women's leadership conference at Bryn Mawr College. In attendance were about 80 women, all high-level administrators, from a wide range of institutions of higher education.

Because the group was all women, there was a content piece based on the work of Deborah Tannen, an expert in the different communication styles of men and women. Prior to the presentation of this content area, the theater troupe presented a scene designed to introduce the content and invite participants into the presentation. Because of the actors' familiarity with the participant group and the program content, they were able to anticipate a scene that would have relevance for the group and introduce content. There were four actors on site for this session, two men and two women.

The scene started with actors playing the four people responsible for planning an event on a college campus. During the enactment, the male actors began acting in ways that were illustrative of how Tannen described men as communicators. And the women in the scene began acting in the ways that she described as typical of women. As the scene played out, the session participants were able to see the connection between cross-gender communication and the possible conflicts that could be generated. As the group saw themselves and others with whom they work in the characters, they started to react, mostly with laughter. A few exhibited a heightened desire to rectify the situation depicted by the actors. After watching the enactment for five minutes, the group participants were engaged and eager to explore the topic more fully. The use of theater also allowed the women to release some of the feelings they carried related to the topic and their own experiences. This purely experiential format for generating discussion and learning about conflict has proven to be an effective training technique and a tool for building trust and strong relationships.

THE LEARNING ORGANIZATION

> *The technology-driven enterprise demands a new leadership paradigm— one that creates a far stronger, more genuine link between the achievement of corporate objectives and the employee's realization of his deepest, often unexpressed, intensely personal growth needs. Thus, rather than the mere promise of greater corporate status and power, followership is borne of belief in the leader's true understanding and caring for the employee's holistic being and welfare, and thus flows from greater intimacy.*

> —KENDALL A. ELSOM, JR., PRESIDENT, CEO GENESIS
> CONSULTING PARTNERS

In *The Fifth Discipline*, Peter Senge introduces five new component technologies, or disciplines, that "are gradually converging to innovate learning organizations."[20] They are systems thinking, personal mastery, mental models, building shared vision, and team learning. According to Senge, organizations that practice these disciplines are adaptable, self-organizing, and have the potential to "continually enhance their capacity to realize their highest aspirations."[21]

The Five Disciplines

Systems Thinking   As described in Chapter 2, systems thinking takes the approach that to have impact, the organization needs to be viewed in its entirety with recognition that the whole is greater than the sum of its parts. While one participates in a system, it is sometimes difficult to see the overall pattern and how that pattern changes over time. Since parts of organizations are connected by numerous interactions, the effect on other parts may take years to play out.

Traditional approaches tend to view each part in isolation, often never getting to some of the deepest issues. Senge defines systems thinking as "a conceptual framework, a body of knowledge and tools that has been developed over the past fifty years, to make the full patterns clearer, and to help us see how to change them effectively."[22]

Personal Mastery   Senge defines personal mastery as "the discipline of continually clarifying and deepening our personal vision, of focusing our energies, of developing patience, and of seeing reality objectively."[23] As someone might strive for master status within a trade, mastery is a special level of proficiency or self-actualization. It is a foundational element of the learning organization since "an organization's commitment to and capacity for learning can be no greater than that of its members."[24]

Unfortunately, this is where many organizations fall short, leading to vast untapped potential. Most people enter business full of optimism and energy. But after a number of years, they become disenchanted and just put in their time until retirement with minimum effort. Therefore, it is critical for management to hire and inspire toward the goal of each member striving for personal mastery.

Mental Models   Senge defines mental models "as deeply ingrained assumptions, generalizations, or even pictures or images that influence how we understand the world and how we take action."[25] A majority of these models are unconscious and have existed since childhood. Yet they pervade every thought, word, and action.

The first step in dealing with mental models is to look within oneself. Then the organization must create a safe place for members to participate in compassionate scrutiny and influence through the process of "inquiry and advocacy."

Building Shared Vision   One thing that all successful organizations have in common is a shared vision. Made up of shared goals and values, a shared vision has the capacity to bring "people together around a common identity and sense of destiny,"[26] according to Senge. It unleashes creative energy and fuels innovation by rallying diverse members in a shared vision that galvanizes the organization. It "involves the skills of unearthing shared 'pictures of the future' that foster genuine commitment and enrollment rather than compliance."[27]

Team Learning   The success of organizations to learn is based on the ability of the teams to learn. The team must connect and share through dialogue while suspending assumptions and learning to trust each other. Blocks such as fear, apathy, and defensiveness can undermine learning. Therefore, safe and open communication is essential.

Team learning has the power to enhance capabilities for innovation and creativity. But to maximize the benefits, the learning must be shared. Many teams of brilliant individuals have produced mediocre results due to lack of interaction and integration.

Practicing team learning is not about copying a model. Many new management innovations emerge as "best practices." But most organizations adopt and implement the ideas in a piecemeal fashion. Toyota is a great example of a company that uses a systems approach. Many companies copy Toyota's kanban system. But they fail to see how all the parts work together in a way that is unique for Toyota.

The Fifth Discipline

Senge points out that "[i]t is vital that the five disciplines develop as an ensemble."[28] This is truly a time when the total is greater than the sum of its parts.

Based on that truth, "systems thinking is the fifth discipline." Without a systemic approach, the coherence necessary to be adaptable is lost. "For example, vision without systems thinking ends up painting lovely pictures of the future with no deep understanding of the forces that must be mastered to move from here to there."[29]

Organizations that embrace systems thinking must also practice "the disciplines of building shared vision, mental models, team learning, and personal mastery to realize its potential." Each of these disciplines plays a role in powering the system. Shared vision builds a group commitment to the future. Mental models provide the openness necessary to unveil the limitations present in the organization. Team learning improves the members' skills to create and take action on an organizational level. And personal mastery encourages the self-reflection, healing, and personal growth necessary to fully participate in an adaptable organization.

Finally, learning organizations offer amazing potential for creating their future. Based on the new science, a learning organization is creating its future by shifting how individuals perceive themselves and their world.

A New Global Organization

As stated earlier, the information explosion coupled with advances in technology and globalization are placing stress on organizations to adapt. Companies stuck in the old hierarchical structure often are based on closed systems with separate units defined by activities and offerings. The organizational management chart looks like a tree with each position branching off from the one above.

A dynamic, emergent organization, however, has an organizational chart that is very nonlinear. It bears more resemblance to a network of relationships or groups of overlapping circles. This living-systems model enables an optimal flow of information leading to higher resiliency and innovation.

Chapter 7 offers some guidance for individuals taking on a leadership role in adaptable organizations.

NOTES

1. Margaret J. Wheatley, *Leadership and the New Science* (San Francisco: Barrett-Koehler, 1992), 118–119.
2. Edwin E. Olsen and Glenda H. Eoyang, *Facilitating Organizational Change* (San Francisco: Jossey-Bass/Pfeiffer, 2001), 2.
3. Dee Hock, "Transformation by Design," *What Is Enlightenment*, No. 22 (Fall/Winter 2002), 134.
4. Olsen and Eoyang, *Facilitating Organizational Change*, 3.
5. *Id.*, 3.
6. *Id.*

7. "Total quality management" as defined by the International Organization for Standardization (ISO). Available at http://en.wikipedia.org/wiki/TQM
8. *Id.*
9. Peter M. Senge, *The Fifth Discipline* (New York: Currency, 1990), xii.
10. *Id.,* xii.
11. Jeffrey W. Bennett and Steven B. Hedlund, "In a Slump? Realign, Don't Re-Engineer," www.strategy-business.com/press/enewsarticle/22710.
12. Christopher Laszlo and Jean-François Laugel, *Large-Scale Organizational Change* (Boston: Butterworth Heinemann, 2000), 25.
13. *Id.,* 24–25.
14. Melissa Hoffman, "Transformation by Design, An Interview with Dee Hock," *Enlightenment Magazine,* No. 22 (2003), 131.
15. Laszlo and Laugel, *Large-Scale Organizational Change,* 25-29. The quotes that follow in this section are all from Laszlo and Laugel's book.
16. Margaret J. Wheatley and Myron Kellner-Rogers, *A Simpler Way* (San Fransisco: Barrett-Koehler, 1996).
17. Ronald Heifetz and Donald Laurie, "The Work of Leadership," *Harvard Business Review* (January-February 1997). Available at www.ncsl.org.uk/media-f7b-97-randd-leaders-business-heifetz.pdf.
18. Peter Coveney and Roger Highfield, *Frontiers of Complexity: The Search for Order in a Chaotic World* (New York: Fawcett Columbine, 1995).
19. Julie Roberts Ph.D., "Leading with Heart and Soul," Manuscript.
20. Senge, *The Fifth Discipline,* 6.
21. *Id.*
22. *Id.,* 7.
23. *Id.*
24. *Id.*
25. *Id.,* 8.
26. *Id.,* 9.
27. *Id.*
28. *Id.,* 11.
29. *Id.,* 12.

Leadership

When we motivate, we serve ourselves first.

—Lance Secretan, Author and leadership coach

In highly adaptable organizations, everyone plays a leadership role from time to time. However, certain competencies are essential for those in key leadership roles, especially when an organization is seeking a higher level of adaptability.

The Conscious Leader

To become a leader, you must first become a human being.

—Confucius

A conscious leader is best described by defining what it is not. According to leadership consultant Lance Secretan, consciousness is the opposite of rationalism:

The rational mind believes that:

- Success is always measured in material terms.
- Self-worth is measured in comparison to others.
- Feelings are private and should not be expressed in the workplace.
- The single bottom line is the main arbiter of success.
- Anything that cannot be scientifically proven is not real or valuable.
- We are each separate and must compete.
- The world is dangerous and we must always protect ourselves.
- Violence and aggression are necessary for survival and safety.

- Notions like love, eco-interdependence, spirit or soul, absolute truth, and the divine are the province of philosophers, idealists, and the naïve—not business people.[1]

The rational mind is firmly entrenched in the Newtonian model of science, which is insufficient when it comes to thriving in a volatile economy. As Secretan puts it:

> The rational mind describes compassion and caring for people as touchy-feely soft stuff. The conscious mind sees compassion and caring for people as the juice—even the purpose and necessity of life. The rational mind reasons that an imbalance between work and life is the means that is justified by the ends. On the other hand, the conscious mind understands that everything in the universe, including work and life, must be balanced, that there is a season for everything. The conscious mind therefore balances thinking and feeling, profit and people, wisdom and learning, ego and spirit, now and the future, rich and poor, the sacred and the secular. The fully conscious leader is an evolved being.[2]

Organizations that strive to be highly adaptable in the turbulent times ahead will be those with conscious leaders at every level.

SOCIAL INTELLIGENCE

If there is any great secret of success in life, it lies in the ability to put yourself in the other person's place and to see things from his point of view—as well as your own.

—HENRY FORD

The human brain offers fascinating insights into how leaders can leverage the new science.[3] Based on the latest research in social neuroscience, a person who feels empathy for someone else is able to become attuned to the other's mood. The result is resonance. The two brains become attuned as if they are part of the same system. This idea has powerful implications for leaders, as it follows that truly "great leaders are those whose behavior powerfully leverages the system of brain interconnectedness."[4]

Natural leaders are those who easily connect with others. Individuals can improve their leadership abilities by finding "authentic contexts in which to learn the kinds of social behavior that reinforces the brain's social circuitry. Leading effectively is, in other words, less about mastering situations—or even mastering social skill sets—than about developing a genuine interest in and talent for fostering positive feelings in the people whose cooperation and support you need."[5]

Tuning In

The process of tuning in occurs through the activation of *mirror neurons*, which are widely distributed throughout the brain. They operate as a "neural Wi-Fi" that facilitates our navigation of the social world by picking up the emotions of others and sharing their experience.

This point has powerful implications for leadership style. It suggests that leaders can succeed while being very demanding, as long as they foster a positive mood. In fact, certain mirror neurons are designed to detect smiles and laughter and often prompt smiles and laughter in return. Leaders who elicit smiles and laughter stimulate bonding among their team members. Research shows that "top-performing leaders elicited laughter from their subordinates three times as often, on average, as did mid-performing leaders."[6]

Intuition

Great leaders often say they make decisions from the gut. While some discount this concept, neuroscience steps in again to suggest that intuition is, in fact, in the brain. Intuition is produced by neurons called *spindle cells*. These cells are characterized by their large size (four times that of other brain cells). Their spindly shape, with an extra-long branch that allows them to attach to many cells at the same time, enables spindle cells to transmit thoughts and feeling to other cells more quickly. "This ultrarapid connection of emotions, beliefs, and judgments creates what behavioral scientists call our social guidance system."[7] This ability to take a thin slice of information and make a split-second decision has proven to be very accurate as shown in follow-up metrics. The ability to intuit while tuned in to others' moods offers very accurate radar.

Other neurons that play a role in our social intelligence are called *oscillators*. The oscillator neurons coordinate movements between people who are attuned to each others' feelings. It explains the phenomena experienced in dancing or a drumming circle. And it plays heavily in nonverbal communication, as this connection enables one to look in a certain direction or adjust position by the actions of another.

Dan Goleman, author of *Social Intelligence*: *The New Science of Human Relationships*, and Richard Boyaztis, author of *Becoming a Resonant Leader*, share their behavioral assessment tool, the Emotional and Social Competency Inventory. "It is a 360-degree evaluation instrument by which bosses, peers, direct reports, clients, and sometimes even family members assess a leader according to seven social intelligence qualities."[8] Goleman and Boyaztis worked with the Hay Group to develop the following list of behavioral assessments:

Empathy

- Do you understand what motivates other people, even those from different backgrounds?
- Are you sensitive to others' needs?

Attunement

- Do you listen attentively and think about how others feel?
- Are you attuned to others' moods?

Organizational Awareness

- Do you appreciate the culture and values of the group or organization?
- Do you understand social networks and know their unspoken norms?

Influence

- Do you persuade others by engaging them in discussion and appealing to their self-interests?
- Do you get support from key people?

Developing Others

- Do you coach and mentor others with compassion and personally invest time and energy in mentoring?
- Do you provide feedback that people find helpful for their professional development?

Inspiration

- Do you articulate a compelling vision, build group price, and foster a positive emotional tone?
- Are you lead by bringing out the best in people?

Teamwork

- Do you solicit input from everyone on the team?
- Do you support all team members and encourage cooperation?

PARADOX OF EMPOWERMENT

True power is the ability to relinquish control.

—OLIVIA PARR RUD

One of the most challenging aspects of leading in the new model is giving up the need for control. And yet with the complexity of business today, it is impossible to micromanage from the top. Years ago, the chief executive officer (CEO) could do the job of practically every person in the company. Today, it is a totally different story.

As discussed in Chapter 4, John Chambers, CEO of Cisco, did not always entrust decision-making to others. He started out as a command-and-control type. "If I said, 'Turn right,' all 65,000 employees turned right." But he soon realized that the company couldn't grow as rapidly as was necessary under that model. So he and his top leadership team invented a new way to run the business.[9]

Not only is it less effective to operate with a top-down leadership style, but it diminishes so much of the energy, wisdom, and vitality of the organization. In the article "The Paradox of Empowerment," Wayne Baker states that "empowerment means letting go while taking control."[10] Often this requires leaders to transform the work environment by actively changing "the way people work, relate, think, and feel." However, they must also allow time for the new empowerment to "take root, grow, and thrive."

"Like any paradox, the paradox of empowerment is full of traps. It ensnares CEOs who cannot accept or live in the contradiction of taking control and letting go. Such CEOs become abdicators or meddlers. Those who thrive in the paradox become coaches who learn how to cultivate true empowerment."

Abdicators are good at letting go. But they fail to offer guidance or make the fundamental changes necessary to cultivate emergent leadership such as setting goals and establishing empowering processes. Meddlers never really give up control. They say they want self-managed teams, but they often stay too involved and tend to micromanage. This results in team members delegating upward and abdicating responsibility. "Coaches [, however,] know the difference between intervention and interference."

> If the CEO of yesterday's command-and-control corporation was the military chieftain, then the CEO of tomorrow's corporation is the philosopher-king. As a philosopher, the CEO develops the comprehensive theory of the corporation as a society. This theory includes an ideology or system of beliefs about human nature, superordinate goals, and shared values, and it encompasses a vision of a better society—a model of the company tomorrow. As a king, the CEO acts decisively to put theory into practice. This demands not just business but social re-engineering— all the deep interventions necessary to transform the corporation.

Empowering CEOs are experts at tapping into the natural desire of people to work in fulfilling and productive jobs. They know that people are motivated by many things besides money, such as "belonging, mastery, self-esteem, achievement, respect." Meddlers, who generally distrust human nature, feel their employees must be coerced into doing their jobs.

Empowering CEOs create an environment of collaboration and self-direction. They create effective social mechanisms, such as high-level networks that unite and build community.

10 PRINCIPLES FOR LEADING A DYNAMIC ORGANIZATION

> *At the executive level, the rules of the game have changed. Just a few years ago there was no Sarbanes-Oxley, the Internet was in its infancy and corporations were coming to grips with globalization.*
>
> *Managing in a global, technologically driven, and fast-changing economic environment requires a more complex set of skills than those needed by managers in the past.*
>
> *My clients are looking for innovative leaders who can adapt and manage through continuous change.*
>
> —JERRY BERNHART, BERNHART ASSOCIATES

In *Large-Scale Organizational Change*, Christopher Laszlo and Jean-François Laugel define the 10 Principles as guidelines to action that "offer an integrated approach to the main managerial processes of a company: strategy formulation, annual budgeting, investment appropriation requests, controlling, and project management."[11] To support the implementation of the principles in a dynamic organization, they offer some tactics that are designed to work in complex and chaotic environments.

The 10 Principles tackle the central issues of corporate management in the areas of strategy, organization, and execution. However, the focus is on the dynamics involved. Since they are designed to guide dynamic companies that thrive on complexity and instability, they cannot be applied separately. They must be seen as a comprehensive approach. "As a part of a mind-set, the 10 Principles are an effective basis for action that leads to corporate renewal and development of the capability to survive frequent and radical discontinuities in the operating environment."[12]

Principle I: Create Adaptive Strategies

A primary role of management is to define the vision or the overall goals for the company. Generally, the next step is to define the strategy. Traditionally, strategy is set by management and delegated throughout the rest of the organization. However, in a highly volatile global economy, this approach can prove limiting if not devastating when unforeseen circumstances occur.

In a highly adaptive company, management shares the vision and allows the strategy to emerge. A diverse employee base is a real benefit because it allows for a wider range of strategies. The best approach is to have several strategies that can be implemented quickly, given different economic stimuli. "They [management] must do this by visualizing alternative futures on the basis of probability-weighted trends."[13] Doing so may require abandoning past trends, a difficult task for many established businesses.

Companies can take several approaches to prepare for and leverage unforeseen events that demand a change in strategy. One tactic is to design "what-if" scenarios to serve as alternate long-term strategies that ensure adaptability in the face of unpredictable economic forces.

Another tactic is to define business units around a group of skills that provide the flexibility and resources to pursue new opportunities in a volatile economy. Doing so unleashes a creative energy that leads to adaptability and innovation.

A strong Business Intelligence infrastructure is critical to adaptability. Networks designed to effectively transfer information about inventories, staffing, and trends help to eliminate time lag and reduce errors across supply chains and between partners. Dashboards that track daily trends are able to reveal weak signals. The role of revealing weak signals is defined in chaos theory as one that can magnify and transform entire systems during times of instability. Direct interaction between top managers and the rank-and-file is also important. Companies in which leaders connect with employees on a regular basis are much better at noticing weak signals as signs of shifting markets or other changes.

Organizations that access the innate wisdom of their organization to tap into future trends encourage and reward innovation as they simultaneously access and create future market trends.

In traditional organizations, strategic planning usually consists of analyzing and applying past trends to the future. "The statistical quantification of past trends, the rigor of mathematical models, and the fact of including hard historical evidence in a structured framework remain important to the strategy-formulation process. But they also can stifle creativity and block insights about future trends."[14] While this method works well in a stable economy, it can suppress creativity and inhibit adaptability in economically volatile times. If structures are solidly built on past trends, many organizations are not resilient enough to survive a quick change in market trends.

Principle II: Maintain Long-term Identity while Repositioning

Advances in technology and global connectivity have combined to unleash a host of new opportunities for companies of all sizes. As organizations become adept at morphing their strategies to take advantage of these opportunities, they gain strategic benefit by establishing and maintaining a long-term identity that speaks to their core strength. This ability to change also protects companies from failure if their existing business is marginalized or deemed untenable by government legislation, new technological innovation, or other unforeseen events. By building and communicating an identity vision, organizations are able to leverage their ability to "differentiate themselves from competitors, motivate their employees, and build lasting relationships with customers."[15]

Several approaches can help leaders reposition their business while maintaining their overall identity. Defining a transcendent vision allows a company to redefine aspects of its business while maintaining its overall identity. SAS, for example, is a global Business Intelligence Solutions company that started out creating software for statistical analysis. A SAS user was someone who knew how to write SAS code. Today, SAS has broadened its scope and evolved into a leader in Business Intelligence solutions with an emphasis on business analytics. With SAS, anyone within the organization can access information to gain knowledge about their business through simple graphical user interfaces (GUIs). But the vision of the company as one that helps businesses turn data into knowledge still rings true for SAS.

To ensure success when adapting strategies, organizations should keep an eye on customer value while taking advantage of all the internal knowledge as well as market indicators to determine which new activity or group of activities will serve future needs of customers.

Another consideration is to reduce reliance on forecasting tools and statistical methodologies. In a volatile economy, these tools are only marginally useful. Companies that are thriving today are leveraging the concepts of chaos theory and complexity science. These concepts include "better monitoring of trends in the external environment, regular reevaluation of the broader industry configuration to see where margins are highest (to see which players are making the most money), scenario planning, pattern recognition, improved ability to pick up weak signals in the environment, and rapid and coordinated decision-making."[16] By focusing on the future rather than on past patterns and accomplishments, the application succeeds by tapping into the innovative spirit of the organization.

Principle III: Compete for Industry Sustainability

The longevity of any company is dependent on the sustainability of the industry. Measures to increase the sustainability of suppliers, distributors, subcontractors, and even direct and indirect competitors promote the long-term viability of the industry. While there is still competition between businesses on certain levels, the overall win–at–all–costs model is giving way to a more win–win philosophy. For example, companies have been known to request legislation that limits all players from certain practices that put the industry at risk.

A win–win approach to business will ultimately enhance industry sustainability. The pursuit of profit that ignores the health of the community or the environment ultimately destroys the entire system.

Companies can take several steps to improve industry sustainability. Forming partnerships to enhance collaboration among competitors can be very effective for tasks such as technology development, financing, and setting standards. In addition to adding benefit, partnerships can increase flexibility, free resources, inspire innovation, and disperse risk.

As industry sustainability degrades, companies may be subjected to increased regulation and possible negative publicity. By projecting these costs and incorporating them into their planning, companies are in a position to set the standards for their industry. This can lead to a positive company and industry image while improving long-term industry sustainability.

Companies can create their own standards that look to the future needs of their industry. In an age of instant communication and corporate scrutiny, companies that establish policies for the long-term benefit of the industry get the immediate benefit of positive press. With the recent awareness of corporate malfeasance, consumers often reward companies that "do the right thing." As other companies adopt the behavior, the market increases and everyone wins.

Principle IV: Use Strategic Inflection Points

A strategic inflexion point, a term coined by Andrew Grove, former CEO of Intel Corporation, "occurs when a company is confronted by an innovation of revolutionary significance (force 10x) that affects the entire industry in which it operates."[17] Minor shifts, such as price drops and changes in purchase behavior, challenge companies every day. Strategic inflexion points, however, force companies into seismic shifts or extinction. As our economy becomes more unpredictable, strategic inflexion points are increasing in frequency. By developing adaptability and resilience, organizations can leverage the opportunities these strategic inflexion points present.

Chaos dynamics says that strategic inflection points represent decision points or bifurcations for many organizations. At this point, companies must adapt in order to survive. The status quo is no longer viable.

The long-term success of an organization in times of volatility depends on its ability to take advantage of each strategic inflection point better than its competitors. There are several ways to leverage this opportunity.

Organizations are better able to perceive key shifts in advance of competitors by tapping into their front-line employees. The "sales staff, warehouse managers, customer service representatives, product developers, scientists, or purchasing agents are often the first to sense"[18] these changes.

When top leaders see continuation of the status quo as unviable, they may decide to generate a period of transitional chaos. Clear, frequent, and comprehensive communication is essential during these times. If employees are kept in the dark about what is happening, fear increases and positive energies that support innovation and cooperation shut down. At a time when it is often the most difficult, people need to be heard. Communication about the status and expected outcome must flow freely in all directions.

Disorder is a strange or chaotic attractor that can unleash powerful forces for change within an organization. However, when faced with an unforeseen strategic inflection point, top leaders are challenged with maintaining a delicate balance. By dispersing control and supporting the organization as it self-organizes within the new paradigm, the company survives and grows in resilience.

Principle V: Link Transformation to Shareholder Value Creation

Shareholder value has long been the single measure of company value. However, as organizations are exposed to continuous uncertainty, they need to behave more like living systems to survive. The survival of living systems "is measured according to strict criteria of adaptability and fit with the sustainable environment."[19] However, there are some challenges when managing shareholder value in a complex and unstable competitive environment:

- In a highly volatile economy, the accuracy of measures such as discounted cash flow and expected losses is diminished. It is difficult for highly adaptive companies to predict how much their core business might change in a few years.

- It is difficult to capture the value added from a company's management style or decision-making capabilities. "During rapid transformation, change processes become more influential in determining financial performance than either structure or traditional processes."[20]
- Companies are beginning to see the impact on cash flow from connecting with other groups, such as their communities, partners, and the environment. Quantifying this value continues to be challenging.

In summary, the method of calculating economic value added must be "modified to integrate perpetual transformation rather than one-time (or periodic) shareholder value initiatives in managing a business portfolio."[21]

The next actions are designed to assist companies in determining shareholder value in a complex and volatile environment.

- *Develop different cash flow scenarios.* Organizations will be in a stronger position if they develop different cash flow scenarios for multiple futures based on the best estimates of what will change and how the market will behave in the next few years. The actual exercise of scenario building and the resulting discussion are more important than getting the estimates exactly right. The flow and exchange of ideas is valuable in generating the preparedness for the next phase.
- *Link shareholder value at every phase.* When new business lines or other opportunities emerge through the adaptive process, it is essential to link shareholder value at every phase and ensure "sufficient coherence among strategy, finance, organization, and implementation."[22]
- *Focus on growth strategies.* Such a focus is essential, even if it requires actions such as downsizing, restructuring, and reengineering, when an adaptive company is experiencing a major transformation.

Principle VI: Develop Ambitions Greater than Means

The limits you create will be real to you until you learn to step beyond them. Then, you will look back at the reality you used to inhabit, wondering how you were able to stand its narrow confines.

—PAUL FERRINI, AUTHOR AND SPIRITUAL TEACHER

Companies looking to engage in perpetual transformational opportunities are most successful when they set their ambitions much higher than their means. As people participate in the vision, energy is released that inspires innovative ways for reaching the goal.

People who feel passionate about the vision step up to be leaders. Others wait until the goal seems more tenable before they engage. A few resist and may add to the instability. However, if handled skillfully, the contrasting tensions can assist the transformation.

It is becoming increasingly apparent that companies that do not stretch their vision will be surpassed by the competition. These actions can assist companies to stretch their vision and prepare people for perpetual transformation:

- *Express a vision or strategic intent to members of the organization that leads to breakthrough thinking and action.* By allowing the participants to embrace a grand vision, leaders naturally align themselves and move beyond what was once considered impossible.
- *Disperse control.* The complexity of a major shift in vision requires top leadership to disperse control. By sharing the vision and empowering the participants, the idea takes on an energy of its own. The role of leadership is to continually share the vision, provide support, and celebrate accomplishments.
- *Stay focused and harness energy.* In large, complex organizations, many transformative processes may be happening at the same time. The key to success is to stay focused and harness the energy created by the overall goal. A simple rallying cry, slogan, or watchword is helpful to thread the varying activities and maintain high spirits.
- *Discuss change and introduce points of inflection.* Introducing a new vision when most members of an organization are satisfied with the status quo may prove to be futile. Most organizations are more susceptible to major shifts in focus during times of crisis. Starting a conversation about what might happen if the market shifts drastically can begin to prepare members for change. Introducing an artificial point of inflection is another option for stimulating receptivity.

Principle VII: Design Decision-Making Systems for Self-Organization

An efficient and effective decision-making system is critical to survival in a complex, volatile economy. Organizations must develop processes that encourage self-organization. Doing so requires an open sharing of the vision, the free flow of information, and strong communication between all levels of management on down.

Decision-making is one area where rigor and precision are beneficial in an otherwise fluid atmosphere. Respect for people's time must be balanced with ensuring that everyone has a voice. Creative incentive packages, such as the ones discussed in Chapter 4 regarding collaboration, enhance emergence of self-organization.

Complex organizations require a variety of decision-making styles. Some are designed for day-to-day operations while others focus on long-term issues. For example, formal decision-making regarding important issues of management, such as strategic planning, annual budgeting, and executive committee meetings, is typically well designed and structured. Formal, nonperiodic decision-making designed to handle unexpected situations may also follow a set format. Formal decision-making is used when a decision is needed with regard to a major restructuring, new directions, or investments and crisis management. Since formal decision-making covers a variety of areas and is not planned very far in advance, the attendees may not be known ahead of time. These types of meetings are more common in complex organizations that aim to adapt quickly to market changes. Informal decision-making can happen anywhere. It is important for leaders to be aware of the effect of limited input on their decisions. Managers who want to promote self-organizing, team-based, distributed decision-making must recognize their power to influence through their conversational style and remind others that their opinion is just one of many that deserves consideration.

To foster self-organization, a company must guide its decision-making to resemble that of an entrepreneurial enterprise. For example, reducing the presence of top management in the day-to-day operations is a good first step. Combined with an effective information exchange through every level of the company hierarchy, this shift ensures that the flow of information goes beyond the typical sharing of knowledge to include daily insights, ideas, and issues as they arise.

Self-organizing companies need teams that have a broad range of skills that represent a microcosm of the company. Such companies can adapt more quickly due to competent leadership and decision-making at many levels.

Learning by doing serves large companies by reviving the entrepreneurial spirit. New challenges inspire people to connect with others to find solutions and increase learning. This leads to faster adoption of new ideas that energize the workforce and unleashe innovation.

Complex organizations that share decision-making and accountability must also share compensation. Many financial instruments to associate compensation with performance exist, such as employee stock purchase plans, cash bonuses, and stock options. One creative practice by Thermo Electron is the practice of spinouts. The company "hands over day-to-day control of newly formed subsidiaries and fistfuls of share options to the staff. The stock has returned 20% per year since the practice began."[23]

Chapter 9 discusses some very specific steps for effective decision-making in an adaptive organization.

Principle VIII: Fluidify the Organizational Structure

The flow and accessibility of information is critical in complex organizations, especially those with global reach. The best structures are those that avoid rigidity. Community-based organizations are structured to optimize collaboration between horizontal units while requiring minimal input vertically. Their network structure facilitates the flow of information and task allocations, leading to maximum adaptability.

The level of localization or decentralization depends on the conditions necessary for self-learning. The goal is to allow a structure to emerge that optimizes the ability to make rapid and relevant decisions. These structures will evolve over time as the organization grows and diversifies. Decision-making is delegating to the front line with a mechanism for self-learning. Management does not set the goals and means. Rather, it sets the overall aim and allows each organizational unit to determine its own path through communication and collaborative decision-making.

These tactics facilitate the development of a fluid structure within a learning organization:

- The creation of multilevel project teams supports a community-based structure. Senior management should delegate resources and objectives to the lowest possible level. Performance should be measured on both a team and an individual level.

- Continually changing demands can lead to unclear reporting rela-tionships. To facilitate learning, the organization should clearly define accountabilities while tolerating some lack of clarity. This becomes more natural as companies experience the value of community-based structures. Specific objectives and defined responsibilities lead the process while maximizing flexibility and learning.
- Horizontal information flow and communication is very important. Within community-based organizations, information flows freely. Interconnectedness is facilitated by a plethora of communication devices. Therefore, the challenge moves from information avail-ability to discretion and relevance.

Principle IX: Use Organizational Instability to Catalyze Learning

Organizations that succeed in leveraging instability unleash enormous amounts of energy for fueling innovation and adaptability. As situations present themselves—such as a new competitive threat or loss of invest-ment money—management must maintain a delicate balance between reacting too quickly and resorting to old patterns.

Working in a culture of constant instability can be stressful, especially when it is new to the organization. Because of years of experience with the stable, predictable model, many managers resist moving to a model of permanent instability. What is required is a delicate balance between main-taining enough discomfort for learning and productivity to be optimized while avoiding the risk of demotivation, paralysis, and complacency.

Some tactics are well suited for fueling innovation and adaptability. One is to make sure that every member of the organization knows the truth about the difficulties facing the company. Holding people account-able is important. Doing so might include publicizing risk taking to high-light successes and explain shortcomings while avoiding blame. During times of stress, typically 20 percent of employees step up to be change agents. Another 20 percent resist or retreat. By raising the visibility of the change agents, the other 60 percent typically follow their lead.

Encouraging diverse points of view enhances adaptability. Discussions that support opposing points of view often trigger ideas that can be advance warnings of needed transformation.

To maintain the energy and loyalty essential to adaptability, organizations should design and share relevant metrics. A strong vision accompanied by clearly communicated roles and responsibilities will lead to accountability. With distributed decision-making in a rapidly changing environment, success metrics must be clear and equitable.

Principle X: Reenvision Leading: From Command and Control to (R)Evolutionary Influence

Motivation is the art of getting people to do what you want them to do because they want to do it.

—DWIGHT EISENHOWER

In contrast to years of hierarchical management, leaders in adaptable organizations play a more subtle leadership role. They are the visionaries who envision a future that seems impossible today. They inspire, empower, and motivate others to make decisions. They manage the flow of information and communicate extensively. They take the broadest possible view and encourage collaborative problem solving.

> The term *(r)evolutionary influence* is used to capture these qualities. The evolution of complex systems is guided by probabilistic influence rather than deterministic control. When discontinuities arise, leaders must occasion a revolution by declaring a future others may not see as possible, and get alignment in the organization so that actions forward that future.[24]

The leadership model in the adaptable organization is more egalitarian. A manager might admit to not knowing an answer or even know the answer but still delegate that executive decision to someone on the front line. Rather than being the solver of all problems, the leader's role is to disseminate decision-making by engaging the whole organization in the bidirectional sharing of information and knowledge.

Some powerful tactics facilitate and encourage evolutionary influence. Leaders must be willing to let go of control, take calculated risks, and envision the impossible for themselves and the organization. To maintain an environment of perpetual transformation, they must be willing to accept a higher risk of failure. This is achieved by treating everyone in the organization like a valued member of the team. True dialogue and information flow are necessary to facilitate communication. Conflict is managed effectively, leading to the generation of new ideas and energy.

Referring back to fractals, it is essential to see the system in its entirety. Each decision must be linked to the larger context. Some decisions may be suboptimal for a small group but still serve the larger good. The survival of the system depends on the quality of the relationships of each of its parts.

TAPPING ORGANIZATIONAL WISDOM

Organizational leaders who hope to adapt and thrive in a volatile economy must access the innate wisdom of the organization. Doing this includes discovering unconscious competence.

Unconscious competence is the deep expertise that often goes unrecognized and unrecorded in knowledge-based organizations. Carl Gaertner, a business analyst with a major financial services company, has been applying psychological principles to business settings for the last 22 years.

In the contribution that follows, Gaertner offers insights and tips to facilitate organizational learning. His comprehensive approach leverages the competency of effective communication.

Discovering Unconscious Competence

In the business world, functional behaviors relate to optimal decision-making. The decision makers may be project team members, managers, or customer-facing associates. Capturing the lessons learned from teams and best practices of project teams after implementation is practical for business continuity and can serve as a catalyst to innovation. In addition, it is sometimes prudent to tap into the deeper recesses of knowledge in which the subtleness of decision-making behavior occurs.

Expertise is developed from years of practice in which trial-and-error learning develops heuristic knowledge. *Heuristic knowledge* is the rule-of-thumb knowledge that provides favorable business outcomes most of the time. It goes beyond the procedural and the business operations manuals.

Sometimes experts use mental shortcuts to arrive at conclusions quickly. Other times, they will trust their intuition to look beyond the surface of a situation to dig deeper to find the root cause. The ability to interpret and apply strategic directives is an area in which practical experts excel beyond average performers. Beyond speed and quality, experts shine in areas of customer satisfaction and risk mitigation. They are able to optimally balance customer benefits while protecting the company assets.

Therapeutic Interviewing in Business   Psychotherapy is proven to help people struggling with personal issues and sometimes serious dysfunctional behaviors. The prognosis for the client is excellent when the therapist is highly competent and motivated to grow, and the methods are appropriate for him or her. Just as a surgeon would not use a scalpel outside of an operating room, an ethical counselor would not practice psychotherapy outside a counseling session. Neither physical nor psychological wounds are intended for public awareness.

Because of their success in unveiling hidden behaviors, therapeutic interviewing and active listening skills are powerful tools for uncovering unconscious competent behaviors for business purposes. They are efficient techniques for learning from customers, subject matter experts, and business partners. Much of this learning occurs during informal conversations. However, it is often valuable to schedule interview sessions for the sole purpose of learning from experts.

Approach to Harvesting Business Knowledge   A substantial amount of valuable business knowledge is stored in the minds of key individuals within an organization. The business knowledge is reflected in experiences, goals, concepts, processes, and decisions. The challenge for the people assigned to gathering business knowledge is identifying this knowledge and making it available for others to use to make informed decisions.

The use of a disciplined yet flexible approach for interviewing business partners from a corporate perspective and subject matter experts from an operations perspective ensures the capture of the strategic decision-making knowledge and heuristic (rule-of-thumb) knowledge necessary for reaching business objectives.

*People don't care how much you know, until they know how much
you care.*

—CARL GAERTNER

Establishing Trust   Trust is the foundation for effective knowledge sharing. Rapport is established by meeting people where they are. Trust follows relationship-building activities. The knowledge-harvesting method helps us to overcome the obstacles of knowledge sharing.

Openness is essential for establishing trust. Self-disclosure elicits self-disclosure in others when safety and security is assured. Withholding judgment of mistakes and guaranteeing privacy will build the confidence in others that it is okay to reveal their deep thoughts and opinions. Providing a safe environment in a business setting for this type of interaction is difficult to accomplish but worth pursuing.

Most human interactions tend to begin at a safe and nonthreatening level. They seldom progress to a level that is highly intimate and revealing. For most interactions, a shallow level of openness makes sense. However, deeper conversations are needed to determine how someone else thinks and makes difficult decisions. By modeling the behavior to the next inner level of openness, the interviewer motivates the interviewee to share at a deeper level.

Barriers to Sharing Knowledge

People Talk Fast and Think Faster   The human mind stores knowledge for rapid processing of information, not for explanation. The mind stores knowledge to get things done, not to tell others why. People think much faster than they can talk, and they talk faster that we can listen and remember. When probing questions are asked early in the interview process, it may feel like an abruption. This may unwittingly cause the expert to shut down. It is better to take notes related to key concepts and wait for an opening to probe deeper in follow-up interviews.

Productive Thoughts Are Often Unconscious   A great deal of valuable knowledge gained by experience is unconscious to the individual who has the knowledge. Experts do not know that they know. They make decisions and assumptions so quickly that they often do not realize the steps they perform automatically. When they share their thought process for the first time with others, they often skip many important steps.

Using a variety of active listening techniques and questions helps to meet the experts where they are. When the expert is seen concentrating before answering a question, allow the silence to expand. Moments of silence allow for deeper access to knowledge.

Listening Requires Discipline   Often people consider listening to be a soft skill. While the soft aspect of listening relates to the delicate nature of relationship building, softness does not mean that it is easy to listen. Effective listening requires discipline and desire. People really need to work at becoming great listeners. Preparing the mind to listen and creating the will to listen is crucial for staying focused.

Remembering Is Tough and Not Always Natural   Capturing knowledge is hard work. People think faster than they talk. People talk faster than the listener can write or type. Short-term memory is also a problem in retaining knowledge unless memory joggers are created. Building group memory diagrams or artifacts while interviewing subject matter experts facilitates long-term memory.

Research in human learning and memory reveals two concepts that describe the difficulty in remembering large volumes of information:

1. *Proactive interference*—what is learned before interferes with what is learned later.
2. *Retroactive interference*—what is learned later interferes with what was learned before.

What happens with the information in the middle? It is lost unless mitigation measures are taken.

Taking breaks helps restore the memory. In most situations, experts begin to fatigue after 50 to 75 minutes of interviewing. If a session goes longer, the expert may become too exhausted to share more knowledge. Taking breaks allows everyone to refresh their memory. It gives people more opportunities to process the beginning and ending thoughts of the session.

Patience Is Needed to Find the Solution—Resisting the Urge to Analyze   Analysis of the knowledge captured must wait until solid rapport is established and mutual understanding of concepts is shared. It is often better to resist the urge to analyze. As people begin to share knowledge, they use language that makes sense to them first and to others second. Thought processes can be triggered effectively only by using familiar terms. Introducing technical jargon will inhibit the flow of thoughts. Asking what and how questions first helps people to think creatively. Asking why questions can stifle free association of ideas; therefore, why questions should be used sparingly at the beginning of the relationship.

Four Stages of Developing Expertise

The Johari Window, originally used for improving communication, is a useful map to help us understand the process for developing expertise.[25]

1. *Unconscious incompetence (novice).* You do not know what you do not know.
   - If you have never picked up a golf club, you likely will not be aware of the fundamentals, including grip, posture, and stance.
2. *Conscious incompetence (trainee).* You know what you do not know.
   - When you take your first golf lesson, your instructor would make you aware of the importance of grip, posture, and stance to help your golf swing. You will know what you need to learn.
3. *Conscious competence (proficient).* You know what it takes to perform the task effectively, but in order to perform the task, you have to think about every step.
   - After several lessons, you have become aware of what you need to do have a consistent golf swing. You have to really think about what you are doing. It has not become second nature for you yet. You are able to explain to others what works and why it works. You have not yet become an expert.
4. *Unconscious competence (expert).* You do not know what you do know.
   - You have been working on your golf swing for years. You are able to swing the club with great velocity and consistency. When faced with adversity, you automatically know how to handle it.

You have tremendous difficulty in sharing your strategy with others because it is so automatic for you. You are not consciously aware of why it worked for you.

Understanding Unconscious Knowledge

The challenge for facilitators when interviewing is making comfortable the process of moving from unconscious competence to conscious competence.

The difficulty with changing from unconscious competence to conscious competence relates to the various ways experts structure their knowledge and their frustration with not being able to explain their reasoning path. Expert knowledge is structured for rapid processing of information, not for explanation. People store knowledge in their minds in a variety of ways, including stories, scripts, scenes, sequential data, and hierarchies.

Understanding how people think will help you become more effective during an interview. People do not always know why they do things the way they do them. Patience during the interview is critical because people store knowledge in their minds in a variety of ways. A variety of interviewing techniques are needed to gather this knowledge.

Theoretical Approaches to Counseling Applied to Harvesting Business Knowledge

By combining the humanistic, cognitive, and psychodynamic psychological approaches for counseling purposes, the client's goals can be achieved. Similarly, by using these approaches for collecting business knowledge, strategic decision-making knowledge and heuristic (rule-of-thumb) knowledge necessary for reaching the business objectives is captured.

The humanistic approach is a person-centered approach to therapy. The therapist extends unconditional positive regard to the client. Offering acceptance of what is being said encourages the client to continue talking. Acceptance does not necessarily mean approval or condoning behavior or decisions. It helps you develop rapport and trust with the client.

The cognitive approach emphasizes internal mental processes. By evaluating how people think, it is easier to unveil the problem-solving thought process. Understanding how humans store knowledge helps to develop questions that trigger their thoughts. This approach helps find the key terms, processes, and business rules for designing business diagrams and detailed documentation. It also enables the creation of mental models that represent the detailed heuristic knowledge used by subject matter experts that can be automated into business rules engines.

The psychodynamic approach encourages stream of consciousness expression. The goal is to identify the step-by-step decision-making process that is so automatic to clients that they are often unaware of all the steps. Clients are asked to start with a blank slate and to let their imaginations run wild while their unvarnished thoughts and opinions are captured. These thoughts and opinions will trigger deeper discussion in later sessions.

To be an effective interviewer, it is not necessary to fully understand these theoretical approaches. These approaches support the *listen, understand, and analyze sequence* that is discussed later in this section.

Preparing Your Mind to Listen   In order to be attentive during a conversation or an interview, you need to clear your mind of distractions and be mentally prepared to focus. When you are feeling anxious about your inexperience with interviewing in a new situation, take extra time to prepare anxiety-reduction techniques. If you find yourself preparing the next question instead of listening, practice active listening techniques.

Sometimes being distracted by personal concerns can be overwhelming. If you are worried about all of your personal and work responsibilities, create a task list and prioritize the urgent and important tasks to help you focus. When you are hearing too much information too quickly, use a whiteboard, or flip chart, or other group memory devices.

Prepare Your Heart to Listen   As you prepare yourself mentally to focus on the other person (interviewee), creating your desire to listen will enhance the experience. One of the best gifts you can give to another person is your undivided attention. You are letting that person know he or she truly matters to you. People feel special, unique, valued, respected, and honored when full attention is granted to them. How is it that you can give this great gift? We know that we cannot give out of emptiness. We cannot give anything that we do not have. As you take time to prepare to interview someone, reflect on a time when someone gave you undivided attention. Remember how you felt as the person showed you respect and honor. This brief reflection time will likely enhance your capacity to give your full attention to the other person.

Developing rapport is the process of building goodwill and trust through mutual education and problem solving. When you allow the person you are interviewing to select the topics for discussion, you are meeting that person where he or she is in that moment. You are beginning to synchronize your mind with that person. When you allow the person to talk on a subject as long as needed, you are connecting with the person's timing. It may feel as if you are on the same wavelength.

As you model openness, develop rapport, and offer a safe environment for authentic dialogue, you are setting the essential foundation for establishing trust. Along with perseverance, this level of trust will ensure the capacity to overcome the barriers to sharing knowledge.

Harvest Business Knowledge Overview

A disciplined yet flexible approach for harvesting knowledge is helpful for discovering the unconscious competence of the key people within an organization. Discipline relates to patiently listening, and the use of open-ended questions allows deep knowledge to surface. The approach is flexible because it uses a variety of active listening and questioning techniques to acquire the knowledge. As in-depth conversations continue to spiral, there are many opportunities to introduce new topics. With the knowledge harvesting approach, a comfort level with the *listen, understand, and analyze sequence* increases.

Listen, Understand, Analyze Sequence   When you are rewarded for being a problem solver, patience in finding a solution may seem awkward. As you patiently listen, you are resisting the urge to analyze. Listening is a prerequisite to understanding. Understanding is prerequisite to analyzing. You cannot apply knowledge without understanding, and you cannot understand without listening.

You begin each interview session by listening. Listening is a nondirective interviewing style that puts the interviewee in control of the topics and allows knowledge to flow on the interviewee's own terms without direction. Understanding occurs as you interpret responses during the interview. Analysis involves evaluating responses and directing the interviewee with a set topic and specific questions.

Relationship Building by Listening   The primary goal for your first session is relationship building by developing rapport with the expert. When the expert is doing most of the talking, your session is flowing. A comfortable topic for beginning a session is a familiar business scenario. You ask the expert to discuss a common case involving a decision. As you develop rapport with the expert, you are gaining an overall understanding of his or her thought process and collecting topics for future discussions.

"Who" and "what" questions are nonintrusive triggers for eliciting broad thinking and knowledge sharing. Avoid "why" questions, because the first session should not feel like an interrogation. Asking "What was the purpose of your decision or action?" is a gentle way to ask why without appearing to question the expert's rationale.

You may consider activities that promote stream-of-consciousness expressions, such as mind mapping. To produce a simple mind map, draw a circle with a word or phrase inside the circle in the middle of a whiteboard or posterboard. The phrase in the circle is the key concept you want to learn more about. Ask the expert what comes to mind when he or she thinks of the word or phrase in the circle. The expert shares thoughts, and you write these around the circle. The thoughts become topics for future session.

You may use gentle listening techniques, such as verbal nudges or probes. With a verbal nudge, you make quick statements, such as "And then, tell me more . . ." With a verbal probe, you may ask, "What happened after you said . . . ?" Your goal is to let the experts know you are listening and to keep them talking.

Interactive Communication by Understanding   After listening to experts express thoughts in their own words, you will need to confirm your understanding of what you have heard. You may need to connect experts' terms to words that are familiar to you. The objectives for this stage of interviewing are to understand how experts organize thoughts, identify conclusions, and detect gaps in their thought process.

"How," "when," and "where" questions will sharpen your understanding by adding context to the concepts you heard earlier. You may ask the expert to talk about a unique experience, case, or situation. These experiences are sometimes referred to as war stories or critical incidents. Experts tend to love sharing these stories because they are filled with emotional memories. These cases may represent situations in which they were burned by their decision and learned from the outcomes. These stories are defining moments for them. These scenarios differentiate an expert from other highly skilled performers.

Your active listening style becomes a bit more sophisticated at this point in the interview cycle. You may ask the expert to explain the meaning of a word. Confirmation will help you validate or correct your understanding. Paraphrasing is rephrasing the content of the interviewee's reply. Reflection is rephrasing the emotional aspects of the interviewee's reply.

Analytical Communication by Using Probing Questions As you refine your understanding of the expert's knowledge, you are analyzing the collected knowledge by using probing questions. You validate the accuracy of the knowledge you have collected, clarify ambiguity, and verify the adequacy of the details. When the knowledge is accurate, the context is clear, and it is made available for others to use, a tremendous return on investment can be realized.

Your interviewing style becomes directive. Now you may ask "why" questions that may seem to challenge the expert's knowledge. "Why" questions are appropriate when you have a solid rapport, you trust each other, and your intention is to be sure your representation of the knowledge can be explained and used by others.

You are relating to the expert in a whole-brain manner. Your left brain helps you analyze and evaluate actions. Your right brain fosters acceptance and appreciation for the knowledge you have gained and for the relationship. When experts sense you understand them mentally and emotionally, the level of the dialogue becomes very deep and meaningful.

You may facilitate the knowledge by organizing it in a business rule form. A logical premise and conclusion is sometimes expressed as an "if–then" statement. Sometimes rules are represented by expressing the conclusion of the decision first followed by the criteria for reaching that conclusion. Decision tables help sort out many factors that lead to various conclusions based on values of each factor.

The distinguishing conclusions approach is particularly helpful to clarify ambiguity. When the expert arrives at two similar decisions, you can draw out the distinctions in each decision path. By writing each conclusion on the bottom of a whiteboard, then asking what factors helped the expert arrive at each conclusion, you may identify some of the same factors and some unique ones.

Let us consider an example of someone planning a family outing. They are deciding on two options: an amusement park or a minor league baseball game. For both options, the expense budget is moderate. When the factor of extended family (aunts, uncles, grandparents) participating was announced, the option was a minor league baseball game. When only the parents and children were participating, then the option was an amusement park.

You could impose a constraint by changing one of the variables and ask, "What if friends were going instead of the extended family? Would your decision change?" Early in the decision process, what–if analysis impedes thought flow, but when you need to apply the knowledge, what–if is appropriate.

Some active listening techniques help the expert focus on main topics. Clarify by asking for more information to refine a point. You may summarize two or more paraphrases or reflections that condense the client's messages. Topic scheduling designates a topic for later within the current discussion. Topic deferral designates a topic for discussion at a later time. Using these techniques during an initial session may interrupt the expert's thought flow. To accomplish the objective of reuse, you need to keep the expert focused.

The analytical communication phase yields deep knowledge and reusable wisdom. The relationships between the concepts and categories are visibly connected. You understand when order and hierarchy are relevant. You also realize when decisions can be made independent of order. When you have identified the intermediate conclusions, the steps in the problem-solving process, you have revealed the unspoken thoughts. You have discovered the expert's unconscious competence.

Harvesting Business Knowledge Approach Summarized Using a disciplined yet flexible approach for interviewing leaders can preserve knowledge assets and share wisdom throughout the organization. The interview approach involves right- and left-brain awareness. Right-brain mindfulness reinforces the "being" nature of relationships, while the left brain captures the "doing" aspects of work that produces favorable outcomes. Results-focused behaviors are optimized by relationship building. As relationships are strengthened, best practices are broadly shared, and the collective decision-making abilities are elevated.

▦ NOTES

1. Lance Secretan, "Spirit at Work: The Conscious Leader," February 12, 2001. Available at www.industryweek.com/ReadArticle.aspx?ArticleID=2084.
2. *Id.*
3. Daniel Goleman and Richard Boyatzis, "Social Intelligence and the Biology of Leadership," *Harvard Business Review* 86, No. 9 (September, 2008), 74–81.
4. *Id.,* 76.
5. *Id.*
6. *Id.,* 77.
7. *Id.*
8. *Id.,* 78.
9. Interviewed by Bronwyn Fryer and Thomas A. Steward, "Cisco Sees the Future," *Harvard Business Review* 86, No. 10 (November 2008), 74.
10. Wayne Baker, Ph.D., "The Paradox of Empowerment," 2000. Available at www.humaxnetworks.com/Print/p-paradoxarticle.html. The quotes that follow in this section are all from Baker's article.
11. Christopher Laszlo and Jean-François Laugel, *Large-Scale Organizational Change* (Boston: Butterworth Heinemann, 2000), 36.
12. *Id.,* 38–39.
13. *Id.,* 43.
14. *Id.,* 51.
15. *Id.,* 57.
16. *Id.,* 62.
17. *Id.,* 70.
18. *Id.,* 72.
19. *Id.,* 79.
20. *Id.,* 80–81.
21. *Id.,* 81.

22. *Id.*, 84.
23. *Id.*, 104.
24. *Id.*, 124.
25. Joseph Luft, *Group Process: An Introduction to Group Dynamics* (Palo Alto, CA: National Press Books, 1963), 10–12.

PART THREE

Models and Practices

CHAPTER 8

Systems Thinking

The leadership we need next cannot try to escape the complexity of the world but has to develop a capacity for effectiveness that acknowledges that the fundamental reality is one of inherent unity. That's why the primary revolution that we need is a spiritual revolution as opposed to a political or an economic one.

—LEO BURKE, DIRECTOR OF EXECUTIVE EDUCATION,
UNIVERSITY OF NOTRE DAME

BASICS OF SYSTEMS THINKING

As discussed in Chapter 2, systems thinking is the application of systems theory in organizations. Peter Senge, author of *The Fifth Discipline*, describes it as "a framework for seeing interrelationships rather than things, for seeing patterns of change rather than static 'snapshots.'"[1]

In today's business environment, the amount of information being created is far greater than at any time in history. And there appears to be no end in sight. The beauty of systems thinking is that it is ideal for managing dynamic organizations that are rich in information.

Mechanics of Systems Thinking

Reality is made up of circles but we see straight lines.

—PETER SENGE, *THE FIFTH DISCIPLINE*

Most businesses have a plethora of sophisticated tools for forecasting and analysis, the results of which are fed into elegant strategic plans.

However, they often fall short in achieving business breakthroughs because they are designed to handle detail complexity. A more pervasive dynamic is one in which the effects are subtle and measured over time; it is called dynamic complexity.

Dynamic complexity takes on various forms. It is present when the short-run and long-run effects of an intervention are dramatically different. Or when an action has one effect on one part of a system and a different effect on another part of the system. Or when obvious actions or interventions produce nonobvious outcomes.

As Senge puts it, "The real leverage in most management situations lies in the understanding of dynamic complexity, not detail complexity."[2] Consider the dynamic interplay of forces in the U.S. economy. As witnessed in the financial collapse of 2008, a new type of investment that entered the system caused an eventual imbalance that wreaked havoc on many innocent parties.

Unfortunately, the typical approach to increasing complexity is increased analysis. Senge points out that "Simulations with thousands of variables and complex arrays of details can actually distract us from seeing patterns and major interrelationships."[3] Most people tend to battle complexity with more detailed solutions. However, this is the opposite of systems thinking.

Senge says "The essence of the discipline of systems thinking lies in a shift of mind. It requires seeing interrelationships rather than linear cause-effect chains, and seeing processes of change rather than snapshots."[4]

Feedback Loops

One of the basic principles of systems thinking is feedback. Many Business Intelligence–centric organizations are built around information. The problems arise when information is seen as a static state. According to Meg Wheatley, first introduced in Chapter 2:

> Information organizes matter into form, resulting in physical structures. The function of information is revealed in the word itself: in-*formation*. We haven't noticed information as structure because all around us are physical forms that we can see and touch and that beguile us into confusing the system's structure with its physical manifestation. Yet the real system, that which endures and evolves, is energy. Matter flows through it, assuming different forms as required. When the information changes (as when disturbances increase), a new structure materializes.[5]

The free flow of information is the very lifeblood of organizations. And the larger the company, the more critical it is to keep it flowing. As information moves, it becomes self-generative. As information is sent, received, and processed, new information is created. In this model, feedback loops take on a different meaning. Traditional feedback loops were designed to measure deviations from the norm. The goal was to detect problems or ensure compliance, thereby ensuring the stability of the system. However, to accommodate an adaptive system, positive feedback loops are necessary. These may create short-term disturbances, but they magnify information that creates the impetus to move a system forward.

SYSTEMS VIEW OF BUSINESS ANALYTICS

In the next contribution, Dave Wells, a consultant, mentor, and teacher in the field of Business Intelligence (BI), provides insights into applying systems thinking to BI.

Overview

Many of today's BI programs focus intensely on analytics. The business wants scorecards, dashboards, and analytic applications, and the technology to deliver them is mature. Still, companies struggle to deliver high-impact analytics that are purposeful, insightful, and actionable. The key to high-impact analytics is a strong connection with cause and effect—the essence of understanding *why* and deciding *what next*. Systems thinking offers the cause-and-effect connection. It holds the key to real analytic value that is derived through insight, understanding, reasoning, forecasting, innovation, and learning.

Systems Theory

The key to understanding is to look beyond analytics and think about systems. Not specifically computer systems, although computer systems are one type to which systems theory can be applied. But systems theory applies just as readily to human, organizational, and business systems.

Fundamental truths for all systems regardless of their type include these assertions:

- A system is a collection of interacting parts.
- Behavior of any part is influenced by interaction with other parts.

- A system boundary defines the set of parts that comprise a system.
- A system may interact with things outside of its boundary.
- External interaction is less influential of system behavior than internal interaction.
- Behavior is understood by examining the entire system, not individual parts.

Systems Thinking: Applied Systems Theory

Systems thinking applies systems theory to create desired outcomes or change. It offers a unique approach to problem solving that views problems as part of an overall system. Traditional problem-solving approaches tend to focus on one or a few parts of a system, believing that changes to those parts offer a solution. The systems-thinking approach focuses less on the parts and more on interactions and influences among them as the core elements of problem solving.

Understanding of systems is achieved through identification, modeling, and analysis of relationships and interactions among the parts of a system—a distinctly different and more in-depth analysis than is possible with structural models of a system. Systems modeling is performed by representing the parts of a system and the interactions among those parts.

The most basic concept of systems theory is that a system is a collection of interacting things. The use of the word *thing* avoids the context-based connotations that might occur with terms such as *entity, object*, or *component*.

Things in a system are of many types. They may include (but are not limited to) entities that are familiar to data modelers, objects that are familiar to object-oriented systems analysts, and components as they are understood by software developers. Things in a business system encompass artifacts such as resources, capacities, limits, gaps, goals, desires, actions, results, plans, processes, rules, standards, and much more.

Influence is a behavioral characteristic of interaction. Interaction between two things in a system is directional—one thing has influence on another thing. System behavior is important to understand why things happen in a system and to predict what may happen in the future. Analysis of influences is the key to understanding system behavior.

Systems Thinking Models: Causal Loop Diagramming

Visually representing system behavior is widely practiced in systems thinking with a causal loop diagram (CLD). Causal loop diagramming is a form of cause-and-effect modeling. The diagrams represent systems and their behaviors as a collection of nodes and links. Nodes represent the things in a system, and links illustrate interactions and influences.

Influences are of two types—same direction and opposite direction. A same-direction influence means that the values of two things move in the same direction when change occurs: *When employee morale increases, employee productivity goes up.* An opposite direction influence means that the values move in opposite directions: *When employee stress increases, employee productivity decreases.* Exhibit 8.1 illustrates how these two examples are modeled. Note that a plus (+) indicates same direction and a minus (-) is used for opposite direction.

The diagramming technique is called causal loop diagramming because real understanding comes from understanding the system as a whole. Cause and effect is typically not linear; it is circular with a sequence of influences producing a feedback loop. Loops are closed structures that represent a sequence of system interactions without a beginning or an end. A loop may contain any number of interactions greater than one. Feedback is a characteristic of loops in systems.

Feedback is a process by which the results of an activity or action are returned to the actor in a way that influences the behavior of that actor. Positive feedback occurs when the cumulative effect of all interactions in the loop is one of growth, amplification, or acceleration. Positive feedback loops are often called reinforcing loops. Negative feedback occurs when the cumulative effect of all of the interactions is stabilization or

| Employee Morale | + Employee Productivity − | Employee Stress |

EXHIBIT 8.1   INFLUENCE AND DIRECTION OF VALUES

equilibrium. Negative feedback loops are also known as balancing loops or goal-seeking loops.

Exhibit 8.2 illustrates both kinds of feedback loops. Note that the kind of feedback loop—positive or negative—is indicated using a polarity symbol at the center of the loop. Polarity describes the positive or negative feedback property of a loop. Determining loop polarity is relatively easy. Simply count the number of subtractive interactions in the loop. An odd number indicates negative polarity, and an even number, positive polarity.

Individual feedback loops are a step toward understanding cause and effect, but they only scratch the surface. Often the interactions among loops provide real insight into system behaviors by breaking down stovepipe views of the parts of a system. Exhibit 8.3 illustrates this principle with only one minor change to the diagrams shown in Exhibit 8.2. The new model shows a connection between the two feedback loops. Finding these kinds of connections is the first step to developing a holistic view of a system.

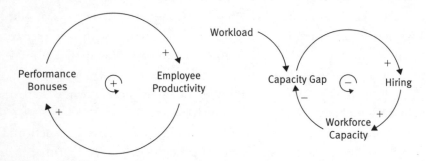

EXHIBIT 8.2   **POSITIVE AND NEGATIVE FEEDBACK LOOPS**

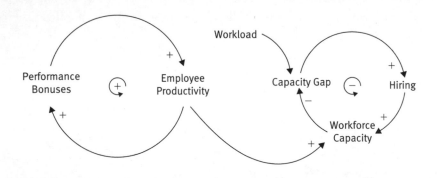

EXHIBIT 8.3   **MODELING A SYSTEM**

In reality, a system consists of many loops and many interactions among those loops. It is that total system view that helps to achieve depth of understanding and real insight into the behaviors of complex systems. The intersection nodes—those that participate in two or more loops—are the core of system complexity, and they provide the greatest opportunity to discover side effects, hidden influences, and unintended consequences.

Determining the boundaries of a system model can be challenging. Every system is a part of some larger system. Therefore, it is possible to continue modeling infinitely. The time to stop modeling is when enough knowledge and information has been acquired to satisfy the purpose of the model. Stopping too quickly, however, presents a risk that side effects and unintended consequences might be overlooked. Exhibit 8.4 illustrates the nature of this challenge.

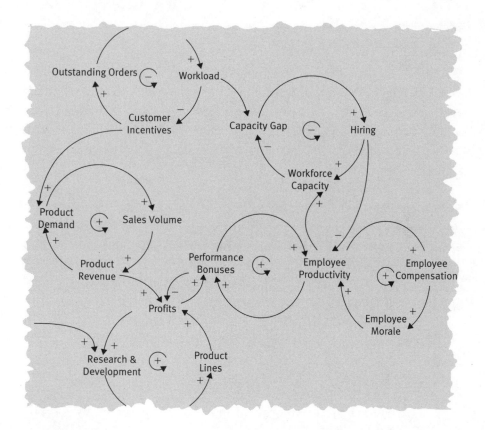

EXHIBIT 8.4   SEEKING SYSTEM BOUNDARIES

Systems Thinking and Business Analytics

This section provides only a brief introduction to systems thinking, a subject that is deep, complex, and very much related to business analytics. Only by understanding systems dynamics can the most meaningful measures emerge to deliver analytics that are purposeful, insightful, and actionable. Sometimes business analytics means measuring things, but more often it means measuring interactions and influences.

The discipline of systems thinking includes several archetypes—generic models that represent recurrent patterns in systems. The names of the archetypes are fascinating in themselves: accidental-adversaries, fixes that fail, drifting-goals, tragedy of the commons, and so on. But even more interesting is the clear and certain relationship that exists between these archetypes and the patterns seen in time-series analysis.

Recurring Patterns in Systems

System archetypes—the recurring patterns that are found in systems—show a strong relationship to patterns found in time-series analysis. Virtually every business analytics system analyzes data over time and presents the analysis as time-series graphs. Creating the graphs is relatively easy. Finding meaning in them is frequently more challenging. This is where system archetypes are valuable.

System Archetypes   Nine system archetypes are widely recognized in systems theory. Each archetype describes a generic structure that can be generalized across many different settings. The underlying relationships are fundamentally the same regardless of the system or setting in which the archetype is found. Each of the archetypes is described next using causal loop diagramming.

Accidental-Adversaries   Localization with system-wide suboptimization typifies the accidental-adversaries archetype. Exhibit 8.5 illustrates the archetype as a causal loop model. It is characterized by:

- Two distinct local reinforcing loops exist, represented by localities X and Y.
- Each locality behaves locally to contribute its own success.

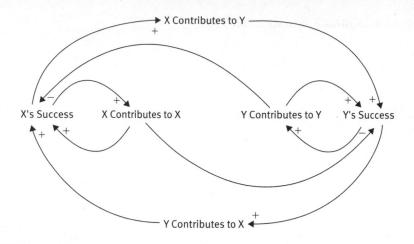

EXHIBIT 8.5   **ACCIDENTAL-ADVERSARIES CAUSAL LOOP DIAGRAM**

- X locality behaves cooperatively to contribute to the others' success.
- The two cooperative links create a system global reinforcing loop.
- X's local actions to contribute to X's success have unintended consequences that inhibit Y's success.
- Y's local actions to contribute to Y's success have unintended consequences that inhibit X's success.
- Overall system potential is limited by the effects of unintended consequences of local optimization without global system awareness. The value of the global reinforcing loop is diminished.

As a sociocultural example, consider the conflicting goals and activities of national security versus workforce economics as they relate to U.S. immigration policies. In a more business-oriented scenario, consider an example where two people are managing separate but related software development projects. Cooperatively they have agreed to develop shared and reusable software components, where practical. Yet each of them, when faced with schedule pressures or conflicting needs, chooses to build local custom components.

In behavior-over-time analysis, accidental-adversaries graphs as two activities—X and Y—which both experience accelerating growth early in the time scale. As local optimization limits success potential of both

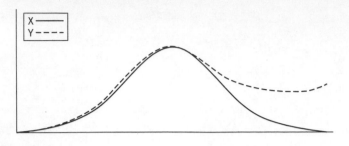

| EXHIBIT 8.6 | **ACCIDENTAL-ADVERSARIES GRAPH** |

activities, they each decline in the later stages of the time scale. Exhibit 8.6 shows the graphical pattern of accidental-adversaries.

Drifting-Goals Lowering the bar describes the common effect of the drifting-goals archetype. Exhibit 8.7 illustrates the archetype as a causal loop model. The characteristics are:

- Two separate balancing loops exist.
- The two loops intersect at a common gap.
- One loop contributes to the desired state, and another, the current state.
- The gap simultaneously influences action and causes pressure to adjust the desire—in essence to change the goal.
- As the desired state is distorted, the influence on action mutates.
- Ultimately the balance that is achieved has little relationship to the initial desired state.

Consider this scenario: A company is scheduled to negotiate its sales revenue budgets annually. In one year, actual revenue would significantly exceed the budget, creating pressure to increase budget in the following year. The higher budget in the second year caused actual revenue to fall short of budget, creating pressure to reduce the revenue budget in year three. What are the implications of this seesaw budgeting pattern continuing over several years?

In behavior-over-time analysis, drifting-goals graphs as mildly oscillating patterns of both the current state and the desired state. Current state increases slightly over time, as desired state experiences a slight decrease.

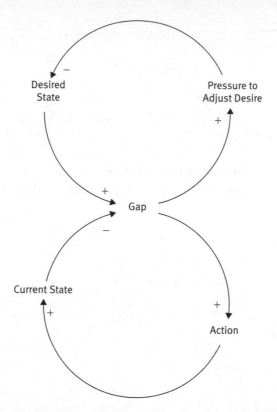

EXHIBIT 8.7   **DRIFTING-GOALS CAUSAL LOOP DIAGRAM**

Eventually equilibrium is reached and both states flatten at a level that is less than the original desired state. Exhibit 8.8 shows the graphical pattern of drifting-goals.

Escalation   Competing for dominance best describes the nature of the escalation archetype. Exhibit 8.9 illustrates the archetype as a causal loop model. The characteristics are:

- Two separate balancing loops exist, identified here as X and Y.
- The two loops intersect at a common gap, which is defined as relative results.
- The results of action in each loop influence the desired state of the other.

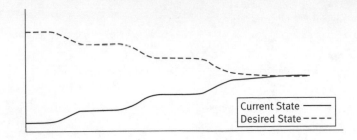

Current State ——————
Desired State - - - - -

| EXHIBIT 8.8 | **DRIFTING-GOALS GRAPH** |

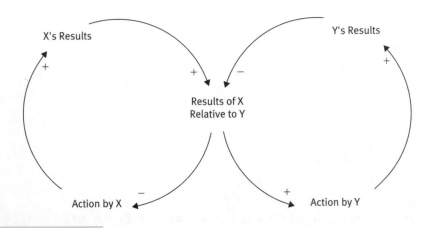

| EXHIBIT 8.9 | **ESCALATION CAUSAL LOOP DIAGRAM** |

- The results of action in each loop influence the drive for action in the other.
- The cycle repeats with no apparent end.

The cold war is an obvious sociocultural example of escalation. Competitive pricing is a common business-oriented example. It is common for retailers to advertise that they will match any competitors' price. What would be the eventual outcome if two retailers each established a policy of beating the other's best price by 5 percent?

In behavior-over-time analysis, escalation graphs as two activities—X and Y—that each grow in a stair-step pattern, with each as the driving force for the next growth step of the other. Exhibit 8.10 shows the graphical pattern of escalation.

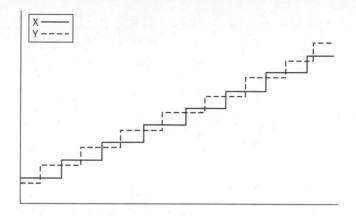

EXHIBIT 8.10   **ESCALATION GRAPH**

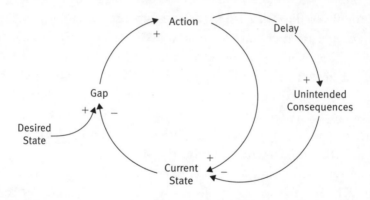

EXHIBIT 8.11   **FIXES-THAT-FAIL CAUSAL LOOP DIAGRAM**

Fixes-that-Fail   The high cost of the quick fix describes the consequences of fixes-that-fail. Exhibit 8.11 illustrates the archetype as a causal
loop model that is characterized by:

- A balancing loop is applied to produce immediate positive results.
- The action of the balancing loop produces side effects in the form
  of undesirable and unintended consequences.
- A time delay exists between taking action and realizing the side effects.
- The side effects impede the current state from migrating toward the
  desired state.

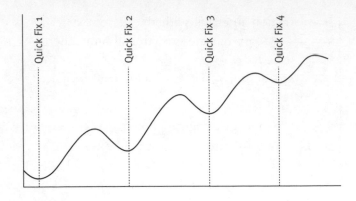

EXHIBIT 8.12   **FIXES-THAT-FAIL**

Free phone promotions in the wireless telecom industry are a sociocultural example of fixes-that-fail. A business-focused example is a company that is losing customers due to long wait times at the customer service call center. To improve customer retention, the company decides to outsource call center operations. The early result is a visible reduction in wait times and a corresponding reduction of customer attrition due to call center waits. After several months, however, the customer retention rate flattens and begins to trend again toward attrition. What may be the cause, and what fundamental solution may resolve it?

In behavior-over-time analysis, fixes-that-fail exhibit an oscillating pattern of increase followed by decrease. Each of the increases coincides with the introduction of a symptomatic solution. Each decrease that follows is the result of unintended consequences of the fix that become visible only after some delay. It is common that the time intervals between cycles decrease over time and that the amplitude of each wave also shrinks. Exhibit 8.12 shows the graphical pattern of fixes-that-fail.

Limits-to-Success   A growth plateau describes the effect of the limits-to-success archetype. Exhibit 8.13 illustrates the archetype as a causal loop model in which:

- A reinforcing loop drives growth of a current state.
- As the current state increases, it interacts with some limiting state in a way that produces a slowing action.

- The slowing action interacts with the current state in a balancing loop that inhibits current state growth and limits the growth effects of the reinforcing loop.
- Rapid growth decelerates, flattens, and may ultimately decline.

One-hour photo developing is an example of limits-to-success where the limiting factor is the emergence of digital photography. Limiting factors may appear in many different forms, including capacity constraints, market saturation, aging product lines, emerging technologies, resource limits, and so on.

In behavior-over-time analysis, limits-to-success exhibit a growth curve that shows early acceleration, followed with deceleration and eventual flattening over time. Exhibit 8.14 shows the graphical pattern of limits-to-success.

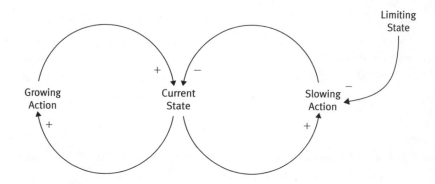

EXHIBIT 8.13   **LIMITS-TO-SUCCESS CAUSAL LOOP DIAGRAM**

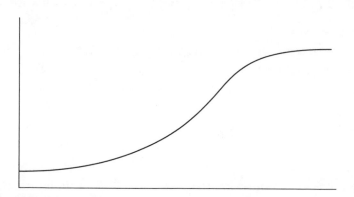

EXHIBIT 8.14   **LIMITS-TO-SUCCESS GRAPH**

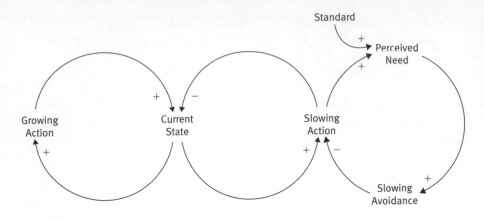

EXHIBIT 8.15   GROWTH-AND-UNDERINVESTMENT CAUSAL
LOOP DIAGRAM

Growth-and-Underinvestment A common variation of limits-to-success is called growth-and-underinvestment. In this archetype, the limiting state is created by failure to invest, often due to short-term pressures such as limited capital. As growth stalls due to lack of resources, incentive to add capacity declines, which causes growth to slow even more. Exhibit 8.15 illustrates growth and underinvestment as a causal loop diagram. Note that a complete limits-to-success model is present. Growth-and-underinvestment have the same behavior over time patterns as limits to success.

Shifting-the-Burden The enduring bandage describes the effects of shifting-the-burden. Exhibit 8.16 illustrates the archetype as a causal loop model that is characterized by:

- A short-term solution is implemented that successfully resolves an ongoing problem.
- The short-term solution is implemented as a balancing loop within the system.
- As the short-term solution is used repeatedly, it diminishes the drive to implement a more fundamental solution.
- Over time, the ability to implement a fundamental solution decreases and reliance on the short-term, symptomatic solution increases.
- Ultimately, the short-term solution may produce other side effects that emerge as new problems.

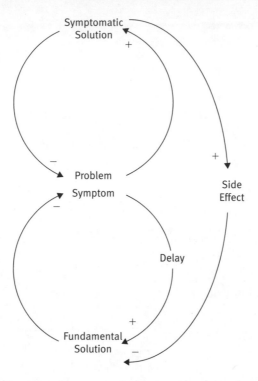

Symptomatic
Solution

+

−

Problem
Symptom

+

Side
Effect

−

Delay

+

Fundamental
Solution

−

EXHIBIT 8.16   **SHIFTING-THE-BURDEN CAUSAL LOOP DIAGRAM**

A common example here is overuse of temporary labor to balance workforce capacity with workload demands. Temporary labor satisfies the immediate need to increase capacity. But, when used repeatedly, the percentage of the workforce that is classified as temporary grows, and many "temporary" workers become a permanent part of the workforce. Ultimately issues of Fair Labor Standards Act compliance, benefits eligibility, and such emerge—sometimes resulting in legal action and financial penalties.

In behavior-over-time analysis, shifting-the-burden shows an oscillating pattern of erratic growth of a symptomatic solution. A corresponding (but not always graphed) pattern of oscillating decline in the viability of a fundamental solution occurs simultaneously. Exhibit 8.17 shows the graphical pattern of fixes-that-fail.

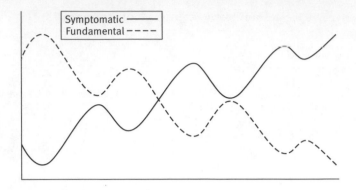

| EXHIBIT 8.17 | SHIFTING-THE-BURDEN GRAPH |

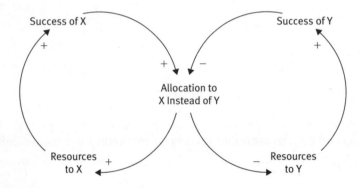

| EXHIBIT 8.18 | SUCCESS-TO-THE-SUCCESSFUL CAUSAL LOOP DIAGRAM |

Success-to-the-Successful   Winners and losers describe the effects of success-to-the-successful, which makes win-win systems difficult to achieve. Exhibit 8.18 illustrates the archetype as a causal loop model that is characterized by:

- Two activities in a system (represented here as X and Y) compete for the same limited set of resources.
- Both activities are represented by reinforcing loops where resources influence success, which in turn influences resources.
- The early success of activity X creates incentive to allocate more resources to X.

- Allocation of resources to X instead of Y increases X's ability to succeed.
- Allocation of resources to X instead of Y decreases Y's ability for success.
- Continuation of the cycle reinforces positive results of X and negative results of Y.
- The combined effect of two reinforcing loops moving in opposite directions is a single reinforcing loop that enhances success of X and inhibits success of Y.
- Ultimately X is sustained while Y fails.

Consider the example of two departments in a company that are competing for priority of information technology (IT) projects. The marketing department needs data and technology to get a 360-degree view of customers and the marketplace and to manage effective marketing campaigns. The research department needs modeling and simulation technology to drive innovation of new products. Both projects are initiated at similar times. In a span of a few months, the marketing department illustrates success with campaign effectiveness metrics. In the same short time span, the research director has only anecdotal justification for the simulation project. The demonstrable success of marketing is reasoned to justify assigning more IT resources to marketing projects, which takes them away from research projects.

Success-to-the-successful graphs as two activities—X and Y—with divergent patterns. The activity to first demonstrate success (illustrated here as X) shows a growth curve, while the other shows a corresponding decline. Over time, the gap widens. Exhibit 8.19 shows the graphical pattern of fixes that fail.

Tragedy-of-the-Commons   Shared resource overload is the nature of tragedy-of-the-commons. Exhibit 8.20 illustrates the archetype as a causal loop model where:

- Two activities in a system (represented here as X and Y) depend on a shared resource of limited capacity.
- Both X and Y grow through activity that produces individual gain, as illustrated by two reinforcing loops.

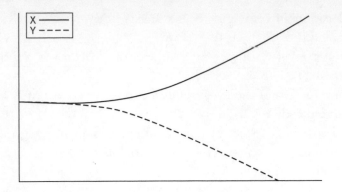

EXHIBIT 8.19   **SUCCESS-TO-THE-SUCCESSFUL GRAPH**

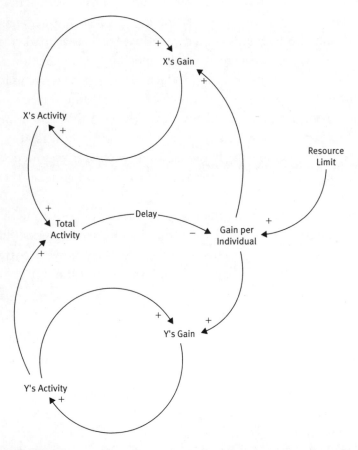

EXHIBIT 8.20   **TRAGEDY-OF-THE-COMMONS CAUSAL LOOP DIAGRAM**

- With growth over time, the total activity first approaches and then exceeds the limited capacity of the resource.
- Growth opportunities for both X and Y disappear when the capacity of the resource exceeded.
- Ultimately (especially for consumables) the resource is depleted, which stalls (or even reverses) growth of both X and Y.

Consider the example of a company that depends extensively on the subject and domain knowledge of one person. Initially that person provides valuable knowledge that fuels growth of programs, products, marketing, sales, and quality. As each area grows, demands on the expert increase to the point where he or she cannot keep pace with demand. Ultimately the demands become burdensome, the job becomes unrewarding, and the expert resigns.

In behavior-over-time analysis, tragedy-of-the-commons illustrates three variables. As seen in Exhibit 8.21, two activities—X and Y—exhibit early and steady incline followed by late and rapid decline. The common resource of limited capacity exhibits rapid growth of demand (coincidental with the growth peak of the two activities) followed by very rapid decline.

Putting the Archetypes to Work   The archetypes described in this section are an effective way to gain insight from analytics. It is useful to understand

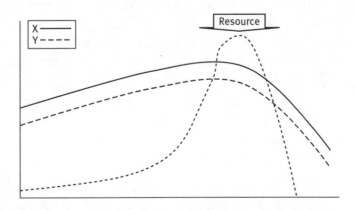

EXHIBIT 8.21   **TRAGEDY-OF-THE-COMMONS GRAPH**

the relationships between archetypes shown as causal loop diagrams and the patterns found in time-series analysis. Whether one is looking at a behavior-over-time graph and asking "Why?" or at a system model and asking "What should I expect?" the archetypes offer a view into the dynamics of systems. Understanding cause-and-effect relationships really is the key to gaining insight through analytics.

Making Cause and Effect Measurable

This section examines stock-and-flow models—the systems thinking tool specifically designed to answer *how much*.

Stocks and Flows   The causal loop techniques described in previous sections help to understand influences among the things in a system. But they make no distinction between the transient things and those things that accumulate. Yet things that accumulate are often the most important to examine when analyzing a system. They are quantifiable and provide the means by which influence can be measured. Understanding the dynamics of things that accumulate in a system is central to modeling and simulating system behaviors. Stock-and-flow models are designed to meet this need.

The things that accumulate in a system are called stocks. A *stock* is an accumulation of something in a system—either concrete and tangible things (i.e., dollars or widgets) or abstract and intangible things (i.e., knowledge or morale). Tangible stocks are accumulations of consumable resources. Intangible stocks are accumulations of catalytic resources.

A stock changes through the influences of flows. A *flow* is an action that influences a stock by increasing or decreasing the quantity of the stock. Flows are of two kinds: inflow, which increases the accumulated quantity, and outflow, which decreases the quantity.

The relationships of stocks and flows are graphically represented using stock-and-flow diagrams. Exhibit 8.22 shows a simple stock-and-flow diagram for the accumulation of workforce capacity.

The diagram notation is:

- The stock is illustrated as a rectangle—in this example, *workforce capacity* based on FTEs (full-time equivalents).
- The arrows indicate two flows: *hiring* and *workload assignment*. Inflow and outflow are designated by the directions of the arrows.

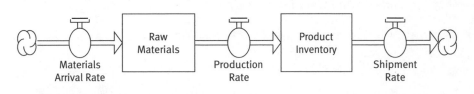

EXHIBIT 8.22   STOCK-AND-FLOW DIAGRAM

EXHIBIT 8.23   COMPOUND STOCK-AND-FLOW SEQUENCE

- The containers on the arrows illustrate how each flow is quantified—*hiring* becomes *hiring rate* and *workload assignment* becomes *workload assignment rate.*
- The "clouds" at each end of the diagram mark the boundaries of the problem space. They indicate that the flow *hiring rate* arrives from somewhere beyond the scope of the diagram and that the flow *workload assignment rate* travels to a place beyond the scope of the diagram.

The rest of this section builds on the simple example shown in the workforce capacity model. It is important to mention, however, that stock-and-flow models are not always as simple as one stock with two flows. Stock-and-flow sequences may involve more complex and interrelated stocks and flows, as shown in the materials to shipment sequence illustrated by Exhibit 8.23.

Measurement of Stocks and Flows   Measurement is a key concept of stock-and-flow modeling. Stocks are always measured as units—dollars, items, and so on. In this example, the measurement unit for workforce capacity is employee full time equivalents (FTEs). Flows are measured as rate of flow, which is expressed as units per time period. Flow measures for this example might be FTEs hired per week for *hiring rate* and FTEs assigned per week for *workload assignment rate*. Consistency of measurement

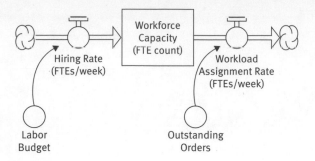

EXHIBIT 8.24   **CONVERTERS IN STOCK-AND-FLOW DIAGRAMMING**

within a stock-and-flow sequence is important. Measuring workforce capacity as FTEs and quantifying flows as headcounts would make little sense. It would be similarly nonsensical to measure the inflow on a weekly basis and the outflow as a monthly amount.

External influences often affect the rate of a flow. In stock-and-flow modeling, these influences are known as converters. (The term *converter* may seem odd for this concept right now. However, it is standard stock-and-flow terminology and will make sense later.) Connectors link converters to flows as shown in Exhibit 8.24.

- *Labor budget* is a converter that affects hiring rate.
- *Outstanding orders* is a converter that affects workload assignment rate.

From Causal Loop to Stock and Flow   Causal loop diagrams will likely be the initial method to analyze system dynamics, with stock-and-flow modeling used where quantification is needed. A stock-and-flow diagram typically examines a portion of a causal loop model to distinguish stocks from flows and to determine how each is measured. Exhibit 8.25 uses a causal loop model to illustrate how causal loop extends to become stock-and-flow diagrams.

A systematic process of working from a CLD to create stock-and-flow diagrams uses these seven steps:

1. Identify critical behaviors of the system—those that are problematic, under study of analysis, or central to the goals and strategies of the organization.

2. Identify the stocks that participate in critical behaviors of the system—those things that are accumulated in the system upon which critical behaviors are dependent.

3. Name each stock with a term that is quantitative but not comparative. The example in Exhibit 8.25 adds "FTE count" to the name "workforce capacity" to make it quantitative. But it does not say "more workforce capacity," which is comparative language.

4. Examine every link to each stock to determine if it becomes a flow. If the influence is one that changes the accumulated quantity of the stock, then it is a flow.

5. Add each flow to the diagram expressing the influence as units over time or rate of flow. The example translates "hiring" CLD to "hiring rate" and "workload" to "workload assignment rate."

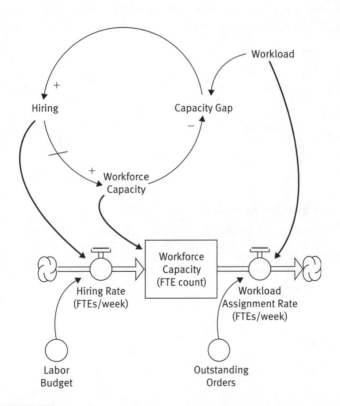

EXHIBIT 8.25   FROM CASUAL LOOP TO STOCK AND FLOW

6. Examine each flow in context of the system-wide CLD to identify links that are converters—influences that regulate or otherwise
   affect the rate of flow. Labor budget and outstanding orders are
   converters in the example.
7. Mark the boundaries—start and end—of the model.

The act of creating stock-and-flow models from causal loop diagrams
also serves to test the causal models and make them more complete. It
is common, for example, to discover influences previously not modeled
when analyzing rate of flow and identifying converters that affect the rate.

Multiple Stocks and Flows   It is possible—even probable—to derive
many stock-and-flow sequences from a single causal loop model. When
this occurs, valuable insights can be derived by identifying the interconnections among stock-and-flow sequences. Interconnections occur when
a flow in one sequence acts as a converter in another sequence. Exhibit
8.26 illustrates an example of interconnected stock-and-flow sequences.

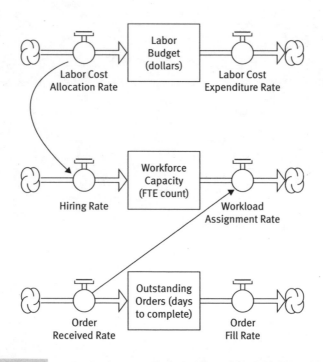

EXHIBIT 8.26   **MULTIPLE INTERCONNECTED STOCKS AND
FLOWS**

Labor budget is a stock whose inflow is *labor cost allocation rate.* The cost allocation rate is a converter that affects *hiring rate,* which is an inflow to *workforce capacity.* Similarly, *outstanding orders* is a stock with the inflow of *order received rate.* In both instances the converter link is a flow-to-flow connection. The stock itself is never used as a converter. The result of this analysis is greater insight that may add understanding and detail to the CLD.

Here is where the term *converter* begins to make sense. The units of measure vary among the three stock-and-flow sequences. *Labor budget* is measured in *dollars. Workforce capacity* is measured in *FTEs. Outstanding orders* is measured as *days to complete.* A conversion formula is needed to describe the influence of labor cost allocation dollars upon hiring rate FTEs—in other words: How do dollars convert to FTEs? Similarly, there is a need to determine how *days to complete* is converted to FTEs for the influence of *outstanding orders* upon *workforce capacity.*

Business Intelligence Connection

So what does all of this have to do with business analytics? The most obvious connection is the use of stock-and-flow models as the basis for predictive modeling and computer-based simulation. The quantitative nature of these models—stocks measured as units and flows as units per time period—make it practical to define simulation models and apply simulation and predictive analytics tools effectively.

But further consideration suggests that the BI connection is much deeper than simulation and prediction. The power of BI is in the ability to deliver insight, gain understanding, enable reasoning, support planning, and drive innovation.

- *Insight* is a clear and deep perception of a complex situation or condition—the ability to "see inside" the situation. Insightful analytics are those that create the ability to look inside deeply enough to understand the causes of a situation or condition. Stock-and-flow modeling provides a tool for greater insight through analysis of system behaviors.
- *Understanding* is the ability to perceive, discern, and distinguish. Distinguishing stocks from flows, units from rates, and causes from effects certainly enhances understanding of how a system behaves.
- *Reasoning* is the ability to identify root causes, to understand cause and effect, and to logically develop conclusions based on that

understanding. Quantifying influences and thinking through questions such as how dollars convert to FTEs undoubtedly advances the capacity to reason about system behaviors.

- *Planning* is the ability to determine a course of action based on understanding and reasoning. The value of insight is limited unless analytics can help to determine what to do next. By extending understanding and reasoning, stock-and-flow modeling enhances planning capabilities.

- *Innovation* is the ability to create something new and different—a device or a process—through study and experimentation. Innovation often occurs by combining or connecting existing things in different ways. Stock-and-flow modeling provides a means to study a system in new and different ways. And simulation certainly has a role in experimentation.

The example shown in Exhibit 8.27 is identical to that of Exhibit 8.26 with only one exception. The model in Exhibit 8.26 does not link *order received rate* to *labor cost allocation rate*—the converter that is shown as a dotted line.

This example illustrates:

- Insight to see that labor cost budgeting is not currently influenced by the rate at which new orders are received.
- Understanding to recognize that this situation isolates labor budgets from the realities of workload dynamics, which is a fundamental cause of the gap between workload and workforce capacity.
- Reasoning to conclude that the gap will improve if order received rate becomes an influence to determine labor cost allocations.
- Planning that is required to define a course of action through which labor cost allocations are influenced by orders received.
- Innovation to establish a new process through which order received rate influences labor cost allocations, which in turn influences hiring rate and narrows the gap between workload and workforce capacity.

Final Thoughts

Systems thinking is a mature discipline with roots dating back to 1961.[6] It is widely known and practiced in many areas where understanding of

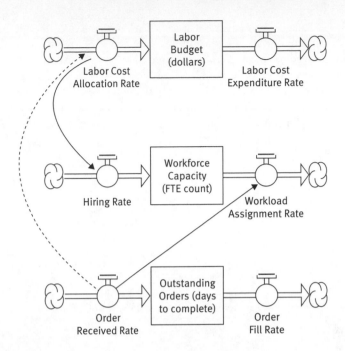

<table>
<tr><td>EXHIBIT 8.27</td><td>INSIGHT AND UNDERSTANDING THROUGH STOCK-AND-FLOW MODELING</td></tr>
</table>

cause and effect really matters—areas such as manufacturing, process control, industrial systems, and organizational dynamics. Business Intelligence has the same critical need to understand cause-and-effect relationships. It does not make sense for BI practitioners to reinvent the wheel. The BI community needs to learn and adopt the practices of systems thinking. The time has come for systems thinking to become a central discipline of business analysis.[7]

NOTES

1. Peter M. Senge, *The Fifth Discipline* (New York: Currency, 1990), 68.
2. *Id.,* 72.
3. *Id.*
4. *Id.,* 73.
5. Margaret J. Wheatley, *Leadership and the New Science* (San Francisco: Berrett-Koehler Publishers, Inc., 1992), 104.

6. Randy Urbance, "System Dynamics: Tackling the World's Complexity." Available at http://web.mit.edu/esd.83/www/notebook/SystemsDynamics.pdf.

7. For further reading, please see the following books: H.B. Asher, *Causal Modeling,* 2nd ed. (Beverly Hills, CA: SAGE Publications, 1983); Charles F. Haanel, *Cause and Effect* (Whitefish, MT: Kessinger Publishing, 2007); Jay W. Forrester, *Industrial Dynamics* (Cambridge, MA: MIT Press, 1961); David Luenberger, *Introduction to Dynamic Systems: Theory, Models, and Applications* (New York: John Wiley & Sons, 1974).

CHAPTER 9

Holacracy

You never change things by fighting the existing reality. To change something, build a new model that makes the existing model obsolete.

—BUCKMINSTER FULLER, INVENTOR, DESIGNER, POET, FUTURIST

Mastering every competency goes a long way to creating an environment through which an adaptable, resilient organization can emerge. However, considering the ingrained habits from many years of working in an old model, real effort is often required to change day-to-day activities that allow a different relationship with work.

EVOLVING THE ORGANIZATION

Six years ago, Brian Robertson, entrepreneur and creator of Holacracy™[1], asked the question, "How can we live and work together in a fuller, more embracing, more powerful way?"[2] He was not looking for another incremental improvement or new techniques within existing models and structures; he wanted "an entirely new tier of organization and shared meaning, one which rewrote the most basic rules of human engagement."

With the question in mind, he had his goal. The rest of the journey consisted of staying focused on the question, testing different practices, and seeing what emerged. He decided to create a company within his current expertise, software development, to serve as a test bed for answering his question. Hence, Ternary Software was born.

As he and his team ventured into uncharted territory, they held the question as an ever-present imperative while they built the company. Along the way, they ran into all the usual challenges of building an organization and working together, from how to organize and govern to how to plan and manage projects. But they refused to turn to the usual solutions. They refused to lessen the pain of an ad hoc approach by adopting solutions they knew would be helpful but partial. Instead, they held the pain and let it wash over them—they would carry it, feel it, and dwell in it. They walked a razor's edge between letting the pain kill them and mitigating it too early with typical solutions. And every time they went through this pattern, they developed a deeper understanding of the pain. At this point, in Robertson's words, "something remarkable would happen: a piece of our answer would emerge—we'd find a way to resolve the usual organizational challenge at an entirely new level."

They repeated this process again and again over many years. Each challenge they overcame showed them a new piece of the answer, and so they wove it into an emerging tapestry of a new way of living and working together. After a while, it became clear that each piece related to all of the others—each aspect of the emerging organizational practice was reinforced by all of the other aspects, creating a powerful whole-system shift from the existing organizational paradigm.

Organizational Challenges

As they began their journey, they quickly ran into all the typical challenges faced by a growing organization. They learned that whenever two or more people work together toward a common aim, they will organize to do so somehow—organization now exists. Even before they discussed or officially recognized that organization, it was there, and with it came questions and expectations. Questions such as:

- Who will make which decisions? How? Under what limits and with what input?
- Who will tell whom to do what? When and how, and under what limits?
- Who will handle what work, and what processes will we follow to do the work?
- When and how will we deviate from the established process, and who will make that call?
- How will we go about answering all of these questions anyway, and how and when will we update the answers as our situation changes?

They also found that answers to these questions were actually operating in the organization, even before they had ever discussed them. Along with these implicit answers came more specific expectations, which were often also implicit. For example, participants may expect their coworkers to arrive at meetings on time, or their managers to provide coaching and feedback when needed, or their administrative assistants to fax something on request. Whenever there are relationships with others to pursue a common aim, it is natural to have expectations—in fact, expectations are an essential aspect to working together effectively to reach a shared goal.

Thus, an effective approach is needed for answering these key organizational questions.

Existing Options

Robertson and his team started by considering their existing options. In a modern corporation, there is a limited democracy in place externally: The shareholders elect board members by voting their shares, and the board in turn appoints a chief executive officer (CEO) by majority vote. From there, all decision-making and expectation setting is autocratic, and the CEO has near-supreme power. Typically the CEO delegates some of power to managers, creating what is akin to a feudal hierarchy. This hierarchy steers the organization through top-down, predict-and-control planning and management. Those lower in the hierarchy have virtually no voice except by the good graces of those above, and they have no official way to ensure that key insights or information they hold are incorporated into plans or policies. Robertson and the team had seen firsthand how limited this system can be—even at its best, it tends to be inflexible to change and ill-equipped to artfully navigate the complexity most businesses face today.

Their real challenge, of course, was not in seeing the weaknesses of the modern approach but in coming up with a worthwhile replacement. They saw some companies attempting to skip an explicit power structure or use only a minimally defined one. That may work to a point, although with no explicit power structure in place, one will implicitly emerge over time. Decisions need to be made, and they will be made in one way or another; social norms will develop. The best one can hope for at that point is a healthy autocratic structure of some sort, although more often organizations, using this approach end up with something far more insidiously dominating and ineffective.

So, they considered running the organization via consensus. That does not scale at all, and the time and energy required often is so impractical that the system is bypassed for most decisions. That leaves the same problems as having no explicit structure and sometimes even worse, as consensus can pull people toward an egocentric space. What about some kind of internal democracy, they wondered. Democracy often results in the same challenges and inflexibility as autocracy but with a higher time cost. To make matters worse, the majority rarely know best. In addition to the other downsides of autocracy, the democratically run company is stuck with ineffective decisions.

While each of these approaches has some merit, none is highly effective at harnessing true self-organization and agility throughout the enterprise. None provided the answer, and so the team began building their own approach, bit by bit.

Integral Approach

Fortunately, the founders had a few ideas of where to begin searching for a better way. They all shared a rich background in using several psychological models to better integrate human differences. The models they used and the methods they practiced were extremely deep—well beyond the more common approach of using less holistic models just to label and stereotype. Through their work at this deeper level, they came to see that different type patterns tended to naturally tune in to different aspects of reality. Each resonated with different fields of very real information and value. And they saw firsthand the powerful results that came when an organization learned to effectively harness and integrate even a few of these fields of information simultaneously.

They sought to go a step beyond that—to find a way to simultaneously harness and integrate the value with which every single unique pattern naturally resonated, even the ones that seemed opposite or conflicting. As just one example, some people prefer to integrate as much information as possible to get the best result possible. And some prefer to make quick decisions to get an achievable result now. On the surface, these styles look at least partially in conflict, and usually in organizations they are. And yet the group's gut feeling told them that they did not have to be and that finding a way to integrate styles would lead to vastly improved organizational effectiveness, not to mention a compassionate and embracing environment within which people of all types could work and flourish.

In addition to embracing and harnessing the value to which each type pattern resonates, they also sought to create an organizational environment capable of working effectively with the interiors of individuals and the cultures in which they exist. In other words, it encompassed emotions, aspirations, purpose, values, shared meaning, language, and so on—all those wonderful internal aspects of being human and in relationships with others. They also put a strong focus on the exterior behaviors: practices, systems, and processes that are the more typical emphasis in the modern business world. As they began to grow the company beyond the initial founders, they brought on board people at different stages in their life's journey and saw firsthand the value in eliciting the best from all of them. And so the act of embracing folks at any stage or space of individual development became a goal, and other similar goals arose over time as well. Although they did not have the language for it when they started the company, they later came to realize that they sought a more *integral* approach to living and working together, and their journey would uncover exactly that.

INTRODUCING HOLACRACY

In the following contribution, Brian Robertson discusses the origins, structure, and practice of holacracy.

What Is Holacracy?

Holacracy is not a model, idea, or theory. Holacracy is a practice. However, unlike an individual practice, Holacracy is an organizational practice expressed through the individual members for the benefit of the organization. Holacracy defines the organization as a separate entity. While there are many benefits to the individual members, the focus and purpose of the practice is to strengthen the organization.

Holacracy enters a new tier of organization and culture that is previously unexplored. Fortunately, those organizations practicing Holacracy have begun to map some of the contours of this new territory. Their experience can be summed up in this way:

> [Holacracy] is about living and working together in the fullest possible way, and evolving the organizations and cultures we exist within to the

next step along their natural evolutionary journey. It is about embracing everything we've learned so far about human organization and culture, and at the same time seeking to fundamentally transcend all aspects of our current organizational and cultural norms. It is about regrouping around a profoundly deeper level of meaning and capability, so that we can more artfully navigate the increasing complexity and uncertainty in today's world, while more fully finding and expressing our own highest potential. Holacracy is about relating and organizing in ways that enable and sustain this quantum leap—a shift to a new level of organization and culture as fundamental as the leap from the feudal systems of old to the democracies of today.

Overview of Holacracy

At the highest level, Holacracy has four major aspects.

Organizational Structure   Holacracy aligns the explicit structure of an organization with its more organic natural form, replacing artificial hierarchy with a fractal "holarchy" of self-organizing teams (circles). Each circle connects to each of its subcircles via a double link, where a member of each circle is appointed to sit on the other circle, creating a bidirectional flow of information and rapid feedback loops. Each circle governs itself by uncovering the roles needed to reach the aim of the circle and assigning circle members to fill them.

Organizational Control   Holacracy enhances organizational agility by improving the methods used to control organizational activities. It aids rapid and incremental decision-making with maximal information, so the organization can continue to move forward as new information emerges. And when it is not clear what decisions and actions are required, Holacracy encourages individuals to take solitary action using their best judgment, accept ownership of the impact, and help the organization learn from the experience.

Core Practices   Holacracy's core practices include regular circle meetings for both governance and operations. Governance meetings help to define how individuals work together—they facilitate uncovering and assigning the roles needed to reach the circle's aim. Operational meetings help get work done—they facilitate effective planning and execution of the circle's day-to-day business. In addition to the core practices, Holacracy includes add-on practices, or "modules," which address many specific organizational processes, from hiring to budgeting to project management.

Shared Language and Meaning Holacracy injects powerful mental models and concepts into the organizational culture, creating a body of culturally shared language and meaning that facilitates ultra-high-bandwidth communication beyond ego.

ORGANIZATIONAL STRUCTURE

Roles and Accountabilities

In many organizations, accountability is often vague if not nonexistent. However, in organizations of any size, there are many webs of accountability. For example, a single person might be accountable to his or her manager, coworkers, direct reports, and customers. Whether formalized or not, these points of accountability underlie the integrity of the organization.

The person to whom one is accountable is important. But the specific actions or clarity around what each person is accountable for is the real issue. When there is not mutual understanding around this, interpersonal strife ensues. When different expectations exist around "for what" each individual is accountable, it leads to important needs being dropped and frustration from all parties. If there is no clear and compelling mechanism to sort out any misalignment of expectations directly with each stakeholder, then playing politics becomes an effective path to working around the system. This results in interpersonal drama and wasted energy. Often the misalignments of expectations are unconscious. Individuals turn to making up stories about each other and assigning blame, which quickly feeds into a downward spiral.

When there is an effective process and supportive culture in place to clarify each other's expectations, however, the frustration of misaligned expectations is channeled into an opportunity for organizational learning and evolution. Politics lose their utility, and personal drama gives way to an explicit discussion of what accountabilities are reasonable, fair, and effective.

From Accountabilities to Roles   In Holacracy, an *accountability* is one specific activity on which the organization is counting. It typically begins with an "-ing" verb, such as "facilitating a daily meeting," or "faxing documents on request," or "managing overall resource allocation for the company." Whenever accountability is defined, it is also immediately attached to a role.

Roles in Holacracy hold multiple related accountabilities in a cohesive container. The list of explicit accountabilities is detailed and granular, specifically to avoid the "title trap"—thinking expectations are explicit just by creating a job title or a place in the management hierarchy. More often than not, these approaches just add to the politics and personal drama. In Holacracy, the title of a role is secondary, merely a label; the real meat that describes the role is the list of explicit accountabilities.

One Step at a Time . . .   With the detailed accountabilities used in Holacracy, any given role may have dozens of accountabilities, and any given individual may fill multiple roles. If accountabilities are defined up front, they are often based on past experience. In an ever-changing economy, this puts organizational progress in danger of grinding to a halt, as its members come up with a list that is soon to be out of date or just plain wrong from the start. Holacracy seeks to clarify accountabilities over time, as tensions actually arise from unclear implicit accountabilities or conflicts between roles. The accountabilities are clarified at the exact time they are needed. No sooner, no later. If no tensions arise from the lack of an explicit accountability, then there is no need to make accountability explicit yet. (This is an example of Dynamic Steering in action, a topic covered later in the chapter.)

Filling Roles   Whenever a new role is defined, it is then assigned to a member of the organization to fill and execute. This assignment formally gives that member control to do what is needed to enact the accountabilities of the role, within any defined limits. (Accountability always goes with control.) It also gives others in the organization the reasonable expectation that they can ask the individual to be responsible for any of the role's explicit accountabilities. That account may just be "I consciously chose to drop it for now in favor of this other priority." As long as it is a conscious choice, people are fulfilling their "account"-ability. Although their action can be appropriate, it may be a clue that something else is needed. In that case, someone else is accountable for ensuring that that individual is a good fit for the role. Along with that accountability comes the control to change the assignment.

Differentiating Role and Soul   In our modern organizational culture, individuals and the roles they fill are largely fused. It is difficult to separate emotions about *people* from emotions about the *roles* they fill. Sometimes the conflicts that arise in organizational life are actually clashes of the *roles* involved, yet they are mistaken for clashes between the people filling those roles. At other times, conflicts arise despite the fact that there are actually people underneath the roles we fill—people with passions and emotions and values and purpose. Sometimes modern organizational culture ends up reducing every person to little more than the function they fill in the organization, omitting their soul entirely.

A handful of more progressive organizations have recognized this danger and the importance of honoring the people side of the fusion of people and their roles by trying to downplay or throw out roles entirely. But in reality, roles are still needed. Individuals still count on each other for certain things whenever they are working toward a common aim. Roles and accountabilities exist, and denying this reality does not help to move beyond the fusion of roles and people.

Holacracy's approach focuses on clearly differentiating individuals from the roles they fill. An amazing thing happens as this process unfolds: Members of the organization are able to understand and honor each other more fully as individuals, while we all see more clearly what is needed from each role to meet the organization's aim, separate from what the people need as individuals. This differentiation helps us more deftly navigate and address human issues, by more clearly seeing the inherent perfection of the individual, the inherent perfection of the role, and the mess that sometimes ensues when the two do not line up well. Once this differentiation is clear, we can begin to more effectively integrate the people and the roles, and thereby help both thrive and evolve together.

Circle Organization

A "circle" in Holacracy is a self-organizing team. Each circle has an aim (purpose) and the authority to define and assign its own roles and accountabilities. Each circle has a breadth of scope that it focuses on;

some circles are focused on implementing specific projects, others on managing a department, and others on overall business operations. Whatever the circle's level of scale, the same basic rules apply.

Defining a "Holon" and "Holacracy"

A "holon" is a whole that is also a part of a larger whole. The term was coined by Arthur Koestler, Hungarian philosopher and author of the *Ghost in the Machine*, from the Greek *holos*, meaning "whole" and *on* meaning "entity," and was further expanded on by integral philosopher Ken Wilber.

Examples of holons are everywhere. For example, atoms are wholes in their own right, and they are also parts of molecules, which are parts of cells, which are parts of organisms, and so on. In a company, specific project teams are parts of a broader department, and departments are parts of the broader company.

Each series is an example of a holarchy, or a nested hierarchy of holons of increasing wholeness, where each broader holon transcends and includes its subholons. That is, each broader holon is composed of and fully includes its subholons yet also adds something novel as a whole and thus cannot be explained merely as the sum of its parts.

Each circle is a holon—a whole self-organizing entity in its own right, and a part of a larger circle; for example, a whole project team circle may also be a part of a department circle. Like all holons, each circle expresses its own cohesive identity—it has autonomy and self-organizes to pursue its aim. Regardless of the specific area or level of scale a circle is focused on, it makes its own policies and decisions to govern that level of scale ("leading"), it takes some actions or produces something ("doing"), and it collects feedback from the doing ("measuring") to guide adjustments to its policies and decisions, bringing each member full circle into a self-organizing feedback loop.

An Example   Exhibit 9.1 shows a view of a holarchic circle structure for a software development organization similar to Ternary Software. Note that each broader circle transcends and includes its subcircles, except for the board, which is a bit of a special case (discussed later).

Compare this to the same company's organizational chart in Exhibit 9.2. Holacracy does not make this traditional organizational chart obsolete,

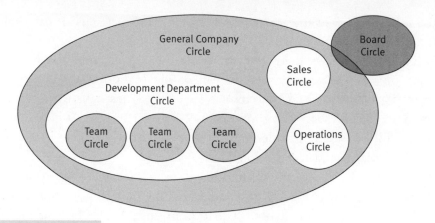

EXHIBIT 9.1   **TERNARY HOLARCHIC ORGANIZATIONAL STRUCTURE DIAGRAM**

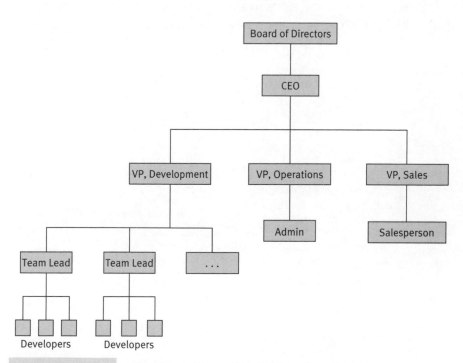

EXHIBIT 9.2   **TERNARY TRADITIONAL ORGANIZATIONAL STRUCTURE DIAGRAM**

although the view of the organization is now incomplete (and it has a subtly different meaning within Holacracy's cultural context).

Exhibit 9.3 brings these two views of the organization together by overlaying the circle structure on top of the traditional organizational chart. This is really the same view as Exhibit 9.1, just taken from a different angle. This view also shows how a manager serves as a connection or conduit between a broader and more focused circle. (Note how both circles overlap the manager role.)

Although the processes within and between each self-organizing circle will be different from typical organizations, notice how the overall organizational structure is not all that surprising. At the broadest level, the board of directors and the chief executive officer (CEO) form a *board circle*, integrating the concerns of the outside world into the organization. Below that, the CEO and the department heads (the executive team) form a *general company circle*, with scope over all cross-cutting operational functions and domains, except those specific functional areas that are delegated to department subcircles (*sales circle*, *operations circle*, and

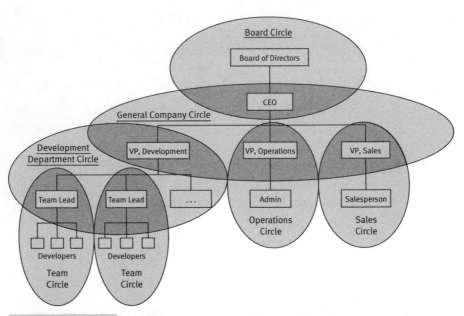

EXHIBIT 9.3   **TERNARY TRADITIONAL ORGANIZATIONAL
CHART WITH CIRCLE OVERLAY**

development department circle). One of the departments is large enough to go one step further and break itself into various *project team circles*, each owning a different set of client engagements. Of course, this is just one example for one company—any given organization will look different, and even the same organization will evolve dramatically over time.

Double Linking   Decisions and operations of one circle are never fully independent of others. Each whole circle is also a part of a broader circle and shares its environment with the other functions and subcircles of that broader circle. So a circle cannot be fully autonomous—the needs of other circles must be taken into account in its self-organizing process. To achieve this, a subcircle and its supercircle are always linked together by at least two roles (and two individuals filling those roles). Each of these two link roles takes part in the governance and operational processes of both connected circles.

One of these two links is appointed from the supercircle to connect to a subcircle. This is called a "lead link" role in Holacracy and is akin to a traditional manager (although there are differences, functionally and culturally). A lead link is accountable for aligning the subcircle's results with the supercircle's needs.

The other half of the double link is appointed by a subcircle to connect to its supercircle. This is called a representative link role in Holacracy ("rep link" for short). Like the lead link, the rep link forms part of the membrane between two circles. The role itself is quite different from anything we are used to in a modern organization, although it bears some similarity to a lead link (but in the opposite direction). A rep link is accountable for ensuring that the supercircle is a conducive environment for the subcircle, by carrying key perspectives from the subcircle to the supercircle's governance and operations.

Rep Links in Action   Rep links are a crucial part of a Holacracy. They provide rapid feedback from the perspective of someone who really knows what is going on at the street level and often provide key insight to the managers and CEO.

In a traditional company, it is wise for a CEO to consider the impact of his or her proposals on lower levels in the organization; and if something is missed, you know whom everyone will blame. With Holacracy in place, managers can focus just on their level of scale and trust the rep links to catch any issues and help to craft a proposal that is workable for all parts of the organization.

And when a rep link misses something, folks in subcircles do not look at the CEO as the guy from above doing stuff to them; instead, they look to their rep link as a conduit for improving the situation. It is the rep link's accountability to ensure the subcircles needs are met, not the CEO's.

Rep links help free management from having to deal with organizational politics, leaving them much more time and energy to focus on moving the organization forward.

This double linking continues throughout the holarchy of the organization. Continuing the previous example, Exhibit 9.4 shows the addition of rep links on our software company's organizational chart—each circle has appointed one of its current members to also serve as a rep link to the supercircle. (The lead link is already shown, as the "manager" in the traditional organizational chart view.)

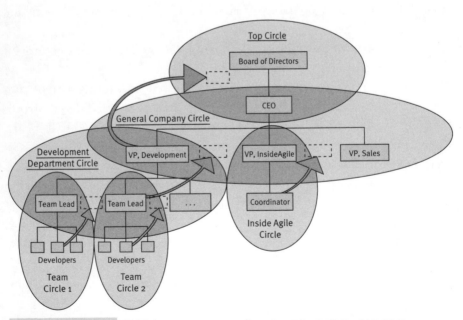

EXHIBIT 9.4   ORGANIZATIONAL CHART WITH CIRCLE OVERLAY AND REP LINKS

Requisite Organization   Once an organization adopting Holacracy has all the basics in place, a new series of questions about Holacracy's structure often arise. How does one know what specific circles an organization should have, and into how many levels these should be organized? How does one know what specific accountabilities should exist within the organization, which role should own which accountabilities, and which circle should own which role? Does it matter? The answer is a strong *yes*, it definitely does matter. This is an issue in any organization, with or without Holacracy. But with Holacracy in place, the organization's ability to both find and harness an effective structure seems to increase significantly.

Holacracy suggests that, at any given time, an organization has a naturally ideal or "requisite" circle structure that "wants" to emerge. And within that circle structure there seem to be requisite roles and accountabilities. In other words, the organization is a natural holarchy that has emerged over time and will evolve with time. This requisite structure is not an arbitrary choice. Finding it requires detective work, not creative work—the answer already exists, it just needs to be uncovered. This discovery process feels a lot less like explicit design and a lot more like listening to and becoming attuned with what reality is already trying to tell you—what naturally wants to emerge.

The benefits of doing this listening are significant. The closer our explicit structures mirror these natural structures, the more effective and trust-inducing the organization becomes. As members align with the requisite structure, the organization feels increasingly "natural," and self-organization becomes easier. Circles feel more cohesive—they have healthier autonomy and clearer identity and more clear-cut interplay with other circles. Each circle more easily performs its own leading, doing, and measuring, with its supercircle able to focus more comfortably on specific inputs and outputs rather than the details of the processing going on within. Roles and accountabilities become clearer and more explicit, and it becomes easier to match accountability to control. Aligning with requisite structure dramatically eases and enhances everything Holacracy seeks to achieve.

ORGANIZATIONAL CONTROL

Among the most fundamental paradigm shifts in Holacracy is its approach to maintaining organizational control. This shift permeates all of Holacracy, and understanding other practices often takes considering them within this context.

Dynamic Steering

Most modern decision-making and management is based on attempting to figure out the best path to take, in advance, to reach a given aim (predict), and then planning and managing to follow that path (control). A commonly used software engineering metaphor is appropriate here: "It's like riding a bicycle by pointing at your destination off in the distance, holding the handlebars rigid, and then pedaling your heart out. Odds are you won't reach your target, even if you do manage to keep the bicycle upright for the entire trip."

In contrast, if you watch someone actually riding a bicycle, there is a slight but constant weaving. The rider is continually getting feedback by taking in new information about the present state and environment and constantly making minor corrections in many dimensions (heading, speed, balance, etc.). This weaving is the result of the rider maintaining a dynamic equilibrium while moving toward an aim—using rapid feedback to stay within the constraints of the many aspects of the system. Instead of wasting a lot of time and energy predicting the exact "right" path up front, the rider instead holds a purpose in mind, stays present in the moment, and finds the most natural path to the goal.

Organizations that replace detailed up-front analysis and prediction with continual incremental adaptation with real data enjoy many benefits, including significant efficiency gains, higher quality, more agility, increased ability to capitalize on ideas and changing market conditions, and, perhaps most ironically, far more control. And the dynamic approach achieves these business benefits while meeting human and social needs at a level far beyond the traditional approach.

It is important to note that transcending the predict-and-control model is not at all the same as just "not predicting," no more than riding a bicycle is a process of "not steering." It is about attuning to an appropriate telos (purpose) and being fully present in the here and now. It involves steering continuously in a state of flow with whatever is arising. Doing this across an organization requires an enabling structure and a disciplined process of continually taking in feedback and adapting across multiple people and multiple semiautonomous teams. Surfing the emerging wave of reality is extremely tricky. Doing it without getting swept away in the tide requires an entirely new approach to organizational steering, and the cultural environment to support it.

Present-Moment Awareness   When dynamic steering is done well, we enable the organization to stay within present-moment awareness and act decisively on whatever arises within that moment, like a master martial artist or an experienced Zen monk. All the benefits and grace individuals find from this present-moment awareness are available to our organizations as well. And when the organization is acting from this flow state, the echo effect on the individuals working within can be extremely powerful indeed.

Rules of Dynamic Steering   There are three key rules to effective dynamic steering:

1. Any issue can be revisited at any time, as new information arises. Steer continually, whenever needed.
2. The goal at any given moment is to find a *workable* decision, not the "best" decision. Make small workable decisions rapidly, and let the best decision emerge over time.
3. Present tensions are all that matter. Avoid acting on predictive tensions while delaying decisions until the last possible moment.

Rapid feedback is critical to effective dynamic steering—it is hard to dynamically steer a bicycle with your eyes closed! Feedback allows our plans to be imperfect at the start of a journey and quite good by the end. It gives us the data we need to adjust our planned route based on the actual territory encountered, rather than trudging forward blind with nothing but a map of what we thought the territory might look like.

Rule #1   Critical to both Holacracy as a whole and dynamic steering in particular is the rule that *any issue can be revisited at any time*. Dynamic steering requires quick decisions based on the aim of the circle and the facts at hand. Knowing that any issue can be revisited as new information arises prevents getting bogged down by predictive fears or trying to figure everything out up front (see rule #3). This prevents wasted time and energy speculating about what "might" happen and instead adapting rapidly—the minute reality reveals what actually is happening. It also leads to a lot less agonizing over the "perfect" decision and makes it easy to just try something and see what happens, knowing that the course can be altered.

Rule #2   The goal at any given moment is not to find the best possible decision but merely find a workable one—the best decision is not the one predicted in advance, it is the one that emerges into reality over time. Dynamic steering facilitates quick starts with something workable. Then better decisions are reached by listening to reality and adapting constantly as new information arises. Avoiding the trap of trying to find the "best" decision up front frees a circle to swiftly move from planning a decision to testing it in reality and integrating the resulting feedback.

Practiced together, the rules of dynamic steering remove a lot of the fear inherent in decision-making. Removing that fear is critical to boosting organizational agility while spending a lot less time in the decision-making processes. Essentially, dynamic steering results in *less* time in decision-making, not more.

Rule #3   When predicting the future, participants often experience fear. If they are stuck with the results of their prediction, as they often are in modern organizational life, then that fear is also *useful*. "If riders are only able to steer the bicycle once at the beginning, then they better be scared of the ride, and spend considerable time up front predicting the right path. And even if they can steer along the way, if that process takes considerable time and energy, then forget about adapting quickly to opportunities that arise along the journey—riders are lucky just to get to the destination intact."

In contrast, holding an aim in mind while living fully and continually in the present is not frightening. To the extent that the members of the organization can hold an aim in mind, fear is no longer useful. Dynamic steering makes it safe to just try something and to revisit issues whenever any potential fears begin to actually manifest. Where many individual transformative practices focus on helping individuals operate from a space beyond fear, Holacracy shifts the fundamental context to one that reduces the degree to which fear arises in the first place. This facilitates much more useful and fulfilling emotional reactions toward both the process and results of decision-making and allows organizations to seize opportunities in their environment that might otherwise be missed.

Failure   Failure is often considered a key principle behind dynamic steering. When you don't know what to do to succeed, just do something to fail. A "failure" at one level of scale is just new information and an opportunity to learn and succeed in the bigger picture.

As Thomas Edison famously said of his early experiments, he did not fail, he just learned thousands of ways not to make a light bulb. Rather than waste time and energy ensuring he "got it right the first time," he simply emphasized getting started, failing fast, and learning fast from that failure. Failing fast at that level of scale allowed him to succeed more swiftly in the bigger picture.

Integrating Predict and Control   Finally, note that there are times when predictive steering makes sense. Integrating future possibilities into present decision-making makes sense if both the probability of a costly outcome is uncomfortably high and there is no opportunity to safely adapt later, once new information becomes available. In other words, if the business path is fixed with no opportunity to steer, and the decision will have a significant impact on the business, it makes sense to incorporate predictive measures. For example, if an organization is deciding on an expensive 10-year lease on office space without the ability to change or renegotiate the lease at a later date, then up-front prediction is crucial.

That is not the whole story, however. Often it is possible to turn what would otherwise be a situation requiring predictive decision-making into one that allows dynamic steering, simply by creating a way to add feedback and steering points along the path. For example, at Ternary, all processes and contracts with clients and vendors are intentionally built to allow and harness dynamic steering. The key is to break down otherwise large commitments, so that small decisions are made incrementally and each decision is deferred until the last responsible moment. Each incremental decision considers feedback and measurements from prior decisions. Of course, doing this can be quite challenging, and it is not always practical; when the situation absolutely calls for it, sometimes the dynamic thing to do is to use a predict-and-control model. In this sense, dynamic steering adds to and yet also fully includes predictive steering methods—it is a broader, more encompassing paradigm.

Integrative Decision-Making

Imagine flying an airplane and ignoring one of the key instruments: "Well, the airspeed indicator and altimeter say we're doing fine, so the fuel gauge is outvoted!" Of course this makes no sense—we all know the fuel gauge is tuned into a different field of information from the others—and yet this pattern plays out time and time again in modern organizations. It is very easy to forget that, like the instruments on our airplane, people are often tuned in to very different fields or types of information. Yet when we look closer, we often find there is at least some value or core truth in anything anyone perceives.

With the speed and demands of modern organizational life, it is not surprising that the perspectives of others are often ignored. However, if an effective and rapid process is in place that brings together and integrates those perspectives that really are important to integrate now, it is possible to build a more complete picture of the present reality. And a better picture allows for more powerful actions that take into account more needs and more constraints of the situation—in other words, it helps to avoid the danger of ignoring the fuel gauge at precisely the wrong time.

Holacracy provides a tool for exactly this kind of rapid integration of key perspectives: integrative decision-making. This rapid decision-making process systematically integrates the core truth or value in each perspective put forth while staying grounded in the present-tense focus provided by dynamic steering. As each key perspective is integrated, a workable decision tends to emerge. The best decision is determined when each member of the circle making the decision sees no objection to proceeding with the proposed decision, at least for now. An "objection" is defined as a tangible present-tense reason why the proposed decision is not workable right now—why it is outside the limits of tolerance of some aspect of the system. Thus, objections belong to the circle—they are not the individuals' personal objections. As long as objections have surfaced, the process continues to refine the proposed decision by integrating the core truth in each perspective.

Short-Format Integrative Decision-Making Process Several facilitation formats are available for integrative decision-making. The short-format process, used when a circle member has both a tension to resolve and a specific proposal to offer as a starting point for integration, is discussed here. The process comprises five steps.

1. *Present proposal.* The proposer states the tension to be resolved and a possible proposal for addressing it. Clarifying questions are allowed solely for the purpose of understanding what is being proposed. The facilitator immediately cuts off discussion and reactions, especially reactions veiled in question format (e.g., "Don't you think that would cause trouble?").

2. *Reaction round.* The facilitator asks each person in turn to provide a quick gut reaction to the proposal (e.g., "Sounds great," "I'm really concerned about X," etc.). The facilitator ruthlessly cuts off discussion or cross-talk of any sort—this is sacred space for each person to notice, share, and detach from his or her reactions, without needing to worry about the potential effect of sharing them.

3. *Amend or clarify.* The proposer has a chance to clarify any aspects of the proposal he or she feels may need clarifying after listening to the reactions or to amend the proposal in very minor ways based on the reactions. (Only trivial amendments should be attempted at this stage, even if clear shortcomings were pointed out.) Again, the facilitator cuts off discussion.

4. *Objection round.* The facilitator asks each person in turn if he or she sees any objections to the proposal as stated. Each person states any objections briefly, without discussion or questions. The facilitator lists all objections on the board and cuts off discussion of any kind at this stage. If the objection round is completed with no objections surfacing, the decision is made and the process ends.

5. *Integration.* If objections surface, once the objection round is complete, the group enters open dialog to integrate the core truth in each objection into an amended proposal. As soon as an amended proposal surfaces that might work, the facilitator cuts off dialog, states the amended proposal, and goes back to an objection round.

Beyond Consensus Using integrative decision-making is not seek-ing consensus—in fact, decision-making and seeking consensus are barely comparable. Consensus-based processes typically ask whether people are "for" or "against" a proposal, or perhaps whether anyone "blocks" it. Integrative decision-making, however, does not focus on personal support at all, one way or the other—it is totally orthogonal to that. An "objection" is not a statement that someone will not sup-port a decision, nor is "no objection" a statement that someone is "for" it. It is simply a statement about whether someone sees something in a proposal that is outside the limits of tolerance of any aspect of the system.

This is a critical distinction—asking people if they are "for" or "against" something tends to push them into an egocentric or highly personal space. Integrative decision-making asks them to speak from a more impersonal (or transpersonal) space about what is actually needed and workable for the collective aim. The process acknowl-edges and honors whatever emotions arise within the participants and then helps them to move beyond the emotions—to make them objects in their awareness. Each participant is asked to view his or her emo-tion without being controlled by it. Once participants are no longer stuck in the charge of their emotions, they can use their personal emo-tions as clues to why a proposed decision may really be outside a key limit of tolerance for the system. Personal emotions become sources of valuable information but not decision-making criteria in and of themselves.

Thus the focus shifts from personalities and emotions to the issue itself and the organization's aims. This process achieves the value in a consensus-based approach without the baggage, by recognizing that the best way to get the best decision is to continually listen to and integrate present-tense perspectives raised by the individuals involved. No one's voice is crushed, and yet egos are not allowed to dominate. The integrative decision-making process helps people meet and interact in a state beyond fear and ego; a group engaged in it has a palpably different feel and usually gener-ates far better results.

With integrative decision-making, it often feels like the people inv-olved in the process are not actually making the decisions per se. They are holding a space, listening to reality, and allowing the creative force of evolution itself to make the decisions—*through* them, not *from* them. These distinctions are all very difficult to describe and perhaps hard to believe, although this is the best interpretation based on the experience of those practicing integrative decision-making to date.

The Enemy of Good Enough   A common problem that arises in organizations is where someone just does not see how a proposed decision makes sense or addresses an issue. How does Holacracy facilitate understanding so the decision can move forward? And a related question: How does Holacracy facilitate the emergence of the better decision when people disagree on the form that it ought to take? The simple answer is it does not. Holacracy sets a very different threshold for decision-making, one that does not create space for this kind of conflict in the first place.

As discussed earlier, the threshold of decision-making in Holacracy is merely the discovery of a "workable" decision. Organizational dysfunction occurs whenever any part of the organization lacks sufficient control to ensure its own effective operation (when it lacks "requisite control"). So a "workable" decision is simply one that maintains the ability to effectively control the organization. This method entirely bypasses the tricky and wasteful business of finding agreement among participants of the "better" or "best" decision. Holacracy does not seek a decision that fully takes into account all perspectives, merely a decision that takes into account the minimally sufficient perspectives required to ensure the continuation or restoration of requisite control.

Going back to the original questions, there is no need for everyone present to understand all aspects of a decision or even why it makes sense. They just need to have confidence that the decision will not undermine any part of the organization's ability to function effectively—to control itself. There is rarely a need for anyone to be convinced of anything, since the goal is not to find the "best" decision.

Practically speaking, when multiple workable options exist, the better decision is often the one that is made more quickly. Quicker decision-making means more decisions can be made, more approaches can be tried, and more can be learned about what really works and what really does not. Requiring only a workable decision can be seen as lowering the bar on decision-making, but, more accurately, it is raising the bar on slow-ing or stonewalling the decision-making process. When participants are allowed to learn rapidly from experience, quality continually improves.

Riding the Evolutionary Impulse   Holacracy expressly pushes against attempts to fully integrate all perspectives at any given moment in time, and yet over time it ends up integrating more than any other process. Consider that it is not actually possible to step back and integrate all per-spectives; no matter how much you integrate, there is always something more still to integrate and more reality still emerging around you—it is never-ending.

Integrating perspectives is a process, an evolutionary one that unfolds through time, not something we step back and "do" at any one point. So what we can do is *be integrating*; we can become an agent for the nat-ural evolutionary impulse at the heart of reality, by riding the emerg-ing moment here and now and integrating what actually arises into that present moment.

In Holacracy, we strive to integrate what needs integrating as it needs integrating—no more, no less, no sooner, no later. The more we can find the discipline and skill required to do this, the more value we can integrate into our reality. It is not about trying to integrate everything instantly; it is about unfolding more value into our reality tomorrow than we had yes-terday while recognizing the inherent perfection of the present moment and the evolutionary process, wherever we may be within it at any given time.

A Whole-System Shift   Holacracy is a whole-system change. Its req-uisite processes and resulting culture are very different from those found in most organizations today. And by looking at any one aspect, it can be very difficult to understand. Each aspect reinforces and is reinforced by the others. If integrative decision-making was added to an organiza-tional culture without implementing the other aspects, it could lead to a slowed or stonewalled decision-making process with predictable tensions.

It is difficult to use integrative decision-making without dynamic steer-ing. It is hard to dynamically steer without the clear view of reality that comes from rapidly integrating key data. And it is hard to rapidly integrate all necessary perspectives if participants fall out of present-moment awareness and try to integrate every fear of what "might" happen in the future. But when dynamic steering leads to integrative decisions, each aspect reinforces the other. Their collective effect is greater still when they are both supported by yet other aspects of Holacracy—hence, a whole-system shift.

Integrating Autocracy   Despite Holacracy's power, most decisions in a Holacratic organization are actually not made directly via the integrative decision-making process. Most of the decisions faced day to day are relatively simple and are made most effectively by one person autocratically. Yet as a rule in Holacracy, the governance decision to give autocratic control over certain operational decisions is always done via integrative decision-making. That is, defining and assigning roles and accountabilities and the type of control that goes with them is done through integrative decision-making. In fact, by default, any accountability assignment also grants autocratic control with regard to that specific issue, unless another accountability exists that limits this control, such as an accountability to integrate other perspectives before making a decision. In this way, integrative decision-making wraps and integrates other decision-making styles, although the authority delegation itself can always be revisited via integrative decision-making, as new information arises.

For example, it is not practical for an office manager to call a meeting every time he or she wants to buy more pencils. So instead, the integrative decision-making process is used to create a role with accountability and autocratic control to make decisions related to keeping the office up and running operationally, within certain purchasing limits. Should this authority ever prove too broad or the limits too restrictive, the policy would be revisited via the integrative decision-making process, and the circle would adapt incrementally.

Individual Action   No matter how well the roles and accountabilities are defined and refined, there will be cases where actions are needed that are outside the role definitions and thus outside official authority. In fact, in the early days of practicing Holacracy, most actions fall outside of defined accountabilities, since the process encourages participants to let their roles evolve over time.

Sometimes the action that someone believes is needed is not just outside of defined accountabilities but actually against them, such that taking the action would require neglecting an accountability outright. In a situation like this, the best action is to consider the information at hand, including deference to existing accountabilities (or lack thereof), use the best judgment, and take action. In Holacracy, this is called individual action.

Individual action directs its participants to do exactly what the organization would want them to do anyway: Consider the information available, use their best judgment from their highest self, and take whatever action they believe is best for the circle's aims. When that action falls outside or even against existing accountabilities, they must be prepared to go out of their way to "restore the balance" from any harm or injustice caused, via a restorative justice system rather than a punitive one. Finally, participants are to take the perceived need for such action to a governance meeting, so that the team can learn from the case study by evolving roles and accountabilities to transcend the need for it next time—in this way, individual action drives organizational evolution.

Recognizing individual action as an expected practice within the organization has a profound effect on organizational culture. It helps participants to avoid getting stuck in all the blame, negativity, and "should haves" that otherwise get thrown around in modern organization. These are all reasonable emotions that get confused for facts about reality; they create resistance to what has already happened and cannot be changed. Resisting the past gets in the way of accepting the present for the perfect moment it is and shifting our energy toward how to move forward effectively. Expecting individual action helps shift from blame and fear of blame to living in the present and courageously facing the future together.

CORE PRACTICES

Governance Meetings

The members of a circle meet regularly to establish and evolve circle governance. Governance meetings focus on uncovering the general roles needed to reach the circle's aim and the specific accountabilities and control required of each, and then assigning these roles to circle members. Attendance is open to all members of the circle, including the representative links elected to this circle from subcircles. These meetings typically are held at least once per month for most circles, and sometimes more frequently.

The focus of a governance meeting is governance, not operations. These meetings are about evolving the pattern and structure of the organization—defining how members will work together—and not about conducting specific business or making decisions about specific issues. That is not to say that all talk of operational issues is avoided—in the spirit of dynamic steering, governance proposals typically are inspired by specific operational needs or events. Whenever something did not go as well as desired, often additional requisite roles or accountabilities are waiting to be uncovered in a governance meeting. Likewise, whenever it is not clear who makes which specific decisions and how, likely a helpful clarification of roles and accountabilities is ready to hatch. (Remember, control goes hand in hand with accountability.)

Still, the key to effective governance meetings is to continually pull the focus back to roles and accountabilities. Without a strong focus and a clear space held for governance, it is easy for an organization to get so caught up in the day-to-day operations that governance just does not happen. Regular governance meetings are essential to the effective practice of Holacracy.

Governance Meeting Agenda   A template agenda for a typical governance meeting looks like this:

Check-in. The check-in is a brief go-around, where each person gives a short account of his or her current mind-set and general emotional state, to provide emotional context for others in the meeting and to help the speaker let go of any held tensions. The facilitator crushes discussion or reactions to others' check-ins. Example: "I'm a little stressed out from the project I'm working on today, but I've been looking forward to this meeting."

Administrative concerns. The facilitator quickly checks for objections to last meeting's minutes and explicitly states the time available for this meeting.

Agenda setup. The facilitator solicits agenda items for the meeting on the fly. (Agenda items are never carried over from prior meetings.)

Participants state agenda items briefly, as just a title, and the facilitator writes them on the board. Once all agenda items are listed, the facilitator proposes an order in which to tackle them and quickly integrates any objections to the order.

Specific items. The group proceeds through each agenda item until the meeting time elapses or until all items have been resolved. Each agenda item uses one of the integrative decision-making processes (e.g., short format, long format, or election format). The secretary captures all decisions (and only the final decisions) in the meeting minutes and in the overall compiled record of the circle's roles and accountabilities.

Closing. The closing is a brief go-around, where each person reflects and comments on the effectiveness of the meeting, providing feedback for the facilitator and others about the meeting process itself. The facilitator crushes discussion or reactions to others' closing comments. Example: "We ended up out of process in discussion several times, and it'd be useful for the facilitator to cut that off sooner next time."

Integrative Elections

Several key roles must be filled in each circle: a representative link to the supercircle, a facilitator to run circle meetings and ensure the group sticks to process, and a secretary to record decisions and maintain an overall compiled list of all the roles and accountabilities of the circle. Circle members are elected to each of these key roles via Holacracy's integrative election process, which seeks to tap the group's collective intelligence to arrive at a best fit for the role. The circle may choose to use this election process for other roles as well—it is helpful whenever a clear best fit for a role is not immediately obvious.

Integrative Election Process   A template for the integrative election process follows.

Describe the role. The facilitator announces the role up for election and the accountabilities of that role.

Fill out ballots. Each member fills out a ballot, without any up-front discussion or comment whatsoever. The ballot uses the form of

"(Nominator's Name) nominates (Nominee's Name)." Everyone must nominate exactly one person—no one may abstain or nominate more than one person. The facilitator collects all of the ballots.

Read ballots. The facilitator reads each ballot aloud and asks the nominator to state why he or she nominated the person listed on the ballot. Each person gives a brief statement as to why the person nominated may be the best fit for the role.

Nomination changes. The facilitator asks each person in turn if he or she would like to change the nomination, based on new information that surfaced during the previous round. Changed nominations are noted, and a total count is made.

Proposal. The facilitator proposes someone to fill the role, based on the information that surfaced during the election process (most notably the total nomination counts). The facilitator may open the floor for dialog beforehand if necessary, although it is usually best just to pick someone to propose and move on without discussion.

Objection round. This round is identical to the objection round for the general integrative decision-making process; however, the nominee in question is asked last. If objections surface, the facilitator may either enter dialog to integrate them or simply propose a different nominee for the role and repeat the objection round.

Operational Meetings

The members of a circle meet regularly in operational meetings to facilitate the effective execution of day-to-day business. Operational meetings deal with the specific business of the organization—they are a forum for exchanging relevant information and making specific decisions that require integration of multiple roles on the circle. All members of the circle are invited to operational meetings, although rep links often will show up intermittently and/or duck out early when the topics are not relevant to their scope.

There are different types of operational meetings, with different rhythms, or heartbeats, ranging from quick daily meetings to annual off-site review sessions. The breadth of scope of each meeting correlates directly with how frequently meetings are held. The next sections present brief descriptions of each operational meeting type.

Daily Stand-up Meetings   Daily stand-up meetings are 5 to 10 minutes, usually near the start of each workday. They serve as a quick integration and coordination point for the day, and typically focus on what each participant did yesterday, what he or she plans to do today, and what integration points arise as a result. The daily nature of these meetings means they are not always practical, but when they are, they can be surprisingly useful time-savers and efficiency boosters.

Tactical Meetings   Tactical meetings typically are held once per week, although the requisite frequency varies from organization to organization and circle to circle. These meetings are for collecting up-to-date metrics relevant to the circle (the data required for effective dynamic steering) and for integrating around specific tactical issues the circle currently is facing. The output of the tactical meeting is a list of action items, which the secretary captures and distributes to circle members.

Tactical Meeting Agenda

Check-in. Identical to the governance meeting check-in round.

Lightning round. One by one, each participant states what he or she plans to work on in the coming week, with no discussion. Each person has 60 seconds maximum, and the facilitator cuts off anyone who runs over time.

Metrics review. Each circle member with accountability for providing a metric presents that metric. Clarifying questions and minor commenting are allowed, although the facilitator will curtail any significant discussion—if discussion is required, the facilitator should add an agenda item for it, and restrict this phase to just getting the data out.

Agenda setup. Identical to the governance meeting agenda setup (again, the agenda for tactical meetings is always built on the fly, with no carry-over from prior meetings).

Specific items. The group proceeds through each agenda item, with the goal of completing the entire agenda before time elapses. (These are swift-moving meetings.) Typically, each item is a brief free-form discussion—tactical meetings do not use the integrative decision-making process, unless someone has an explicit accountability to integrate perspectives around a specific issue before taking action.

Closing. Identical to the governance meeting closing round.

Strategic Meetings Strategic meetings typically are held monthly, quarterly, and/or annually, depending on the organization and the circle. Whatever the frequency, strategic meetings focus on the broad "big" issues facing the circle. They are a time to step back and creatively analyze the big picture. The format of strategic meetings can vary, and unlike governance and tactical meetings, agenda items here are decided in advance to give everyone time to reflect and research prior to the meeting. Typically the number of agenda items is limited to just one or two, even for a full-day strategic meeting; these meetings are about digging deep into the most important issues in front of the circle.

Special-Topic Meetings Special-topic meetings are about addressing one specific topic or agenda item—they are probably the closest thing to what is considered a "normal meeting" in a traditional organization. These meetings often arise when something comes up at a tactical meeting that is too big to fit into that meeting yet is not appropriate to park for possible inclusion in the next strategic meeting. The format of a special-topic meeting depends on the nature of the topic—anything from free-form dialog to one of the longer integrative decision-making formats may work well.

Add-on Practices

Holacracy includes many add-on practices, or "modules," in addition to the core practices just described, covering many functions and aspects of human organization. These include modules for strategic planning, budgeting, compensation, project management, personnel development, hiring and firing, team formation, retrospectives, and much more. Once an organization has adopted the core elements of Holacracy, these add-on modules become increasingly important for getting the most from the practice.

SHARED LANGUAGE AND MEANING

Holacracy injects powerful mental models and concepts into the organizational culture, creating a body of culturally shared language and meaning that facilitates ultra-high-bandwidth communication beyond ego. As with most practices, the intent of Holacracy is not to assert these models and theories as true or to prove them—Holacracy itself is not a model or theory, it is simply a practice. Rather, they are used because their use seems to enhance the value generated from the actual practice. They may guide the practice, or they may help to effectively interpret and put to use the direct experiences that result from the practice.

The component models harnessed by Holacracy include type models, developmental models, organizational space models, integral theory, team dynamics models, and many more. Through the practice of Holacracy, a cultural depth is realized. The culture the practice generates is as profoundly different from our modern norm as Holacracy's organizational structure and dynamic steering is from today's top-down predict-and-control paradigm.

Broader opportunities for the effective use of Holacracy are discussed in Chapter 10.

■ NOTES

1. Holacracy™ is a trademark of HolacracyOne LLC and aspects of the method are patent-pending. However, HolacracyOne is drafting a unique open license allowing end-users to freely practice Holacracy. Those wishing to earn revenue for providing Holacracy-related services will need a license and must meet quality-control standards. Please visit www.holacracy.org.
2. Adapted from Brian Robertson, "Organization at the Leading Edge: Introducing Holacracy™," *Integral Leadership Review* 7, No. 3 (June 2007), www.integralleadershipreview.com/archives/2007-06/2007-06-robertson-holacracy.php.

PART FOUR

Beyond Our Corporate Borders

CHAPTER 10

Possibilities

Nowhere is it more important to understand the relationship between parts and wholes than in the evolution of global institutions and the larger systems they collectively create.

—ARIE DE GEUS, *THE LIVING COMPANY*

A rie de Geus, author of *The Living Company* and a pioneer of the organizational learning movement, says that the twentieth century witnessed an emergence of a new species on earth: large institutions, notably, global corporations. This is a historic development. Prior to the last 100 years, there were few examples of globe-spanning institutions. But today, global institutions are proliferating seemingly without bound, along with the global infrastructures for finance, distribution and supply, and communication they create.

The expansion of this new species is affecting life for almost all other species on the planet. Historically, no individual, tribe, or even nation could possibly alter the global climate, destroy thousands of species, or shift the chemical balance of the atmosphere. Yet that is exactly what is happening today, as our individual actions are mediated and magnified through the growing network of global institutions. That network determines what technologies are developed and how they are applied. It shapes political agendas as national governments respond to the priorities of global business, international trade, and economic development. It is reshaping social realities as it divides the world between those who benefit from the new global economy and those who do not. And it is propagating a global culture of instant communication, individualism, and material acquisition that threatens traditional family, religious, and social structures. In short, the emergence of global institutions represents a dramatic shift in the conditions for life on the planet."[1]

HOLACRACY IN THE WORLD

Chapter 9 introduced the practice of Holacracy as a model for organizing and operating an adaptive, learning organization that is very supportive of systems thinking. In the next contribution, Brian Robertson describes how Holacracy can be used to support positive change in the world at large.[2]

Why Business?

The business world is often the last place people look to spark massive social change, yet business drives the economy, government, and education and wields immense power in today's world. Over half of the 100 largest economies in the world today are corporations, a type of entity that did not exist just a few hundred years ago. Most people spend a massive percentage of their waking time involved in a business of some sort; it is the container for much of the culture we exist within, and it has a dramatic impact on our lives and our personal development. Business is the first type of truly global social organization to emerge in the world—it crosses geopolitical and ethnic boundaries and has real potential to unite our world in a truly global communion. None of this is meant to ignore or excuse the atrocities committed in the name of business, and there have been many. If we threw out early nations once we saw their dark side, we would be back to living in tribes, warring with and enslaving our neighbors. What is needed is to move forward, not backward, and that means embracing the business world and helping it evolve.

Role of the Board

To discuss the connection between a single organization and the broader world, it is necessary to discuss the unique purpose of a board circle, Holacracy's version of a more traditional board of directors. Each individual organization has a board circle at the outside edge of its holarchy. A board circle looks like other circles in most respects—it holds governance meetings using integrative decision-making, and it is doubly linked to the single broadest "normal" circle within the organization, the one that includes the operations of the entire organization within its scope (usually called a general circle or general company circle, akin to an executive team). The chief executive officer (CEO) is the lead link from the board to the general circle, and a representative is elected from the general circle to the board.

Despite the similarities, there are a few key differences. Other circles represent actual levels of natural ("requisite") holarchy that have emerged within the organization. This holds for the most focused circle all the way up to the general circle, which represents the broadest holon currently in existence. The board circle thus does not represent an actual level of scale within the company—the general circle already transcends and includes the entire existing organization. Instead, the board serves a unique purpose: to help uncover and manifest the organization's evolutionary impulse—to act as the voice of the organization's "higher self," and to spur the organization toward its unique telos, or "purpose in life."

Structure of the Board

Traditionally, a board represents the economic interests of the share-holders (in a for-profit entity) or the organization's social purpose (in a nonprofit entity). A major challenge of the traditional approach is that all organizations have both social and economic needs as well as both social and economic impact on the world around them. When the interests of either one dominate the other, the organization runs the risk of missing an important need and limiting overall forward progress. To truly thrive in a sustainable way, the organization needs to integrate well with all aspects of its broader environment, social, economic, and otherwise.

With Holacracy, the board includes roles representing the different needs of the broader environment the organization exists within. The exact roles depend largely on the nature of the organization; they may include a role representing the social environment, another representing the industry the organization works within, perhaps another representing the local community or geography it serves, and another representing the economic environment (including investors' needs, although this is now just one component of uncovering the organization's path, not the sole driving force). Whatever other roles may exist, there is also always the elected representative from the general circle to the board, there to represent what the organization is right now, including its role as a home of sorts to the people who work within it.

With all of these varied roles in place, the board's process becomes one of continually integrating needs and goals from each of these contexts, to find what the world needs the organization to become—to unleash the organization's own free will.

Integrating for Profit and Nonprofit

Holacracy effectively integrates most of the distinctions between for-profit and nonprofit companies. Instead of a major difference in both purpose and control, the distinction becomes a relatively minor one, of just whether the organization has partnered with investors to help reach its overall purpose or not. (Of course, the tax differences still remain, at least until our tax system catches up to Holacracy.)

No longer is it relevant to talk about the "owners" of an organization, no more than it is relevant to discuss who owns you or me—we certainly do have economic responsibilities to the various financial institutions we do business with, but we are not owned by them, bound by their sole autocratic decree. And nor would they want us to be; history has shown that relying on slavery is not as economically advantageous as using a mutually beneficial contract with a free individual.

With Holacracy in place, the organization is freed to govern itself, to find and follow its own unique purpose and higher calling—and to generate economic returns for those who provide needed resources along the way.

Organizational Consciousness

Engaging in a novel practice sometimes gives rise to direct experiences that help extend mental models of reality and trigger new theories to explain experiences that do not yet fit within existing ones. The remainder of this section interprets a recurring experience that seems to be common among experienced practitioners engaged in the practice of Holacracy. Perhaps others will have a chance to practice Holacracy and help to advance the collective interpretation of this phenomenon known as organizational consciousness.

From the root "holarchy," taken literally, *Holacracy* means governance by the organizational holarchy itself—not governance by the people within the organization or by those who "own" the organization, but by the entity itself, by its own "free will." As alluded to earlier, Holacracy seems to facilitate the emergence of a natural consciousness for the organization, allowing it to govern itself, steering toward its own natural telos and shaping around its own natural order. This organizational "will" feels clearly different from the will of the people associated with the organization—just as the organization persists even as individuals come and go, so too does this consciousness. Its subtle voice usually is concealed by a cacophony of human ego, although it can be heard sometimes when people come together in a transpersonal space—a space beyond ego, beyond fear, beyond hope, and beyond desire—to sense and facilitate the emergence of whatever needs to emerge now. When practiced well, Holacracy allows this transpersonal space to arise often and easily within organizations.

Organizational Holarchy   Stepping back for a moment, consider which holarchy is being addressed when referring to "governance by the holarchy." A common theoretical mistake is to think there is a holarchy that goes something like this: atoms to molecules to cells to organs to humans to teams to departments to companies (with a few steps in between). The dilemma is that these are multiple holarchies—teams, departments, and companies are holons in their own separate holarchy, independent from the humans involved. Humans may become members of a team for a while, but they are not parts of it. So, there are two holarchies here—that of an individual human and that of an individual organization. The organization's holarchy goes from accountabilities to roles to circles to broader circles and eventually to the overall organizational entity. This holarchy has nothing to do with the people involved—they just work within it for a while—and confusing them as one holarchy leads to all sorts of trouble.

Accountabilities, roles, and circles are holons within our organizational holarchy, and these all refer to holons that are independent from and structurally unrelated to the humans who may happen to connect into them. And when referencing these accountabilities, roles, and circles, not in the sense of the explicit advertised structure but of the "requisite" structure underneath (which may or may not match the explicit structure), these are naturally emerging individual holons, not just artifacts of human design. Because these requisite structural elements are all nested together in a holarchy that has emerged over time, there now exists a natural individual holarchy in its own right, independent from its role as a social group for humans. (For readers familiar with the integral³ move-ment and associated models, in integral-speak these are the two *upper* quadrants for the individual organization, which serve as a container for—but are not the same as—the *lower* two quadrants of the human experience.)

The I of Organization   The organizational consciousness is a conscious-ness that seems to stem from the *individual* organization, not from the collective human culture or social systems operating within. This con-sciousness, the organization's own individual will, is freed by effectively practicing Holacracy, and it becomes a dominant monad for the organi-zational holarchy (and not at all for the individual members attached to that holarchy). For example, when the board circle decides to change what business the organization is in, all the roles and accountabilities within the organizational holarchy will shift to follow that will, just as the cells in the body have little choice but to go along when someone decides to walk across the room. At the same time, the human members are not bound to this organizational will—they have their own consciousness and make their own decisions, and can always decide to leave the organization if the shift in roles and accountabilities does not fit them well. Yet regardless of what the members decide, the requisite holarchy for the organization has shifted, according to the organization's will.

This insight helps to illustrate that an organization's purpose or telos is neither explicitly created by its members nor is it a collection of the mem-bers' own individual purposes. In a healthy organization, in many ways the members are really just along for the ride as the organizational entity itself strives to embody its own purpose. (More often in today's world, one or more members dominate the organization's own will, completely obscur-ing it in the process.) Sensing an organization's will is very subtle business, but under the right circumstances, it can be directly and tangibly perceived by those with a developed sense for it, and it can be verified by qualified peers.

Aside from this being the best interpretation based on practitioners' experiences, this interpretation is also extremely practical. It diminishes the likelihood of getting paralyzed by the purely relative consensus-seeking trap that results when the members decide that the organization's vision really should be some form of the sum of the members' personal visions. It also circumvents the domination and ego trap that results from thinking that a subset of the members or just one individual should decide on or instill the organization's vision. And this is not just paralysis or domination of the members. Freeing the organization's own will from paralysis and domination opens the door to many more possibilities. Perhaps it generates an entirely new tier of organization.

Worldwide Holarchic Governance

A company is a semiautonomous holon, just like all the subholons within the company (departments, project teams, etc.). For a holarchy to remain healthy, all holons need clear autonomy as a whole and clear responsibilities as a part or member of something larger. The current corporate governance model pushes companies toward unhealthy agency—they are encouraged to ignore responsibilities for communion with the broader world. The impact of this attitude can be seen whenever companies focus on their own growth and profits while ignoring their impacts on the environment or the world around them. It can be tempting to chalk all this up to ignorant or selfish executives. However, that is not entirely fair. Our current organizational and governance systems are set up in ways that push toward this unhealthy agency—it is extremely difficult to work against this momentum in the current model, or even become fully awake to it. The next two subsections explore how these dynamics might shift in a world practicing Holacracy.

The We of Organization   If an organizational entity is an individual in its own right, can multiple organizations come together and form their own collective culture and processes? If they do, will yet another, still-broader, individual organizational entity emerge? I think the answer to both questions is a clear *yes*—whenever there are multiple entities working together toward a common aim, organization emerges. Just as people become members of a company, so too can individual companies become members of broader organizations, such as those representing an industry or social purpose or geographic region. Of course, each of these broader entities can practice Holacracy to tap into its own individual telos and self-awareness as well.

As these organizations of organizations emerge, individual companies can become members and tangibly connect into them to help steer their governance and operations, and they can help the individual company align with their needs and goals. This happens via a cross-organization double link, where the board of the individual company connects with an appropriately focused circle within the broader entity. No longer will the individual company's board circle need to appoint members itself—instead, it will simply establish a double link with a broader organization representing its industry, another representing its specific social purpose, and so on. Each broader organization will appoint one of its members to sit on the individual organization's board, forming half of the double link. The board in turn will elect one of its members—perhaps the CEO—to carry the voice of the company's context into the broader organization's decision-making, completing the double link. The board becomes a focal point for integrating the needs and goals of all of the major environments in which the company operates. Now it is extremely tangible, and the addition of a representative link provides a conduit for feedback that barely exists in today's world.

Toward a Sustainable World Looking forward, this structure has the potential to advance human society profoundly. As this web of organization grows, it can provide a distributed yet integrated capacity to govern our shared resources and move humans toward a more global communion. It radically transforms governance from something that happens on a "big" scale—the Industrial Age design—to something that happens everywhere throughout the system by everyone, at the level of scale they operate at, while enhancing the ability to act as a coordinated and cohesive whole when required. This capacity provides a way to completely transcend many of the massive geopolitical and environmental challenges facing our world—many just dissolve and others at least become possible to address with such a system in place.

Better still, this worldwide holarchic meshwork is built on top of the governments and legal systems that already exist. For that reason, it can emerge incrementally, in its time, until a new integrative governance web spans the world, with every holon at every level of scale honored and accorded appropriate rights and responsibilities. What this might mean for the individuals who live and work within these holarchies is also quite profound. All in all, the potential for both individual and social transformation on a global scale is truly staggering.

In Closing

Grand predictions aside, Holacracy has a long way to go before modern government paradigms can be retired to the history books. It is extremely early in the spread of Holacracy. As it reaches into more types of organizations, there will be new challenges. Over time, the practice will evolve to answer them.

One thing is certain: As the Holacracy movement gains momentum and spreads beyond single organizations, the pioneers at the forefront of this next sociocultural evolution will face new challenges and tough problems, ones for which answers do not yet exist. Fortunately, all the answers are not needed in advance. What is needed is to hold the question and stay present in mind, body, and spirit. Then it is not a matter of creating the right answers but rather just listening to what they already are. It is amazing what emerges once we get out of our own way and truly start listening.

EDGEWALKERS

In the next contribution, Judi Neal, Ph.D., describes a special type of business leader who has the ability to tap into the energy of the organization, its inherent wisdom (or perhaps its quantum field), to unveil what is invisible to others. The individual in this leadership role in an organization is known as the Edgewalker. The Edgewalker skills are essential to reversing the potential negative effects of the global corporation and to creating new business models that support a world that works for everyone.[4]

How to Walk on the Leading Edge without Falling off the Cliff

The complexity of the business world today is astounding. Nothing is predictable. The rules of the game are changing. Just when an organization gets a competitive advantage, a competitor develops a new technology. Just as it thinks it has found the right motivation tool, the values in the workforce seem to shift. Just when it thinks it has found the right geographical area for the expansion of the organization's internationalization efforts, political turmoil erupts.

Yet some people seem to have an uncanny knack for knowing what is going to happen before it unfolds. They are able to create new rules for the game instead of following the rules everyone else follows. They are able to plan a strategy that seems absurd to most people at first and is later called brilliant when it is successful. They are a part of an unusual breed of leaders called Edgewalkers.

An Edgewalker is someone who walks between two worlds. In ancient cultures, each tribe or village had a shaman, or medicine man. This was the person who walked into the invisible world to get information, guidance, and healing for members of the tribe. This role was one of the most important in the village. Without a shaman, the tribe would be at the mercy of unseen gods and spirits, the vagaries of the cosmos. The skill of walking between the worlds has not died out. In fact, it is even more relevant today. Organizations that will thrive in the twenty-first century will embrace and nurture Edgewalkers. Because of their unique skills, they are the bridge-builders linking and facilitating different approaches, strategies, and techniques.

Walking on the Leading Edge

Five key skills form the hallmark of an Edgewalker:

1. Visionary consciousness
2. Multicultural responsiveness
3. Intuitive sensitivity
4. Risk-taking confidence
5. Self-awareness

1. Visionary Consciousness   Edgewalkers begin with *visionary consciousness*. All their other skills are in service of a sense of mission about something greater than themselves. They feel called to make a difference in the world. The visionary skills arise out of a strong sense of values and integrity. Often these values are developed through some kind of painful experience or loss, and the Edgewalker becomes committed to helping other people who may be going through similar kinds of experiences. Typically Edgewalkers have gone through a major personal or career change that requires them to develop new skills that were never needed before. Edgewalkers are the consummate integrators of seemingly unrelated ideas, skills, and fields.

2. Multicultural Responsiveness   Edgewalkers must have strong *multicultural responsiveness*. They are bilingual in the sense that they can understand the nuances of different worlds or cultures. They span conventional boundaries and act as translators. Edgewalkers know how to pick up on subtle cues that are different from their own. They pay minute attention to people different from themselves and have an open, warm curiosity about people from other cultures. They look for commonalities more than differences, and they want to know more about the worlds of others.

3. Intuitive Sensitivity   Edgewalkers have strong *intuitive sensitivity*. They are natural futurists. Because they are avid readers, they are constantly integrating information from many sources and looking for underlying themes and patterns. Like the shamans of old, they have learned to pay attention to subtle, perhaps invisible, signs of potential change. They have an uncanny knack of making the right decisions, often taking action that seems counterintuitive to others. But when asked how they knew what to do in a particular situation, they have difficulty explaining. They reply, "I just knew." Intuitive skills are gained through the practice of deep listening. When listening to others, Edgewalkers listen as much for the unsaid as the said. They also look for coincidences, patterns, or synchronicities that might provide clues to guide them in their decision-making.

4. Risk-Taking Confidence   Another strong skill that Edgewalkers display is the skill of calculated *risk-taking confidence*. Edgewalkers have a strong sense of adventure and experimentation. They are always attracted to the next new thing. Like entrepreneurs, Edgewalkers are easily bored with stability and are attracted to what is over the horizon. They are constantly asking what is next and trying to figure out how to be part of it. Because they are able to walk in two worlds, the world of practicality and the world of creativity, the risks they take to jump into the next new thing are based on information and intuition. Having a clear vision guided by strong values helps Edgewalkers to take risks that might not make sense to others.

5. Self-Awareness   The most important Edgewalker skill is that of *self-awareness*. A principle that Edgewalkers understand is that each person is a microcosm of the whole. Leaders who are Edgewalkers know that if they are experiencing a vision or dream or hunger, it is most likely arising in others as well. The challenge for the Edgewalker is to find others who have the same passion and to work together to make a difference.

Leaders who are Edgewalkers have a strong sense of being connected to something greater than themselves.

These five skills can be taught. However, the leaders who tend to learn best strongly value their own personal development and have low control needs.

Avoiding Potential Pitfalls

Edgewalkers often can get too far ahead of the pack. If this happens, they lose their credibility and the opportunity to influence others to do creative work. It is nice to have someone say you are ahead of your time, but there are few rewards for being too far out there. The most successful Edgewalkers can remain in the real world and can remember established language and values so they can be a bridge to new ideas.

If you feel that you are an Edgewalker, here are some suggestions for monitoring your actions:

1. Watch for signs that you may be getting too far out on the edge; if this seems to be happening, revisit your own past experience, current priorities, and future aspirations.
2. When you have a new idea that you want to implement, talk to people who are likely to disagree with you or try to block you.
3. Create relationships with people who may provide a good reality check.
4. Have patience with people who do not want to move as fast as you do; take time to build relationships with them and specifically ask for their support.
5. Cultivate the skill of honoring people who disagree with you; listen for any pearls of wisdom they have to offer.
6. Be very aware of your highest values and have a strong commitment to integrity. Even if you get too far out on the edge, you will know you are doing it for the right reasons.

If you feel blocked at every turn by people committed to the status quo, consider finding a different organization to work for or even going out on your own. Being an Edgewalker can feel very lonely. Connect with other Edgewalkers for support and inspiration.

Making It Happen

- Write mission and values statements for the work you want to do in the world.
- Read professional material in fields that are unfamiliar to you.
- Listen carefully to what people and the world have to say.
- Trust your instincts about ways you can make a difference.
- Remember to take time to nurture your inner being and to pay attention to the signs you receive.
- Master practicality and common sense, and strive for a command of the creative and visionary skills.
- Bring creative skills to scientific problems.
- Learn a new artistic skill or deepen your involvement in the arts.
- Involve others in your ideas, recognizing different approaches and perspectives.

Conclusion

Edgewalkers are the leaders of the future. They are the corporate shamans who bring wisdom and guidance for their organizations. The Edgewalker is not an easy role to play, but it is one that is essential to the success of any organization. And the rewards of the role are amazing energy and a feeling of aliveness.

ORGANIZATIONS ON PURPOSE

> *Only those who will risk going too far can possibly find out how far one can go.*

> —T. S. ELIOT

Organizations created for a greater purpose seem to naturally embrace a systems approach. Many of the skills essential to running a holistic organization are a natural feature of these companies. This section introduces five Edgewalkers who embrace a holistic approach to business with the hope of doing well by doing good.

Sustainability: Ben Freeman

Although Ben Freeman has been a successful entrepreneur all his life, his interest has increasingly focused on serving the greater good. Early in his career, he created affordable housing for the poor. Gradually he shifted his focus to United Nations Security Council reform in an attempt help it fulfill its charter obligation to "keep the peace." However, this work did not connect with his entrepreneurial nature. So he searched for a business that he could pursue full time. He was interested in creating a business that could generate decent profits while making the world a little better.

An Electric Car   Freeman got an idea that would allow him to pursue his goal and have an effect on world peace. Seeing a connection between the use of gas-powered cars and both global warming and the oil crisis, he worked for about two years visualizing and designing lightweight vehicles with electric motors that drew their power from the sun. At first, he built a heavy-duty tricycle that combined a small electric motor, a solar panel roof, a pedaling assist, and the ability to carry a few hundred pounds of cargo or a second rider. But because a solar tricycle has a limited market, he looked to use the knowledge he gained in designing and making solar tricycles to design a cost-competitive solar car.

After discussions with the National Highway Safety Administration and experts in the industry, a number of breakthroughs enabled Freeman to design a more practical and cost-effective roadworthy solar vehicle. The breakthroughs included:

- Integrating the common design feature of solar cars used in off-street racing
- Combining a solar panel assist with the plug-in electric
- Maximizing the solar panel output
- Integrating side protection, a key safety element of his first solar car invention
- Designing the body to accommodate enough riders for 95 percent of all current car trips
- Conceiving of a plan to overcome the key range problem of all electric cars

Freeman has filed a second patent to capture these ideas. He feels that its widespread use would significantly mitigate climate change and the coming global oil crisis. He is currently working with top government officials and industry executives to bring his design into reality.

Healing: Antanas Vainius

Antanas Vainius is in the business of co-creating companies that support empowered living. gRAWnola™ is the first in a series of food-based companies that is committed to delivering body-ready nutrition through properly prepared foods while at the same time restoring consumer confidence and trust in the pleasure of true nourishment. Loreta's Living Foods, his mother's company, served as an inspiration and learning ground where he got to see the power of true nourishment. It is also an education-based business that delivers nutrient-rich foods designed to empower buyers by reminding them of their ability to feed themselves through small-scale, micro-green cultivation.

Slated to go to medical school as part of his admission into Brown University, Vainius began exploring human potential by studying the necessary sciences to create a dynamic framework for integrating the arts: performance, visual, somatic, spiritual, and culinary. With various degrees from academic, healing, culinary, and arts institutions, he studied both on and off campus, refining this dynamic framework that could accommodate the multidimensional spectrum of human potential.

Experience with his own life-threatening illness allows him to be an invaluable resource to people who want to heal and create an empowering and transformative context in which to see themselves and their lives. He has taken advantage of these experiences to get very intimate with the body's unending drive for wholeness. And he uses these timeless principles as the blueprint for all his commercial enterprises. As a healer, entrepreneur, consultant and writer, Vainius co-creates his companies with the intention of cultivating and harnessing the innate and infinite capacity of the human being's ability to grow, learn, and evolve.

Next, Vainius shares about how he brings his gifts to the corporate world.

Wholeness/Embodiment through Nourishment   I always believed that we are here on this beautiful blue marble to learn, grow, and evolve. While attending a workshop entitled "Sacred Commerce," offered by Terces and Matthew Engelhardt, founders of Café Gratitude, I was deeply affirmed in my own belief that it was possible to create an enterprise powered by learning and personal growth using the energy of personal awakening as its fuel.

From this perspective, the world looks very different. Many conversations and corresponding frameworks need to be reconsidered. For example, how is value defined—our own and others? How do we understand compensation, currency, and exchange of energy, money, time, knowledge, etc.? What is insurance in terms of its value, purpose, and function?

gRAWnola is a manifestation of our commitment to create an empowered way of doing business, adapting traditional corporate structures in service of our mission to educate, inspire, and nourish, as well as create an environment where we as humans can explore and embody our ever-evolving potential using ancient wisdom and modern technologies. Similarly, we integrate modern food technology and ancient food preparation methods to increase the value of our ingredients, creating nourishment that can be the fuel for this type of evolutionary transformation.

The Company   We are actually in the business of transformation, and we just happen to make a fantastic granola bar. We have created a place where people come to play, learn, nourish, and be nourished. The power of gRAWnola is that it satisfies more than just an immediate physical hunger. It invites people to consider that we have appetites beyond the body.

At a time when there is so much confusion about health and nutrition, conditions such as obesity, increasing food sensitivities, and other chronic health complaints show that people are struggling to find foods that truly nourish them. Many ingredients are synthesized, modified, and grown in artificial environments. Foods are being processed in ways that prolong their shelf life but inhibit their nutrient availability and usability. These wondrous yet unrefined industrial developments need to be acknowledged for their ability to produce a tremendous volume of food. Unfortunately, these same technologies often destroy the foods' vitality, leading to a loss of our own body's vitality and potential.

These mass-production methods cannot honor the subtler properties of food. So many of the health benefits, including the recently identified, crucial healing nutrients, are missing. Perhaps most important is the energizing experience of true pleasure that comes from our simple enjoyment of a fragrant, sun-ripened peach. Those healing moments are deep affirmations of the life and vitality within us.

Bringing awareness to the various steps of this process can begin to reveal the gaps that exist in our current food system, as well as bring awareness to our process and how to honor and address those gaps. Having mastered the quantity issue, the quality of the food needs to be brought into greater resonance with the more subtle needs of the body for us as a civilization to experience true well-being.

One part of our educational mission is to help people reconnect with pleasure, and loosen its connection to that which is unhealthy and unsustaining. Being truly nourished offers the eater such an experience. It is an innocent opportunity to reconsider the possibility that pleasure indeed has a very important place in our learning, evolution, and well-being. In fact, I personally believe that true pleasure is one of our internal guidance systems whose awakening is a foundation of our internal culture.

Through our commitment to deliver true nourishment, we seek to inspire and nurture these awakened moments of pleasure. Our edutainment-focused marketing playfully invites the eater to begin to trust the innate goodness of our food—and in time, the people and the world. Our tag line—"So good it feeds the imagination"—embodies an invitation, connects nutrition with possibility and potential, and invites people to dream again. By understanding the increased value of the product, achieved by integrating ancient and modern food preparation techniques, the appeal of our foods is based on sound knowledge instead of compulsion, addiction, or manipulation.

One of our products, which is deliberately seasonally available, and has all fully ripened, ideally local ingredients, gives the eater the opportunity to experience the simultaneous benefit of pleasure and nutrition. This product further expands the definition of properly prepared foods by acknowledging the impact of the natural ripening process on the development of vital and fragile nutrients that yield enormous anti-aging, anti-oxidant, and phytochemical benefits, and boosting overall energy levels. These critical nutrients augment the nurturing pleasure that properly prepared foods offer.

Consciously connecting the energy coming from these properly prepared foods with the arising pleasure honors and trusts the body as our invaluable resource. Within our enterprise, we practice honoring and trusting the body as a way of powerfully engaging with reality so that we as a "corporation" can do the same.

Creating a business driven by embodied transformation seems especially poignant and timely given the intense disconnect with the body that many humans experience. Within our corporate environment, there is a specific intention to heal this disconnect. The practice of being present and fully "in-body-ed" allows for this disconnect to integrate and heal. When one feels whole and empowered, a desire to contribute and make a difference in the world automatically arises.

With this as our "field," we want to make this powerful, inspiring and almost magical food available to everyone, and with it teach people how to feed themselves. Because when you are truly fed, it is easy to be inspired and get down to the business of making your dreams happen—restoring the cycle of creativity and true power.

Gratitude: John Castagnini

After working with many people who had a variety of issues, John Castagnini recognized one overwhelming concept: People are finally able to stop feeling like victims of the challenging events and circumstances in their lives only after they are able to be grateful for these experiences.

Many of the people who sought out Castagnini's help had experienced sexual assault. One by one, he assisted them in becoming grateful for the growth and access to inner strength that emerged as a result of these experiences. These victims of sexual assault shed tears of gratitude as they were able to say, "Thank God I was raped."

This insight led Castagnini to the deep understanding that the underlying concept of gratitude for everything that we experience is the greatest wisdom we can have and the greatest skill we can learn. This was the genesis of his book *Thank God I Was Raped*, from which grew the Thank God I . . .™ book series. It was Castagnini's realization that collecting the inspiring stories would help not only the people who reached an epiphany through telling their stories and feeling gratitude but also countless others who would read these stories in the book.

He realized that one incredible value of the Thank God I . . . series was that anyone, regardless of their life challenges, be it rape, addiction, or some other turning point, can learn from these inspiring stories. Castagnini's professional background and innate compassion stirred this mission to bring the message of gratitude and inspiration to every person on the planet.

As a result, the inspiring and heart-opening Thank God I . . . movement, focusing on a message of gratitude, was born. John and his team offer the Thank God I . . . book series and online Community of Gratitude, as a system for discovering the magical and miraculous healing power of gratitude. The Thank God I . . . series, seminars, and workshops platform focuses on teaching people how to gain this essential understanding.

Next Castagnini shares his thoughts about his process.

The Thank God I Process   In moments of inspiration and love, the mission of our soul is revealed to us. While taking a good look at myself, it dawned upon me how little I knew and how much I truly had to study. I attracted great teachers, who shared priceless wisdom. I discovered that most of the deeper questions in life have answers. I realized that when I was willing to do the work and look past the myths, I began to understand and find the answers.

Life's most important answers are found in pursuing life's most important questions. All of us have this opportunity. Art shared, in whatever form, stems from the union of mind, body, and soul in order to understand and share divinity. When we access this divinity and give ourselves permission to shine, we become more able to share our gifts. I am truly grateful for a lifetime of sharing, through Thank God I. . . .

Empowerment: Julie Roberts, Ph.D., Psychoeducational Processes

Dr. Julie Roberts spent many years working as an organizational development consultant using a systems thinking approach. She now divides her time between leadership training and individual healing work.

Leadership Training   Over 20 years ago, Roberts and her partner, Rod Napier, developed a powerful training to assist individuals in learning how to lead groups or organizations effectively. Known as GLI, the Group Leadership Intensive, the training includes a wide range of experiences where participants practice developing interventions and creative strategies for meeting group goals while freeing the intelligence and energy of the group.

Principle. Participants have the opportunity to practice dealing with a variety of issues that may surface within a group context. Becoming a creative and effective group leader takes practice, keen observation, and a willingness to look at one's own behavior while attempting to move the group forward. At GLI, participants practice putting together a well-designed process and then intervene in creative ways to help keep the group on target.

Goal. This training provides an amazing understanding of groups and how to facilitate them. A significant focus of the program is to provide a better understanding of each individual's strengths and areas of needed development regarding leadership and membership in groups. Leaders have to continually assess what is happening in a group to ensure that the "design" of the moment is actually what is best for the group at that time; they also have to move the group forward. Leaders have to be constantly aware of the time of day, the relationships within the group, possible conflict among the various members, the physical structure of the room, people's energy level, and, of course, how to best utilize the knowledge and skills in the room at any moment in time.

The richness of GLI comes from its focus on design, the practice that each person experiences along with the true evaluation of the impact of each participant as a leader/facilitator. For these reasons, the Group Leadership Intensive is not for the faint of heart. Instead, it is for those who wish to examine their current impact as a leader and practice a new set of skills and a new way of thinking. It is a powerful tool for leaders who want to learn to empower groups to achieve their highest potential.

Energy Healing   Roberts enhances her leadership work with a process she developed to clear people of their subconscious patterns. This technique is powerful for helping leaders remove emotional barriers that prevent them from leading from the heart.

Energy Healing with CLEAR™   Energy healing is a method for eliminating the negative effects of trauma. Trauma occurs from some past event that negatively influences behavior, thoughts, and feelings. It evokes feelings that we want to avoid. When we experience trauma, we do not like what we feel or think, so we try to block it out or avoid it. This process of avoidance actually ensures that the trauma will get stuck in the body because it is never fully processed. And what we resist persists. CLEAR™ (Clearing Limits Energetically with Acupressure Release) is a method for releasing the stuck trauma. It is also useful in relieving depression, anxiety, and phobias, and it helps free individuals from blocks that impact their ability to move forward in life.

For example, one of my clients was depressed for 20 years every summer resulting from a rape in her home on a hot summer night. After six sessions using CLEAR, she was free of her depression. Another example is a client who had posttraumatic stress syndrome and was on medications for anxiety and insomnia. After one session, he went off of all of his medications because he was no longer anxious and could sleep easily. Results are often this dramatic and permanent unless the individual is retraumatized.

CLEAR integrates a number of energy psychology methods. It uses acupressure point therapy, bilateral stimulation, somatic experiencing, clearing of blocking beliefs, and muscle testing. Each of these techniques is explained next.

Acupressure   There are 14 acupressure points on the body, each of which corresponds to various emotions. With CLEAR, light pressure is applied to each point successively while putting one's attention on the issue being cleared. (Some energy psychology methods "tap" on the points—I find light pressure is sufficient.) Brain scans indicate a significant decrease in generalized anxiety disorder after acupressure point treatment.[5] The theory is that stimulation of the acupressure points actually changes the chemistry of the brain so that the alarm response is inhibited.[6] Going through this process naturally raises thoughts and memories associated with the trauma, and it provides insight regarding how the trauma has impacted the person. "Analyzing" clients is not necessary—they naturally process and absorb what is necessary for healing to occur.

Bilateral Stimulation   Bilateral stimulation (called eye movement desensitization and reprocessing [EMDR] in some circles) involves tapping alternately on the body while the patient thinks about the issue of concern. Sometimes the acupressure points alone are not enough to clear the trauma, and bilateral stimulation is necessary. The theory here is that the trauma is frozen in time and is energetically stuck on one side of the body or the other. Alternatively tapping on the body while thinking of the issue frees it for release.

Somatic Experiencing   Somatic experiencing, developed by Peter Levine,[7] is a practice I use with both the acupressure point technique and bilateral stimulation. Levine developed somatic experiencing after watching animals in the wild experience trauma. He noticed that when they cannot fight or flee, animals become immobile (which dulls the senses so they do not feel the pain if they are eaten). And if something scares away the animal that put them into this state, and they are not badly injured, they will lie there processing the trauma as the body twitches and eyes roll. They then get up and walk away.

Levine surmised that because humans think, we avoid this processing. We do not want to experience the feelings and sensations that usually accompany a trauma, because they are unpleasant. We think, "I don't want to feel that; I don't like that feeling, it is unpleasant and I won't be happy if I feel that. I want to get away from that feeling." Our resistance to feeling is what causes the trauma to get stuck. Using somatic experiencing, we are present in the body and "allow" feelings and sensations so that the trauma can "reprocess" and thus be freed.

Blocking Beliefs   Blocking beliefs are thoughts that prevent us from being who we want to be. Beliefs define who we are—they define what we think, how we behave, and the actions we take. Blocking beliefs are created when we experience trauma. We make decisions about ourselves and life when bad things happen to us as children. For example, if I experienced unhappy, angry parents as a child, I might decide that "I am unworthy (of their love); I am a bad person (or I would have gotten their love)." And perhaps I believe that "something is wrong with me." If I was hurt emotionally or physically, I may decide "I am not safe in the world" or "The world is not safe." These beliefs, like the trauma, also get stuck in the system. Untreated, they will impact much of what occurs in life. How can I truly realize my potential if I feel unworthy, bad, unsafe, and as if something is wrong with me? But CLEAR frees these beliefs so desires may be achieved.

Muscle Testing   Muscle testing (also referred to as applied kinesiology) is a way to get honest feedback about what is going on in the body on a physical, spiritual, intellectual, or emotional level. When the body is in the presence of something negative, muscles are weaker than when it is in the presence of something positive. There are many ways to test muscles, but the most common is to press down on an arm, which is held out parallel to the ground. The logical brain is bypassed to get a true reading of what is occurring in the body/mind—a strong response is a "yes" or positive and a weak response is a "no" or a negative. Muscle testing is used to test for allergies, in assessing chiropractic problems, and sometimes by doctors to facilitate diagnosis and prescribing medication. In CLEAR, muscle testing is used to determine issues to clear, blocking beliefs, methods needed to clear, and finally to see if the issue is indeed cleared. Muscle testing allows practitioners to streamline the clearing process and work only on what is necessary to heal.

CLEAR in Action   Women for Women International (WFWI) helps victims of war become self-sufficient in Afghanistan, Bosnia and Herzegovina, the Democratic Republic of the Congo, Iraq, Kosovo, Nigeria, Rwanda, and Sudan. WFWI conducts year-long programs for participants, providing financial aid, job training, rights awareness, and leadership education. They want to also help participants deal with the often severe trauma they experience during war. I adapted CLEAR so that it can be used in groups in one-hour sessions as a part of WFWI's program. In July 2008, WFWI sent me to Nigeria to test CLEAR with its participants to see if it could translate into other cultures and if the women would accept it.

The pilot program in Nigeria was a success. The participants saw CLEAR as very helpful—they said it helped them to feel calmer and more positive about their situations and that they would use it in the future. I have been working with WFWI headquarters (located in Washington, DC) to add CLEAR to their manual. More facilitator trainings will occur in the spring of 2009. After the manual and facilitator trainings are finished, WFWI facilitators in 10 countries will use CLEAR to help victims of war recover from their trauma.

Ending Poverty: Jim Riordan

Jim Riordan is 30-year builder/developer/entrepreneur who promotes alternative, regenerative building and growing methods. He is also deeply committed to spiritual practice. Twenty years ago, he decided to use his

profits to do something good for the world. A voice in his head kept say-
ing, "Go to Africa." He had met many people from Ghana, West Africa,
over the years and was taken with their consciousness and charm. He
took off for Accra (the capital) to offer his expertise in low-cost building
materials. After meeting with government officials, he learned that their
needs were much more basic. They needed water-moving technology
and higher-yield farming techniques. Jim learned that millions of women
spent hours everyday carrying water long distances for drinking and
watering a few plants for food. In the following contribution, Riordan
shares how he is ending poverty in Ghana, one family at a time.

A Bottom–Up Approach to Ending Poverty   The Adopt-a-Family
Program fights poverty, hunger, and global warming in Africa with used
athletic shoes. Perpetual Prosperity Pumps Foundation (PPPF) is a not-
for-profit foundation that helps small farmers lift themselves out of poverty
permanently. When small farmers learn how to increase yields 1,000 percent
on the same land every year, the slash-and-burn rain forest destruction
comes to an end. Pumping systems supplied from the sale of used athletic
shoes allow farmers to irrigate their fields for the first time.

PPPF teaches MORE (Modular Organic Regenerative Environment)
farming, a style that allows farmers to perpetually stay on the same few
acres. Small-farm families are now able to sustain a good income on the
same land while building the soil and strengthening the environment.
The Adopt-a-Family program is 100 percent funded from the sale of used
athletic shoes. We at Adopt-a-Family are asking for American athletic
shoes that will spend years in a closet, and then 100 years in a landfill.

The contribution of 600 pairs of shoes enables an adopted family to
enjoy 12 months of training in regenerative farming practice. Then they
receive the tools and resources they need to earn a perpetual living on one
acre or less. We also provide a wide range of services, including medical
assistance for adopted families, protecting them against malaria and other
diseases.

The M.O.R.E. System (Modular Organic Regenerative Environment)
Modular. MORE systems are micro-enterprise models designed to
increase small-farm productivity while creating a positive regional impact.

MORE farms are adaptable to almost any climate and allow for constant growth while accommodating periodic economic shifts and climate change. MORE systems utilize portable components. Developed MORE farms are expandable sustainable ecoloops.

Organic. MORE systems leave no negative footprint and require almost no energy import. "Organic" means no chemicals of any kind nor genetically modified seeds. All organic fertilizers and pesticides are locally sourced. Solar power eliminates the need for fossil fuels. Farm-produced biofuels will sustain expansion.

Regenerative. The whole becomes greater than the sum of the parts on a developed MORE farm. Biodiversity enhancement strengthens, builds, and protects natural resources. MORE farms offer accelerated permaculture by utilizing natural resources with a vertically integrated approach.

Environment. A MORE farm is an integrated expandable sustainable ecoloop natural living system. MORE systems are small-business microfarm environments. Each modular system within each MORE farm enhances the overall environment. Each MORE farm assists in the healing of the natural and global environment. The MORE systematic approach mimics nature.

Bottom-Up Approach to Eradicating Poverty One Family at a Time   Over 1 billion people exist on small farms on one dollar a day. For the small-farm family, irrigation is the single biggest hurdle to increasing agricultural productivity. PPPF resolves this problem by providing access to irrigation systems and installing bicycle-powered Miracle Pump Irrigation Systems. We call this program "Peddling to Prosperity." If small-scale farmers can move water all year at no cost once the pump is in place, they can sustain a perpetual harvest.

The second hurdle is to make available appropriate seeds, livestock, and technology combined with the proper training in organic regenerative agricultural practice. PPPF solves this problem in two ways:

1. Working with the most qualified training organizations in each country and internationally.
2. Supplying enough technology transfer and livestock to ensure a family income increase of 400 percent or more within the first 12 months and as much as 1,000 percent within two years.

The PPP Adopt-a-Family Program provides the family with:

Farming Support

- Access to irrigation systems.
- A complete Miracle Pump system is installed after the family has been trained in irrigation techniques.
- A quarter-acre integrated vegetable farm is planted utilizing organic growing techniques. A healthy variety of indigenous and exotic vegetables is introduced with all of the seeds and training. Some examples of crops include tomatoes, okra, cabbage, onions, beans, and peppers.
- Three locally bred hens and one cock generate hundreds of eggs and hundreds of birds within the first 12 months. Ducks are provided if more appropriate.
- A pregnant female rabbit and hutch. With proper training, over 400 pounds of rabbit meat will result in the first year.
- One colonized beehive. Honey can be harvested in the second year.
- 100 Leucaena trees are planted around the farm to create a living fence as well as a sustainable supply of firewood and high-protein leaf for livestock feed.
- 50 assorted fruit trees are planted, including but not limited to avocado, citrus, mango, coconut, palm trees, cashew.
- 50 inoculated mushroom bags are provided, allowing for year-round mushroom production.
- A bicycle is given to the family, so members may easily travel to markets and training classes.

Education

For over 12 months the family receives monthly instruction, which includes but is not limited to the above technology and training as follows:

- Women are instructed in how to create a balanced diet with proper nutrition for the family.
- Basic and advanced classes in crop rotation, biodiversity enhancement, permaculture techniques, modular design case studies of MORE, water harvesting, water conservation, and a variety of irrigation techniques.

- Courses in how to access microfinance, financial management, and marketing skills with assistance in identifying markets for their produce.
- Training in networking with cooperative extension services.
- How to structure networks of growers to improve sustained sales to local and foreign markets, thus enhancing revenue generation.
- Training in entrepreneurship and free enterprise eco–microfarm creation. Training in value-added cottage industries, which can be village based and owned cooperatively by the village.
- Free eye and dental screening; HIV education; free malaria medication and bed nets.

The poorest countries will be the hardest hit by climate change. Rainy seasons are becoming unpredictable, and droughts are increasingly frequent. It is forecasted that annual precipitation in the tropics will diminish gradually in the coming decades, forcing massive migration and/or starvation. Future policy will be defined by environmental needs as climate stresses increase.

MORE systems address this main issue with the highest water conservation possible combined with amazing levels of small-farm productivity. Sufficient food production can be sustained even in increasingly harsh climates with MORE. Few other proven models directly address the core issues of world hunger.

MORE farms are highly profitable free enterprise models that work within the parameters of the natural world. There will never be an equitable distribution of fossil fuel, and mechanized agriculture cannot feed the emerging economies of the world. Small decentralized farms strengthen natural biodiversity, which is vital to environmental health and economic growth.

The basis formula is to simplify, clarify, and duplicate a modular small-farm "cookie cutter." We offer MORE as a combination of tried and proven techniques and technologies designed to permanently resolve poverty for the small farmer. With hundreds of families enjoying the benefits of the MORE system, there will be instantaneous adoption by potentially millions.

With entire nations witnessing the benefits offered by the MORE system, a tipping point will be reached, quickly resulting in a paradigm shift in small-farm practice. Dozens of economic models will be designed to accelerate the transition to perpetual prosperity. Thus far we have learned that everyone wants to do less and accomplish MORE.

With over 300 million pairs of athletic shoes headed for the landfill annually, it is possible to collect 1,000 pair a day. At our current rate of expansion, this level of collection will be reached by 2010. Given 1,000 pairs a day, we will be able to expand MORE training across Africa. The World Bank and other organizations have expressed interest in funding MORE systems on a large scale once our first 100 families have become established.

BOTTOM LINE

Is it possible to do well by doing good? That question is increasingly being debated in the marketplace. Consider the philosophy of Adam Smith.[8] In *The Wealth of Nations*, he argued that the best way to build wealth was through the free market. However, he said that it must benefit both individuals *and society as a whole*.

Fortunately, the skills and competencies that are critical for success in a knowledge-based, global economy are innately geared toward serving the greater good. Over the next few years, we will reach a tipping point.

Our hope is that by learning new competencies and embracing business practices that increase our chances for success while nurturing cooperation and collaboration, we can have a positive impact on the world.

■ NOTES

1. Peter Senge, C. Otto Scharmer, Joseph Jaworski, and Betty Sue Flowers, *Presence* (New York: Currency, 2004), 7–8.
2. Adapted from Brian Robertson, "Organization at the Leading Edge: Introducing Holacracy™," *Integral Leadership Review* 7, No. 3 (June 2007). Available at www .integralleadershipreview.com/archives/2007-06/2007-06-robertson-holacracy .php.
3. For more information and resources on Integral Theory, visit http://integralin-stitute.org/.
4. Judith A. Neal, "How to Walk on the Leading Edge without Falling off the Cliff." Available at www.spiritatwork.org/index.php?ACT=43&fid= 20& aid= 5_64FadFTNPrN98bUGH5lg&board_id=1.

5. Joaquin Andrade and David Feinstein, "Preliminary Report of the First Large-Scale Study of Energy Psychology," 2003. Available at www.emofree .com/Research/Research-other/andradepaper.htm.

6. David Feinstein, Donna Eden, and Gary Craig, *The Promise of Energy Psychology* (New York: Jeremy P. Tarcher/Penguin, 2005).

7. Peter Levine, *Healing Trauma: Restoring the Wisdom of Your Body*, audiotape (Boulder, CO: Sounds True, 1999).

8. Carleen Hawn, "The Gospel According to Adam Smith," *Ode Magazine* 6, No. 5 (June 2008), 40.

APPENDIX A

Resources

CHAPTER 1: BUSINESS LANDSCAPE

SAS

SAS, the leader in business analytics and the largest independent vendor in the business intelligence market, helps customers at 45,000 sites make better decisions faster. SAS's innovative business applications, supported by an enterprise intelligence platform, give customers THE POWER TO KNOW®.

www.sas.com

Business Intelligence Network

The Business Intelligence Network™ focuses on business intelligence, performance management, data warehousing, data integration, and data quality, serving these communities with unparalleled industry coverage and resources.

www.b-eye-network.com

CHAPTER 2: MODELS FROM SCIENCE AND NATURE

Living the Field

Living the Field is the only organization in the world to synthesize the discoveries of the very latest frontier science into a coherent theory and a program for modern integrated living.

www.livingthefield.com

Noetic Sciences Institute

The Institute of Noetic Sciences is a nonprofit membership organization that conducts and sponsors leading-edge research into the potentials and powers of consciousness—including perceptions, beliefs, attention, intention, and intuition. The institute explores phenomena that do not necessarily fit conventional scientific models, while maintaining a commitment to scientific rigor.

www.noetic.org

Collective Wisdom Initiative

Scientific research into the phenomenon of collective wisdom is in its infancy. However, a large number of studies have been conducted over the past 30 years that directly or indirectly suggest the nature and effects of collective consciousness and provide a solid starting point for the scientific study of collective wisdom.

www.collectivewisdominitiative.org

CHAPTER 3: EFFECTIVE COMMUNICATION

Robert Knowlton

Robert Knowlton is a developmental coach. Individual development does not happen in a vacuum. It is only through feedback, reflection, and planning that a person, team, and organization will develop. Using advanced communication skills and proven developmental leadership tools, Knowlton helps leaders emerge into their most aware and conscious selves. It is then their job to create the world as they would like it to be. He can be reached at Robert@RobertKnowlton.com.

www.robertknowlton.com

Conversation Agent

Valeria Maltoni helps businesses understand how customers and communities have changed marketing, public relations, and communications— and how to build value in this new environment. As a communicator, she specializes in marketing communications, customer dialogue, and brand management. Maltoni has come to define modern business as a long and open conversation.

www.conversationagent.com

Chapter 4: Collaboration

Resolution Works

As organizations become flatter, more virtual, and more innovative, people need to become self-directed while working within complex webs of collaboration toward common goals. Tools that create partnership and quickly resolve problems in the face of conflict are essential. We need to prevent communication problems. Instead of staying angry and stuck, we need to quickly resolve conflict and return to partnership andproductivity.

www.resolutionworks.org

Advent Management

John Reddish and his associates at Advent help entrepreneurs, top executives, and their teams who want to master growth, transition, and succession get results faster, less painfully, and in ways that work for them. Reddish is a member of the National Speakers Association and the International Coach Federation. He can be reached at 800-726-7985 in the United States, 01.610.388.9335 internationally, or at johnr@getresults.com.

www.thesuccessionplanner.com
www.getresults.com

Eric Brunner

Eric Brunner, SPHR, Manager in the Learning and Development Division of Temple University's Human Resources Department, designs and facilitates competency-based performance management, communication, diversity, conflict resolution, and policy-based antiharassment/antidiscrimination training programs. He can be reached at Eric.Brunner@temple.edu.

Dr. Marie Amey-Taylor

Dr. Marie Amey-Taylor, Director, Human Resources Department, Learning and Development Division, Temple University, is co-coordinator of the university's Leadership Academy and specializes in leadership, management, and supervisory skill development and interpersonal skills including diversity, communication, team building, and conflict resolution. She is also qualified to administer the Myers-Briggs Type Indicator. She can be reached at AmeyTay@temple.edu.

OnTrackAmerica

Michael Sussman is the founder of the nonprofit organization OnTrack-America, which is helping the North American rail industry and government collaborate across agencies, companies, regions, and stakeholder groups. Sussman and his consulting company, Strategic Rail Finance, apply collaborative principles to financing the most challenging situations, creating funding breakthroughs for their clients that incorporate multiple lenders and government entities. He can be reached at msussman@strategicrail.com.

www.strategicrail.com
www.ontrackamerica.org

CHAPTER 5: INNOVATION

Borderless Thinking

Borderless Thinking LLC™ helps organizations and individuals break free from business-as-usual thinking to reimagine what they can accomplish in today's highly competitive marketplace.

www.borderlessthinking.com

Stages of Innovation

Stages of Innovation (SOI) provides solutions for successfully entering new markets, introducing new products, evaluating customer attitudes. . . . whatever customized approach will work to increase business.

www.stagesofinnovation.com

Brandon Rud Design

Brandon Rud Design offers a variety of design services including interior, landscape, theatrical, and event design.

www.brandonruddesign.com

CHAPTER 6: ADAPTABILITY

Alignment Rules

Alignment Rules provides solutions that unveil areas of organizational, departmental, or group misalignment within a company or group of companies.

www.alignmentrules.com

CHAPTER 7: LEADERSHIP

The Group Leadership Intensive

The Group Leadership Intensive is a residential, five-day program for those truly interested in learning how to lead a group or organization. The five days includes a wide range of experiences where participants practice creating interventions and creative strategies for meeting group goals and freeing the intelligence and energy of a group.

www.groupleadershipintensive.com

www.rodnapier.com

LeaderStrengthSystems

LeaderStrength™ Systems, Inc., is a learning and performance organization that focuses on three specific areas: management skills, leadership development, and partnering with learning and performance professionals to expand their expertise and leadership skills.

www.leaderstrength.com

Standing Stone Center for the Healing Arts

Standing Stone Center for the Healing Arts offers guidance and leadership in personal transformation. Dr. Michael Madden facilitates the discovery of your authentic purpose through individual counseling and group process. He enhances his counseling with training and facilitation in the areas of meditation, ritual, and ceremony. His services are offered in person, via phone and e-mail, or are combined with organized travel and wilderness experiences.

www.drmichaelmadden.org

NTL

NTL Institute delivers powerful learning solutions for organizations, leaders, and practitioners who have a clear stake in accelerating individual, team, and organization effectiveness. For over 60 years, NTL Institute has provided training and learning to tens of thousands of individuals and organizations around the world. The NTL global member faculty includes over 300 members who are leading consultants, practitioners, and researchers at the forefront of innovation in organization and leadership development, interpersonal skills and human development, group dynamics, and diversity and inclusion.

www.ntl.org

Bernhart Associates Executive Search, LLC

Bernhard Associates is a nationally recognized and leading recruiter in direct marketing.

www.bernhart.com

Genesis Consulting Partners

Genesis Consulting Partners is a senior management consulting firm that provides executive search and related services to both corporate and individual clients in the pharmaceutical and biotechnology industries.

www.gcpbiosearch.com

The GEM Survey

The GEM Survey™ has been developed to help users make significant improvements almost immediately. Unlike many assessment tools that focus on leadership styles, personality types, and subjective interpretations, the GEM focuses on specific, repeatable behaviors, behaviors that can be learned quickly and practiced.

barbaraglanz.com/gem/

CHAPTER 9: HOLACRACY

HolacracyOne

The purpose of HolacracyOne is to spread the practice and assist others in learning about Holacracy. HolacracyOne offers half-day seminars and deeper, multiday workshops around the world.

The team at HolacracyOne is actively searching for organizations interested in adopting Holacracy and consultants interested in servicing those organizations as well as taking Holacracy to their existing client base.

www.holacracyone.com

CHAPTER 10: POSSIBILITIES

The Corporation—Video

The Corporation explores the nature and spectacular rise of the dominant institution of our time. Part film and part movement, *The Corporation* is transforming audiences and dazzling critics with its insightful and compelling analysis. Taking its status as a legal "person" to the logical conclusion, the film puts the corporation on the psychiatrist's couch to ask "What kind of person is it?" *The Corporation* includes interviews with 40 corporate insiders and critics—including Noam Chomsky, Naomi Klein, Milton Friedman, Howard Zinn, Vandana Shiva, and Michael Moore—plus true confessions, case studies, and strategies for change.[1]

www.thecorporation.com

Please refer to Chapter 10 for details on the following links.

Holacracy in the World

www.holacracyone.com

Edgewalkers

www.edgewalkers.org

Organization on Purpose

Sustainability: Ben Freeman
www.solartricycle.com

Healing: Antanas Vainius
www.grawnola.com

Gratitude: John Castagnini
www.thankgodi.com

Empowerment: Julie Roberts, Ph.D.
www.changeworksinc.com

Ending Poverty: Jim Riordan
www.pppafrica.org

Personal Mastery through Healing

The next businesses offer healing work that aligns the body, mind, and spirit.

---

[1] www.thecorporation.com/index.cfm?page_id=2

PA BodyTalk Center   BodyTalk™ works gently to restore the body's ability to heal itself, safely bringing the systems of the body back into balance, reestablishing the body's lines of communication, and facilitating true healing.

www.pabodytalkcenter.com

Essential Healthcare   Dr. Russell acknowledges the mind–body connection, which substantiates the belief that the mind–body can heal when it has no interference. Dr. Russell's practice is based on removing this interference and reinstating homeostasis, which enables people to heal on all levels of their being.

www.ehealth-center.com

Barbara Friling   Barbara Friling facilitates healing and self-empowerment through multiple healing modalities. She says that by honoring your being and embracing your personal power, you allow yourself to be open to the opportunities and expansive possibilities of your own self-healing.

www.bridgesofhealing.com

A Call to Conscious Evolution

Climate change, economic disparity, educational inequities, geopolitical tensions—these mounting concerns are symptoms of a world that is out of balance. Together we can shift consciousness by co-creating a new way of being.

www.brucelipton.com

B

Suggested Reading

In general, *Harvard Business Review* is a good source for new thinking, trends, and approaches to adaptability as they relate to business. Other sources are listed by chapter. Please note that some books are listed in multiple chapters.

CHAPTER 1: BUSINESS LANDSCAPE

Barker, Joel. *Paradigms: The Business of Discovering the Future.* New York: HarperCollins, 1992.

Blattberg, Robert, Rashi Glazer, and John D. C. Little. *The Marketing Information Revolution.* Boston: Harvard Business School Press, Chapter 15.

Davis, Jim, Gloria J. Miller, and Allan Russell. *Information Revolution.* New York: John Wiley & Sons, 2006.

Friedman, Thomas. *Hot, Flat and Crowded.* New York: Farrar, Straus and Giroux, 2008.

Friedman, Thomas. *The World Is Flat.* New York: Farrar, Straus and Giroux, 2005.

Miller, Gloria J., Dagmar Bräutigam, and Stefanie V. Gerlach, *Business Intelligence Competency Centers.* Hoboken, NJ: John Wiley & Sons, 2006.

Tapscott, Donald. *Blueprint to the Digital Economy.* San Francisco: McGraw-Hill, 1998.

Zakaria, Fareek. *The Post-American World.* New York: W. W. Norton, 2008.

CHAPTER 2: MODELS FROM SCIENCE AND NATURE

Anderson, Philip. *The Biology of Business*. San Francisco: Jossey-Bass, 1999.

Gladwell, Malcolm. *Blink*. New York: Little, Brown, 2005.

Gleik, James. Chaos: *Making a New Science*. New York: Penguin Books, 1987.

Goldberg, Elkhonon. *The Executive Brain*. Oxford: Oxford University Press, 2001.

Holland, John. *Hidden Order*. New York: Basic Books, 1995.

Kellert, Stephen H. *In the Wake of Chaos*. Chicago: University of Chicago Press, 1993.

Laszlo, Christopher, and Jean-François Laugel. *Large-Scale Organizational Change*. Boston: Butterworth Heinemann, 2000.

McTaggart, Lynn. *The Intention Experiment*. New York: Free Press, 2007.

Nicolis, Greĕgoire, and Ilya Prigogine. *Exploring Complexity*. New York: W. H. Freeman, 1989.

Pink, Daniel. *A Whole New Mind*. New York: Riverhead Books, 2005.

Pinker, Steven. *The Language Instinct*. New York: Harper Perennial Library, 1995.

Senge, Peter M. *The Fifth Discipline*. New York: Currency, 1990.

Surowiecki, James. *The Wisdom of Crowds*. New York: Doubleday, 2004.

Wheatley, Margaret J. *Leadership and the New Science*. San Francisco: Barrett-Koehler, 1992.

Zukav, Gary. *The Dancing Wu Li Masters: An Overview of the New Physics*. New York: Perennial, 2001.

CHAPTER 3: EFFECTIVE COMMUNICATION

Bracey, Hyler. *Managing from the Heart*. New York: Dell Publishing, 1990.

Chambers, Harry E. *Effective Communication Skills*. Cambridge, MA: Perseus Publishing, 2001.

Connolly, Mickey, and Richard Rianoshek. *The Communication Catalyst*. Chicago: Dearborn Trade Publishing, 2002.

Galanes, Gloria J., Katherine Adams, and John K. Brilhart. *Effective Group Discussion*. New York: McGraw-Hill, 2004.

Gittell, Jody Hoffer. *Positive Organizational Scholarship*. San Francisco: Barrett-Koehler, 2003.

Isaacs, William. *Dialogue: The Art of Thinking Together*. New York: Currency/Doubleday, 1999.

Krishnamurti. *Talks and Dialogue*. New York: Avon Books, 1968.

Meyer, Christopher, and Stan Davis. *It's Alive*. New York: Crown Business, 2003.

Seashore, Charles N., Edith W. Seashore, and G. M. Weinberg. *What Did You Say? The Art of Giving and Receiving Feedback*. Attleboro, MA: Douglas Charles Press, 1992.

CHAPTER 4: COLLABORATION

Aburdene, Patricia. *Megatrends 2010*. Charlottesville, VA: Hampton Roads Publishing, 2007.

Cameron, Kim S., Jane E. Dutton, and Robert E. Quinn, eds. *Positive Organizational Scholarship*. San Francisco: Barrett-Koehler, 2003.

Coleman, David, and Stewart Levine. *Collaboration 2.0*. Silicon Valley, CA: Happy About, 2008.

Cooperrider, David L., and Diana Whitney. "A Positive Revolution in Change: Appreciative Inquiry." In D. L. Cooperrider, P. F. Sorensen Jr., D. Whitney, and T. F. Yeager, eds., *Appreciative Inquiry: Rethinking Human Organizations Towards a Positive Theory of Change*. Champaign, IL: Stipes Publishing, 1999.

Covey, Steven M. R. *The Speed of Trust*. New York: Simon & Schuster, 2008.

Hammond, Sue Annis, and Cathy Royal, eds. *Lessons from the Field: Applying Appreciative Inquiry*. Plano, TX: Practical Press, 1998.

Kraus, William A. *Collaboration in Organizations*. New York: Human Sciences Press, 1984.

Laszlo, Christopher, and Jean-François Laugel. *Large-Scale Organizational Change*. Boston: Butterworth Heinemann, 2000.

Lencioni, Patrick. *The Five Dysfunctions of a Team*. Hoboken, NJ: John Wiley & Sons, 2002.

Rosen, Dan. *The Culture of Collaboration*. San Francisco: Red Ape Publishing, 2007.

Sawyer, Keith. *Group Genius*. New York: Basic Books, 2007.

Segil, Larraine. *Measuring the Value of Partnering*. New York: AMACOM, 2004.

Tapscott, Don, and Anthony D. Williams. *Wikinomics*. New York: Penguin Group, 2006.

Wheatley, Margaret J., and Myron Kellner-Rogers. *A Simpler Way*. San Francisco: Barrett-Koehler, 1996.

CHAPTER 5: INNOVATION

Barker, Joel A., and Scott W. Ericson. *Five Regions of the Future*. New York: Penguin Group, 2005.

Christensen, Clayton M. *The Innovator's Dilemma*. New York: Harper Business, 1997.

Crandall, Rick, ed. *Break-Out Creativity*. Corte Madera, CA: Select Press, 1998.

Emery, Marcia. *Intuition Workbook: An Expert's Guide to Unlocking the Wisdom of Your Subconscious Mind*. Englewood Cliffs, NJ: Prentice-Hall, 1994.

Glaser, Judith E. *The DNA of Leadership*. Avon, MA: Platinum Press, 2001.

Goldberg, Elkhonon. *The Executive Brain*. Oxford: Oxford Press, 2001.

Herrmann, Ned. *The Creative Brain*. Lake Lure, NC: The Ned Herrmann Group, 1994.

Kriegel, Robert, and David Brandt. *Sacred Cows Make the Best Burgers*. New York: Warner Books, 1996.

Moore, Geoffrey A. *Dealing with Darwin*. New York: Penguin Group, 2005.

Pink, Daniel. *A Whole New Mind*. New York: Riverhead Books, 2005), Introduction.

Sawyer, Keith. *Group Genius*. New York: Basic Books, 2007.

Chapter 6: Adaptability

Bennet, Alex, and David Bennet. *Organizational Survival in the New World*. Burlington, MA: Elsevier, 2004.

Bradley, Stephen P., and Richard L. Nolan. *Sense & Respond*. Boston: Harvard Business School Press, 1998.

Childre, Doc, and Bruce Cryer. *From Chaos to Coherence*. Boulder Creek, CA: Heartmath LLC, 2004.

Clippinger, John Henry III, ed. *The Biology of Business*. San Francisco: Jossey-Bass, 1999.

Coveney, Peter, and Roger Highfield. *Frontiers of Complexity: The Search for Order in a Chaotic World*. New York: Fawcett Columbine, 1995.

Haeckel, Stephan H. *Adaptive Enterprise*. Boston: Harvard Business School Press, 1999.

Heifetz, Ronald, and Donald Laurie. "The Work of Leadership," *Harvard Business Review* (January–February 1997).

Kaplan, Robert S., and David P. Norton. *Alignment*. Boston: Harvard Business School Press, 2006.

Labovitz, George, and Victor Rosansky. *The Power of Alignment*. New York: John Wiley & Sons, 1997.

Laszlo, Christopher, and Jean-François Laugel. *Large-Scale Organizational Change*. Boston: Butterworth Heinemann, 2000.

Napier, Rod, and Rich McDaniel. *Measuring What Matters*. Mountain View, CA: Davies Black Publishing, 2006.

Olsen, Edwin E., and Glenda H. Eoyang. *Facilitating Organizational Change*. San Francisco: Jossey-Bass/Pfeiffer, 2001.

Senge, Peter M. *The Fifth Discipline*. New York: Currency, 1990.

Senge, Peter M., Art Kliener, Charlotte Roberts, Rick Ross, George Roth, and Bryan Smith. *The Dance of Change*. New York: Doubleday, 1999.

Senge, Peter M., C. Otto Sharmer, Joseph Jaworksi, and Betty Sue Flowers. *Presence: An Exploration of Profound Change in People, Organizations, and Society*. New York: Currency Doubleday, 2004.

Wheatley, Margaret J. *Leadership and the New Science*. San Francisco: Barrett-Koehler, 1992.

Wheatley, Margaret J., and Myron Kellner-Rogers. *A Simpler Way*. San Francisco: Barrett-Koehler, 1996.

Chapter 7: Leadership

Beck, Don, and Christopher Cowan. *Spiral Dynamics: Mastering Values, Leadership and Change*. Malden, MA: Blackwell Publishing, 1996.

Bolman, Lee G., and Terrence E. Deal. *Reframing Organizations: Artistry, Choice, and Leadership*. San Francisco: Jossey-Bass, 2003.

Canfield, Jack, Mark Victor Hansen, and Les Hewitt. *The Power of Focus: How to Hit Your Business, Personal and Financial Targets with Absolute Certainty*. Deerfield Beach, FL: Health Communications, 2000.

Carroll, Michael, *The Mindful Leader: Awakening Your Natural Management Skills Through Mindfulness Meditation*. Boston: Trumpeter, 2008.

Collins, Jim. *Good to Great*. New York: HarperCollins, 2001.

Conley, Chip. *The Rebel Rules: Daring to Be Yourself in Business*. New York: Simon & Schuster, 2001.

Covey, Stephen R. *Principle-Centered Leadership*. New York: Fireside, 1991.

George, Bill. *Authentic Leadership*. San Francisco: Jossey-Bass, 2003.

Gladwell, Malcolm. *Blink*. New York: Little, Brown, 2005.

Goleman, Daniel, Richard Boyatzis, and Annie McKee. *Primal Leadership*. Boston: Harvard Business School Press, 2002.

Hawkins, David. *Power versus Force: The Hidden Determinants of Human Behavior*. Carlsbad, CA: Hay House, 2002.

Hawley, Jack. *Reawakening the Spirit in Work*. San Francisco: Barrett-Koehler, 1993.

Laszlo, Christopher, and Jean-François Laugel. *Large-Scale Organizational Change*. Boston: Butterworth Heinemann, 2000.

Luft, Joseph. *Group Process: An Introduction to Group Dynamics*. Palo Alto, CA: National Press Books, 1963.

Menkes, Justin. *Executive Intelligence*. New York: Collins, 2005.

Napier, Rod, and Rich McDaniel. *Measuring What Matters*. Mountain View, CA: Davies Black Publishing, 2006.

Secretan, Lance. *ONE: The Art and Practice of Conscious Leadership*. Caledon, Ontario: Secretan Center, 2006.

Weisbord, Marvin. *Productive Workplaces Revisited*. San Francisco: Jossey-Bass, 2004.

Wheatley, Margaret J. *Finding Our Way: Leadership for an Uncertain Time*. San Francisco: Barrett-Koehler, 2005.

Whiteley, Richard. *The Corporate Shaman: A Business Fable*. New York: HarperCollins, 2002.

CHAPTER 8: SYSTEMS THINKING

Barrett, Richard. *Building a Values Driven Organization: A Whole System Approach to Cultural Transformation*. Boston: Butterworth-Heinemann, 2006.

Gladwell, Malcolm. *The Tipping Point: How Little Things Can Make a Big Difference*. New York: Back Bay Books, 2002.

Hock, Dee. *One from Many: VISA and the Rise of Chaordic Organization*. San Francisco: Barrett Koehler, 2005.

O'Conner, Joseph, and Ian McDermott. *The Art of Systems Thinking*. San Francisco: Thorsons, 1997.

Senge, Peter M. *The Fifth Discipline*. New York: Currency, 1990.

Wheatley, Margaret J. *Leadership and the New Science*. San Francisco: Barrett-Koehler, 1992.

Articles on Systems Thinking in Business. Available at www.managementhelp.org/systems/systems.htm.

CHAPTER 9: HOLACRACY

Allen, David. *Getting Things Done*. New York: Penguin Books, 2001.

Cohn, Mike. *Agile Estimating and Planning*. New York: Prentice Hall, 2005.

Lencioni, Patrick. *Death by Meeting*. San Francisco: Jossey-Bass, 2004.

CHAPTER 10: POSSIBILITIES

Aburdene, Patricia. *Megatrends 2010*. Charlottesville, VA: Hampton Roads Publishing, 2007.

Ardagh, Arjuna. *The Translucent Organization: How People Just Like You Are Waking Up and Changing the World*. Novato, CA: New World Library, 2005.

Carroll, Michael. *Awake at Work: 35 Practical Buddhist Principles for Discovering Clarity and Balance in the Midst of Work's Chaos*. Boston: Shambhala Publications, 2006.

Dyer, Wayne. *The Power of Intention: Learning to Co-create Your World Your Way*. Carlsbad, CA: Hay House, 2004.

Finney, Martha. *In the Face of Uncertainty: 25 Top Leaders Speak Out on Challenge, Change, and the Future of American Business*. New York: AMACOM, 2002.

Guillory, William A. *The Living Organization: Spirituality in the Workplace*. Salt Lake City, UT: Innovations International, 2001.

Gunther, Marc. *Faith and Fortune: The Quiet Revolution to Reform American Business*. New York: Crown Business, 2004.

Harman, Willis. *Creative Work: The Constructive Role of Business in Transforming Society*. Indianapolis, IN: Knowledge Systems, 1990.

Hawley, Jack. *Reawakening the Spirit in Work*. San Francisco: Barrett-Koehler, 1993.

Heermann, Barry. *Noble Purpose: Igniting Extraordinary Passion for Life and Work*. Fairfax, VA: QSU Publishing, 2004.

Krebs, Nina Boyd. *Edgewalkers: Defusing Cultural Boundaries on the New Global Frontier*. Far Hills, NJ: New Horizon Press, 1999.

Land, George, and Beth Jarman. *Breakpoint and Beyond: Mastering the Future Today*. New York: Harper Business, 1992.

Manz, Charles. *Emotional Discipline: The Power to Choose How You Feel*. San Francisco: Barrett-Koehler, 2003.

Mitroff, Ian I., and Elizabeth A. Denton. *A Spiritual Audit of Corporate America*. San Francisco: Jossey-Bass, 1999.

Neal, Judith A. *Creating Enlightened Organizations: A Practical Guide for Implementing Spirit at Work*. East Haven, CT: Spirit at Work Publishing, 2006.

Neil, Judi. *Edgewalkers*. Oxford: Greenwood Publishing Group, 2006.

Rao, Srikumar. *Are You Ready to Succeed? Unconventional Strategies for Achieving Personal Mastery in Business and Life*. New York: Hyperion, 2006.

Ray, Michael. *The Highest Goal: The Secret that Sustains You in Every Moment*. San Francisco: Barrett-Koehler, 2004.

Ray, Paul, and Sherry Anderson. *The Cultural Creatives: How 50 Million People Are Changing the World*. New York: Harmony Books, 2000.

Renesch, John. *Getting to the Better Future: How Business Can Lead the Way to New Possibilities*. San Francisco: New Business Books, 2000.

Roberts Julie. *Change Works with CLEAR, Clearing Limits Energetically with Acupressure Release*. NP: Author, 2006.

Stephen, Michael. *Spirituality in Business: The Hidden Success Factor*. Scottsdale, AZ: Inspired Productions Press, 2002.

Tolle, Eckhart. *A New Earth: Awakening to Your Life's Purpose*. New York: Plume, 2006.

Wedemeyer, Richard A., and Ronald W. Jue. *The Inner Edge*. Chicago: McGraw-Hill, 2002.

Whiteley, Richard. *The Corporate Shaman: A Business Fable*. New York: HarperCollins, 2002.

Whyte, David. *The Heart Aroused*. New York: Currency Doubleday, 1994.

Wilbur, Ken. *The Theory of Everything*. Boston: Shambala Publications, 2001.

About the Author

Olivia Parr Rud is an expert in Data Mining and Business Intelligence (BI). Her interest in organizational alignment grew out of her experience with large companies in highly dynamic markets. She noticed that as they leveraged the benefits of the new BI technologies in the global economy, the challenges they experienced began to form predictable patterns. Through her personal research into the new sciences and related writings by pioneers in systems theory, she began to understand and correlate these patterns. This led to her research in the areas of complexity science, systems theory, and organizational alignment.

Through OLIVIAGroup, she works with organizations to fully leverage the power of Business Intelligence by offering organizational alignment assessments, leadership development, and skill building in the areas of communication, innovation, and adaptability. Her organizational consulting is offered in partnership with leading experts in the areas of leadership development, personal development, and organizational alignment.

In 2001, Olivia wrote *Data Mining Cookbook: Modeling Data for Acquisition, Risk and Customer Relationship Management* (John Wiley & Sons). She has a BA in mathematics from Gettysburg College and an MS in decision and information systems, with a concentration in statistics, from Arizona State University. She is a member of Phi Kappa Phi National Honor Society and Alpha Delta Iota National Honor Society, Decision Sciences, Arizona State University.

Olivia is a spiritual activist with a passion for seeking solutions through a holistic lens. She continues her research in complexity science, evolutionary biology, and spirituality. She lives in Philadelphia where she treasures her family, her friends, and her trees. She can be reached at Olivia@oliviagroup.com.

Index